Playing for the Hoops

The George McCluskey Story

Playing for the Hoops
The George McCluskey Story

AIDAN DONALDSON

Luath Press Limited

EDINBURGH

www.luath.co.uk

First published 2016
Reprinted 2016

ISBN: 978-1-910745-63-2

The paper used in this book is recyclable. It is made from low chlorine pulps produced
in a low energy, low emission manner from renewable forests.

Printed and bound by TJ International, Padstow

Typeset in 11 point Sabon by Main Point Books, Edinburgh

Contents

This work is dedicated to our parents – Joe and Alice Donaldson and John and Teresa McCluskey – and to our families; to Celtic supporters everywhere and to Our Lady, the Mother of Jesus.

Aidan Donaldson and George McCluskey

Acknowledgements

THIS BOOK WOULD not have seen the light of day had it not have been for the help, advice, guidance and encouragement of many people. In particular I would like to thank George himself for his openness, patience and, above all, friendship. I am indebted also to George's wife, Anne, and their children – Leeanne, Barry, Natalie and Ashleigh – for tolerating frequent intrusions into the life of their family in Uddingston by one who arrived as a stranger from Ireland but has since become very much one of the family. Sincerest thanks also to George's brother, John, his sisters, Pat, Jeanette and Teresa and his Aunt Mary who were all rich sources of family stories, and to George's close friends from boyhood, Paul Brannan and John Kirkwood, who were invaluable companions of the author throughout the writing of this work. I am also most grateful to Dr Joe Bradley who has guided me throughout this project. His wisdom, knowledge and passion for illuminating and articulating a greater understanding and contextualisation regarding Celtic FC, its supporters and the Irish diaspora, particularly in Scotland, have played a most significant role in helping me write this book. While it is difficult (indeed impossible) to list all of those who have been part of bringing George's story to print I would like to thank Jim Mervyn, Eddie Whyte, Martin Donaldson, Declan Leavy, Lenny Gaffney, Declan Dunbar, Cormac McArt, Andrew Milne (and his fanzine *More than 90 Minutes*), Celtic Football Club and the countless friends and Celtic minded people who endured, tolerated and (indeed) encouraged my intrusion into their lives. Special gratitude to my wife, Philomena, and my children, Caoimhe, Eadaoin and Grainne, who were so understanding during my frequent absences from 'normal family life'. Finally, sincerest thanks to everyone at Luath Press for their most professional support in turning a manuscript into this finished work.

Timeline

1957   19 September: George McKinlay Cassidy McCluskey born in Hamilton

1973   9 June: Scores winning goal in under-15 Scotland v England at Wembley

1974   July: Signs for Celtic

1975   1 October: Makes debut for Celtic against Valur FC

          1 November: Makes league debut for Celtic against Rangers

1976   18 September: Scores first goal for Celtic in 2-2 draw (v Hearts)

1979   21 May: Scores in dramatic last game of the season when Celtic defeat Rangers 4-2 and win the league

          6 June: Marries Anne Williams

1980   10 May: Scores winning goal in Scottish Cup Final when Celtic beat Rangers 1-0

1982   15 May: Scores two goals as Celtic beat St Mirren 3-0 to win the league on the final day of the season

          29 September: Comes off the bench to score last-gasp winner to put Ajax out of the European Cup in Amsterdam

1983–86 Leaves Celtic and plays for Leeds

1986–89 Moves to Hibernian

1989   August: Signs for Hamilton

1991   December: Wins the B&Q Scottish Challenge as Hamilton beat Ayr in the final 1–0 at Fir Park

1992   August: Tommy Burns signs George McCluskey for Kilmarnock who secure promotion to SPL on the final day of the 1992/93 season

1994   Signs for Clyde and retires from professional football at end of 1995/96 season

George McCluskey is currently a member of the Celtic hospitality team and coach of the under-17 academy.

Personal Introduction by George McCluskey

I FIRST MET Aidan Donaldson in Cassidy's Bar in Belfast about 15 years ago. I had been in Ireland speaking at a function organised by Beann Mhadaghain CSC the day before and it was suggested that I should pop into Cassidy's Bar if I got a chance. So I did and was warmly greeted by the people there. While I was discussing some aspects of Celtic and football, Aidan came into the conversation with a list of facts and statistics to which my response was, 'You must be a bloody anorak, buddy!' There was an embarrassed silence in the bar before Aidan retorted, 'Nobody ever said that to me before, George.' Despite that rather awkward first meeting Aidan and I have become great friends over the years and he's now very much part of our family. Indeed, it is only through our friendship that this work has appeared. It was Aidan's constant cajoling and encouragement that led me to agree to have my story told. His determination, hard work and knowledge have done the rest and I thank Aidan from the bottom of my heart for the wonderful job he has done in getting my story in print.

From the very start I wanted the book to be about my family and friends and everything else that has shaped me to be the person I am. In football biographies the reader often only sees the player and not the real person. I was extremely fortunate to play football for the club I supported my entire life. My great friend Tommy Burns once said (about himself) that he was 'a supporter who got lucky and wore the shirt', and I am sure that the same could be said about me. Coming from a Celtic minded family and community it has been an absolute privilege to have played for Celtic on so many occasions and to have shared in their joy, hopes and dreams – as well as in their disappointments. It is true to say that when you pull on the green and white hoops and run out in front of a packed Jungle you are playing for your family and friends as well as for Celtic and there is no feeling like that. And I wanted to get that sense of club, community and family across in this book.

I have many wonderful memories and made many friends among players and supporters alike. Yet the footballer's life is not always about the great moments and matches. I have had many great moments in football and also many low points too and not just when bitter defeat was experienced. It's only when you hit life's 'bumps' that you really understand who your true friends are and I have been blessed to have been surrounded by so many close friends who have stuck by me over the years. So sincerest thanks and love to the Dollichans, McAteers, McCormacks, Paul Brannan, Gerry Green, John

Kirkwood and all others whose loyalty and friendship means the world to me.

It is to my family that I owe the greatest debt. My mother and father sacrificed so much for all of us when we were growing up and an awful lot to help myself and my brother, John, as we pursued our dreams to play for Celtic. They taught me everything I know and have tried to pass on to my own children. Both Anne and I are proud of each and every one of them as they make their own journey in life. Anne and I have been together since we met in St Catherine's High School 44 years ago. She has been the rock that has kept me going when times are difficult and has made our house a loving, caring and happy place, home for our children and grandchildren. She has the patience of a saint and the wisdom and understanding that has helped me enormously throughout our lives and I thank her most sincerely for that.

God has always played an important role in my life from my childhood to today. I am most certainly not the best Christian in the world but I pray every day for my family, friends and those in need. In particular I pray to Our Lady. It was a teacher at St John the Baptist Primary School called Teresa Maxwell who said that if you ever wanted to ask Jesus for something then you should always pray to his mother since no son would refuse a mother's request. When I think of the two most important women in my life – my own mother and my wife – I am certain that Mrs Maxwell gave a young boy great advice all those years ago. She also told us that her favourite saint was St Jude – the Patron Saint of Lost Causes. St Jude is now one of my favourite saints whom I pray to especially in times of difficulty. I recommend him!

I hope that those who are kind and patient enough to read this book will enjoy it and see part of themselves and their own story in it. The world we live in is a challenging and often confusing place. Yet there are values and gifts that are passed on from one generation to the next. Celtic has always been an extremely important part of my life and continues to be so. So too are my family, friends and community. All of them are intertwined and interconnected. I was indeed a fan who got lucky and played in the Hoops. I also hope by doing that I played for you.

Hail! Hail!

George McCluskey

Preface

QUESTIONS OF MORALITY, greed, vanity and selfishness are never too far from the surface when discussing modern elite football. Some observers argue that these and other influences and dynamics threaten the very future of the world's greatest team game. It seems that menaces and perils also arise from too much televised football, the rise of wealthy celebrity footballers and managers, the destruction of former models of youth development, a perceived decline in creativity and imagination on the pitch via suffocating tactics and a corporate sanitised manufacturing of football fandom at the expense of the originality of community. It has been said by some that elite football is in mortal danger as it sits on a narcissistic fashioned precipice, in danger of falling even deeper into the toxic sea of global capitalism, never to regain previous values and virtues. Is a great cultural, social and community resource passing away for millions around the world?

Partly reflecting such changes, many or most modern footballers' biographies are often superficial, tedious and too obviously commercially orientated. In reality they often constitute stories not worth hearing. Where are the challenging standpoints, principles, views on fundamental aspects of life, meanings, understandings, lessons to be learned? Not every footballer need produce a great piece of art and not every story needs to have lessons for life, but... the word 'boring' seems to characterise so many elite player biographies.

George McCluskey became a footballer at a time in Scotland when many young lads still harboured dreams of playing football because they loved the sport, and often because they wanted to play for the club they saw as representing their community. George McCluskey lived this dream. For many people from McCluskey's geographical, working class, ethnic or religious background, becoming rich and famous simply wasn't on the radar. Indeed, George was part of a generation that had frequently been taught values often constructed as the opposite to those of being rich and famous. For George McCluskey and many others of his ilk, a good number of parents and grandparents lived and taught values steeped in humility, charity, hospitality, decency, respectfulness, good neighbourliness and community.

George McCluskey played for a Celtic team that for most of the 1960s and 1970s had dominated Scottish football, and was simultaneously a principal force in the European arena; winning the European Cup, runners-up and appearing frequently in the quarter and semi-final stages of the premier club trophy in world football. This was also during a long period when other clubs in Scotland, the likes of Dunfermline, Hibernian, Dundee, Glasgow Rangers, Dundee United and Aberdeen among others, all produced stunning results and successes on the European football stage. In addition, Scotland's players filled the ranks of the best teams in England as they too made their mark at national level and in European football.

McCluskey's time at Celtic was also one of club success. Great players, huge crowds, championships, cup wins and exciting European campaigns. However, as McCluskey's biographer Aidan Donaldson rightly points out, success on the pitch isn't everything: to be held in the highest regard by the fans 'requires that a player should have a love and passion for the club as well as knowledge, understanding, appreciation and love for all it represents'. Answering his own enquiry, for Donaldson, McCluskey 'not only played in the hoops – he played for the Hoops'.

All football clubs have some significance to players and supporters. However, few compare to Celtic. The club has a unique genesis story, invoking images of poverty-stricken refugees fleeing Ireland's death-dealing Great Hunger. Subsequent inter-generational experiences were frequently characterised by a confrontation with religious, ethnic, social, economic, cultural and educational marginalisation, discrimination and prejudice – and by the struggle to rise above these racist, bigoted, inhumane and immoral ways and practices.

Many Celtic supporters who are descendants of the Irish emigrants of the 19th and 20th centuries retain a belief – often born from experience, knowledge, insight and understanding – that most or many of the worst excesses of these denials and deprivations are in the not too distant past. These excesses retain a hidden potency that can still negatively affect life chances and choices today if one is known to be a member of the multi-generational Irish-Catholic diaspora in Scotland. After all, a black president in the USA certainly doesn't equate with the end of prejudice and discrimination against non-whites in the 'land of the free and home of the brave'.

Dr Aidan Donaldson's biography of George McCluskey includes numerous insights and experiences that add to our knowledge of not only Celtic as a club, but also that of the offspring of the refugee immigrant community that gave rise to it, and who today remain the most significant ingredient amongst its support. Family, faith, community and their relationship to football threads much of this work. In itself, that makes it a more interesting proposition than many football biographies. Many Celtic supporters will relate to the story of George McCluskey as relayed by Dr Aidan Donaldson. Simply put, this is a story well worth the read.

Joseph M Bradley

Introduction

ON 25 MAY 1967 a young boy in the village of Birkenshaw in Lanarkshire watched his sporting heroes – Glasgow Celtic – win the European Cup final against the highly fancied Inter Milan and become true football legends. That glorious evening in Lisbon during which Celtic became the first British (and, indeed, northern European) side to lift the coveted European trophy is etched in the memory of every Celtic supporter old enough to have watched the match, as well as in the minds of all Celtic supporters who have had the story handed down to them from previous generations. Like most football-daft youngsters, the ten-year-old George McCluskey dreamed that one day he too would wear the colours of his heroes, and for young McCluskey this meant the green and white hoops of his beloved Celtic. It was not only his team, it was his entire family's team, his whole community's team. To run out in front of the 'Jungle' at a packed Celtic Park was indeed the ambition of many from George McCluskey's background and it was not simply a matter of wanting to play football for a very successful club. For people like George McCluskey and the community he belonged to Glasgow Celtic Football Club was much more than just a successful sports team.

Celtic: an identity – not a commercial brand

It was Barcelona FC that coined the slogan '*més que un club*' ('more than a club'). It is an expression that also fits perfectly in the heart and mind of every Celtic supporter. '*Més que un club*' is a feeling of identity that beats to the rhythm of the soul of all Celtic minded people. Celtic is not just a football club – though it is a wonderfully successful one. Celtic represents its supporters – and their hopes, dreams and aspirations – in a different fashion than the vast majority of other major football teams do. Celtic is seen by its fans as an ambassador that extends beyond the field of play. For the founders of the club, and the generations of those who embraced and sustained it, Celtic was – and is – about an identity, a culture and a people. It was created by and for the descendants of those who had fled poverty and starvation in Ireland in the years following the Great Famine (*an Gorta Mor*) of the 1840s and who found shelter in the East End of Glasgow and a plethora of villages, towns and cities throughout Scotland, England and the world. It also, however, represents a world vision and a very specific and positive one at that. To be 'Celtic minded' means having a shared cultural identity and expressing this in an inclusive and open way. The Celtic community has always looked at the world differently – from its founding on 6 November 1887 in St Mary's Hall in the Calton by those such as Brother Walfrid, John Glass and Pat Welsh right up to the present day. After all, it was founded as a charity and not a business or simply a sporting club. While the initial goal was to help to provide food and education for the poor children of Irish emigrants who had fled Ireland during and in the wake of the 'Great Hunger' or 'Famine', the founding fathers – and not least Brother Walfrid – had a vision beyond that initial one. The beneficiaries of Celtic Football Club – the children, their families and community – were not simply to be pitied and helped: rather, they were to be affirmed and, indeed, celebrated.

The leaders of the Irish community who were instrumental in establishing Celtic and driving it forward understood from the outset that they were dealing with something of much greater intrinsic value than a sporting club or a business. Celtic Football Club – unlike many other football clubs – was not a mere distraction that allowed supporters to forget about or escape from the hardship of their lives. Quite the opposite. Celtic has always been the focal point of a community's living, breathing hopes and dreams. When the Celtic players take to the pitch we take our place with them. When they play we play. When they win we win. When they lose we lose. When they celebrate we celebrate. We are them because they are us. Supporters of other teams just don't get it – and there's no surprise in that. To support a particular football team, for many, simply requires attachment and loyalty to that team and its particular set of players at a given time. It rarely goes beyond that. It does not require or inspire that close identification between the values of the club and the values of the supporter. To be 'Celtic minded' is about how you look at the world, your community, yourself and others. In today's globalised world of 'Planet Football' in which supporters – like footballers – are encouraged to transfer their allegiance as money brings 'success' as surely as day follows night, Celtic are truly remarkable indeed, and players who wear the green and white hoops stand out as legends in a world of shallow celebrities. Jock Stein once famously said that 'Celtic shirts don't shrink to fit inferior players'. They were made for players to grow to fit them. Celtic indeed has always produced legends who have 'grown to fit the shirt', and are more than very talented – even exceptionally talented – players.

What is remarkable is that the bond between the players and the fans has endured – and even thrived – in the new commercial reality that defines football today. Of course like every other successful club we have had our share of badge-kissing mercenaries who will swear undying loyalty to the club and its fans one day, even as their agents seek to move them on to to more lucrative contracts elsewhere the next. In spite of this there are many others who, although they are not from a Celtic background or tradition, have come to fall in love with the club and its supporters. Celtic has always celebrated inclusiveness, openness and diversity. The fact that many of those who became 'Celtic greats' – including John Thompson, Bertie Peacock, Ronnie Simpson, Bertie Auld, Tommy Gemmell, Kenny Dalglish and Danny McGrain – came from backgrounds removed from those traditionally associated with Celtic, is a clear demonstration that Celtic Football Club is open to all who wish to share its vision and celebrate with all other like-minded supporters or players its successes – irrespective of social, religious or ethnic background. This 'reaching out and drawing in' has not been undermined with the internationalisation and globalisation of football. It is indeed remarkable and, perhaps, unique that Celtic continues to attract people from diverse backgrounds who become Celtic minded themselves. They arrive having signed a contract as footballers and often become part of the Celtic family. They start to realise that playing for Celtic means something different, something greater, something beyond what they had initially arrived in Glasgow to *do*. Instead they *become*. One suspects that many such as Henrik Larsson, Chris Sutton, John Hartson, L'ubomír 'Lubo' Moravcík and a host of other players who 'came, saw and were conquered by the Celtic spirit' would immediately empathise with the new generation of players who have arrived at Celtic from various corners of the world and have instantly fallen in love with the Celtic family. Players such as these have come to understand that Celtic is *'més que un club'*.

George McCluskey: a Celtic legend

The young boy who watched Celtic on their most famous night all those years ago and who dreamed of playing in front of his friends and family at a packed Celtic Park did indeed manage just that – and on many occasions too. George McCluskey made his way through the ranks of the junior Celtic Boys Club to sign for Celtic at the age of 16. He made his debut at 17 and played for the club for the next eight years before leaving the only club he had ever supported in controversial circumstances in 1983 to go to Leeds. During his time at Celtic George McCluskey made a magnificent contribution to the club and was held in great esteem and admiration by Celtic fans then – and this remains so today. In recognition of his role as a prolific goal scorer George was inaugurated into the Celtic Hall of Fame in 2006. This honour is hugely significant in that, unlike many other sporting accolades which are bestowed by sports writers, journalists, fellow professionals and so on, it is the Celtic fans who decide who should be included in the Hall of Fame.

There have been numerous players of immense footballing ability and commitment who have made significant contributions to Celtic Football Club. Yet in simple terms of ability, commitment and contribution, supporters for George McCluskey's inclusion in this elite group had a very strong case. George was indeed a wonderfully gifted striker who could (and often did) change games, be that with a run into the box, a sudden turn or twist, or simply by arriving in (or creating) a bit of space for himself. He scored many spectacular goals and, crucially, many important ones. George McCluskey possessed those two wonderful and precious abilities that are only found in the most talented of goal scorers – namely that uncanny knack of 'showing up' just at the right time, coupled with lightning-quick reflexes – something which managers pray for and that make the possessor of these rarest of abilities stand out in the eyes and affection of the fans. And George McCluskey most certainly had these most ineffable of talents. His winning goal in the 1980 Scottish Cup Final (the only goal in a hard fought for 1–0 victory over Rangers) typifies the top-class striker's ability to be in the right place at the right time, and to do the right thing. He demonstrated the same earlier that season when he scored the opening goal at Celtic Park in a 2–0 victory over Real Madrid in the quarter-final of the European Cup. His 89th minute strike against Ajax in Amsterdam dumped the great 'total football' side (which included one Johan Cruyff) out of the same competition in 1982. His two goals in May 1982 against St Mirren at Celtic Park when Celtic won 3–0 against the 'Buddies' clinched the league for Celtic on the final day of the season. Many Celtic fans also remember his goal in that unbelievable final game of the season the following year at Celtic Park when 'ten men won the league' with a 4–2 victory against Rangers. All of these – and many more – are of significance to all Celtic and other football supporters. George was brave and never hid from the opposition nor shirked responsibility on or off the field. And he scored when we most needed it.

Yet in spite of this, something much more than football achievements has, rightly, placed George McCluskey in such illustrious company. Place a number of Celtic supporters together and inevitably the conversation will come round at some stage to talk about Celtic 'greats'. It is the same for all supporters of all clubs. Yet, with Celtic fans, the definition of a 'genuine great' of this incredible club is completely different from almost every fan base in the world. Sure, all who are accorded this accolade must have talent, contribution, personality etc, but the Celtic community look for – in fact demand – something more. The words 'legend' or 'great' are not given to anyone who played for and distinguished the Hoops easily. Connection, attitude, commitment, respect and integrity are touchstones for Celtic supporters and any Celtic player (former or present) will be judged by this criteria. Being 'Celtic minded' is not an optional extra that adds to a player's CV: rather, it is a necessary quality that all genuine Celtic greats possess.

George McCluskey has this quality – and has it in abundance. He is a genuine Celtic legend precisely because he is adored and loved by the fans for being what he is. There never was any false kissing of the badge or appearing in the media to proclaim undying loyalty to the club while looking for a move to something bigger and better from George McCluskey. In many ways he epitomised so much of the club's ethos and attitude. Every supporter who has had the privilege of meeting George or any young person who has been coached by him – as well as everyone from outside the Celtic family whom he has encountered throughout the world – cannot have walked away from the encounter without feeling genuinely valued and affirmed. For Celtic fans George McCluskey is simply one of us. For his local community in Uddingston – many of whom he has known for a lifetime – he is a source of inspiration and friendship, one who came from them and remains one of them. For his family George is, like all of the McCluskey clan, a loved and valued member in whom all rightly have a great sense of pride. George McCluskey's story reveals a rich and multi-layered narrative of a tightknit extended family, communities in the West of Scotland and the Irish diaspora and, of course, Celtic Football Club. In a very profound way, the story of George McCluskey opens up the opportunity for many who share that same sense of values, world outlook, community and collective identity to enter the world of Celtic. When George played for Celtic he played for us. He not only played *in* the hoops – he played *for* the Hoops. For so many who hold a place in their hearts for Celtic – and all it has stood for since its inception at a meeting chaired by Brother Walfrid in St Mary's Hall on East Rose Street in the Calton on 6 November 1887 – George McCluskey represents everything that Celtic Football Club are about – community, family, sporting success and celebration and friendship. This is what makes George McCluskey a real Celtic legend.

Early Life In Lanarkshire

The Irish Diaspora and Celtic Football Club

'COMMUNITY' COMES FROM the Latin word *'communitas'* whereby a group of people are bonded together through a conscious shared sense of history, experience and belonging. Strong communities often exhibit similar characteristics as families and recognise and support each other in a similar manner. Members of such communities share common bonds, recognising that commonality and shared identity when they meet. Celtic supporters understand this more than any other football supporters as they regard themselves as part of the worldwide 'Celtic family'. Meet a Celtic supporter anywhere in the world and in any setting and you have met a member of the 'Celtic family'. It is not merely by supporting a certain football club that unites Celtic supporters in the way that, say, being a supporter of Manchester United, Real Madrid or any other global football product makes you, well, a United or Madrid supporter. Being a Celtic supporter is something entirely different. It evokes a sense of identity, history, understanding and world vision completely different from that of supporters of other football clubs. The origins and identity of Celtic Football Club are linked to the Irish immigration that followed 'The Great Hunger' of the 1840s and led some 2–3 million people to flee starvation in the decades that followed. This does not mean that one has to be able to trace one's roots back to this time (although many Celtic supporters worldwide can). Celtic, like the community that gave birth to it, is open to anyone who wishes to embrace the 'Celtic way'. This involves a certain philosophy of playing football based on flair, an attacking style and a flamboyance that others may lack (or sacrifice). It also promotes a very conscious openness to and, indeed, embracing of its fans as evidenced by the club's willingness to 'adopt' two young fans – Oscar Knox (the young lad from Belfast whose courageous struggle against cancer captured the hearts of Celtic fans, authorities and players alike) and Jay Beattie from Lurgan who has become best buddy with one Georgios Samaras and who won the SPFL for Best Goal for January 2015 with his penalty against Hamilton.[1] And, of course, charity. Celtic was founded as a charity and retains a deep sense of social justice and concern for those in need – no matter who they are. There are many factors that shape a community. Some are historical, some are economic or social, while others may be environmental or ecological. Some are relatively minor but, when added together, can contribute to the distinctive character of a particular community. The community that Celtic emerged from was shaped by many factors but one above all else – *'An Gorta Mor'* – 'The Great Hunger'.

Fleeing famine and poverty: from Ireland to the West of Scotland and founding Paradise

The movement of people between Ireland and Scotland has been going on for many hundreds of years and, especially, from counties in the north-west of Ireland such as Tyrone, Derry and Donegal, as well as Antrim and Down. Many of their descendants would come to establish a new life in Scotland many years later. And it was these people who would build something quite wonderful and unique in the slums in the East End of Glasgow that would become famous throughout the world.

'And then came the Irish'

Irish immigration did not begin in 1847 – 'Black '47' as it is still known today. For generations beforehand people from Ireland had been going to Scotland for employment – almost exclusively in the agricultural sector. The work was primarily in picking potatoes and other crops. The offensive and racist term 'tattie hokers' which is still often used to refer to Celtic fans at some grounds in Scotland owes its origin to this migration. For the *'spalpeens'* (as they were known in their native Gaelic) the work was hard, dirty and badly paid. Just like many recent immigrants from Eastern Europe and other less affluent countries who have come to Scotland, Ireland, England and other well off countries in the European Union in search of a better life and who take the jobs that no one else wants, these Irish came, worked and didn't complain. They also went home, back to Ireland. The migrations that took place during these earlier

---

1. Both young Celtic fans from Ireland caught the imagination of the Celtic family and beyond with their warmth, humour and courage in facing challenge and difficulty in their young lives. Oscar passed away on 8 May 2014 after a two-and-a-half year battle with neuroblastoma.

times were temporary and linked to the agricultural season. After the potato harvest was finished the Irish migrants vanished and would not be seen until the onset of the following harvest. At first, their imprint and impact on Scottish society were negligible. Yet some did stay and became essential to the industrialisation of the Scottish economy. In particular there was a need for labour for infrastructure projects such as roads, canals, factories, coal mining, textile and steel industries and the Irish provided an important source of labour. Whole towns sprung up around these industries and significant Irish communities began to emerge within them. In 1831 it is calculated that some three-quarters of the population of Girvan in Ayrshire was Irish-born, while the census of 1841 reveals that some 125,321 (almost 5%) of the population of Scotland was originally from Ireland.

Although the Irish were not unknown in Scotland (or England or Wales for that matter) before the 'Great Hunger' of the 1840s, the scale and impact of the wave of migrants that arrived in Scotland in the famine years and in the decades following that disaster, had an enormous and long-term effect on the west of Scotland. Dr Joseph Bradley points out that the sudden arrival of tens of thousands of Irish refugees had the effect that 'numerous areas in west-central Scotland changed in their religious and social composition as Irish Catholics streamed in.'[2] Scotland absorbed a proportionately higher number of Irish migrants than any other country in the world at that time and most of this migration settled within a 20 mile radius of Glasgow. One further characteristic distinguished this wave of migration from any other that had hitherto occurred. Previous migrants from Ireland had either been (a) mainly Catholic seasonal agricultural workers who came and went each year, (b) mostly Catholic unskilled but physically strong labourers who worked in the mines or were engaged in canal/railway/road building or (c) 'returning' Protestants who originated from within the Scots and English communities that had been part of the British plantation of the north of Ireland and who took the skilled trades to the shipyards on the Clyde or to the textile industries. The Irish who arrived in the aftermath of the Famine were almost all Catholic and many were ill, weak and just about alive. Almost skeletal, these survivors of this traumatic catastrophe, found themselves shunned and treated with suspicion in a foreign land. These migrants had nowhere to go back to. Those tens of thousands who had made the journey to Scotland arrived,

---

2. J Bradley, *Celtic-minded* (Glendaruel: Argyll Publishing, 2004), p. 19.

found a place to live and then began to develop as a community in the villages and towns throughout the west-central belt of Scotland. Bradley describes the harsh reality of the conditions that faced this new wave of refugees in these early years:

> For much of the 19th century, the Irish in Scotland huddled together in the worst parts of towns and cities. They came to Scotland with an alien and often detested Catholic faith and arrived in a land that had played a significant role in what they often perceived as the subjugation and division of their own country. They often constituted the very poorest sections of Scottish society. They were labelled unskilled due to their limitation to mainly manual labour, although their presence was viewed as essential to the progress of the industrial revolution in Scotland and the development of the transport infrastructure, the coal industry and other economic concerns.[3]

One additional feature of this mass migration is that it was a very localised one and that the vast majority of Irish who found their way to Scotland were from the western counties of Ireland that suffered particularly severely from the Great Hunger. These counties included Leitrim, Mayo and Sligo (where a certain Andrew Kerins was born) and, especially, the northern eastern counties of Derry, Tyrone and Donegal. These latter counties are also the counties from which George McCluskey's people came.

As well as being the 'outsider' who threatened to undercut wages to the detriment of the 'native' Scottish worker, the Irish migrants, because of their weakened state on arrival (exacerbated by the crowded and unsanitary housing conditions that they were forced to live in), were regarded as carriers of disease and infections, so much so that typhoid was called 'the Irish fever.' The city of Glasgow at that time was indeed a byword for poverty and squalor. There were outbreaks of cholera in Glasgow shortly after the Irish arrived; first in 1849 and five year later in 1854. In both outbreaks several thousand people perished of the disease – and the Irish got the blame much as victims of leprosy, Ebola and HIV/AIDS also are treated with hostility and fear today. Already weakened by the ravages of the famine from which they were fleeing, the recently arrived Irish suffered greatly and disproportionately during these outbreaks of this

---

3. ibid., p. 20.

deadly and extremely contagious plague. Leaving behind one horror, the Irish in Scotland found another. Salvation had not come easily.

Yet the newly-arrived Irish in Scotland had one thing that helped them to overcome these great hardships and difficulties: they had each other. The values, identity and culture that this community brought with it served it well during these times. These include solidarity and care for those in need, inclusiveness and openness, reaching out to others and supporting one another. All of those of the Irish diaspora who had arrived in Scotland during the middle and later decades of the 19th century would have had first-hand experience of the dreadful suffering and trauma experienced during the Great Hunger and its aftermath. They also would have had a deep sense of injustice and would have regarded themselves as survivors and victims of a national disaster that had been visited onto them. Their collective identity would have been reinforced by their experience in the country in which they sought refuge and survival. Furthermore, their separation from mainstream Scottish society would have been accentuated by profound differences in ethnicity, language, social class and, above all else, religion. In such a heady mix, Celtic was born.

'And then came Andrew Kerins'

The founder of Celtic Football Club, Brother Walfrid (Andrew Kerins), didn't have as his primary purpose the aim of setting up a football club that has become the wonderfully successful and famous club it is today. He was motivated by something much more important than that. A religious brother with the Marist Order, Kerins was deeply moved by the plight of the marginalised and those oppressed by poverty and injustice. While looking on the faces of fellow Irish immigrants in the East End of Glasgow Brother Walfrid would have been struck by how their wretched conditions conflicted with their God-given human dignity and decided to act. Everything he did in relation to establishing and developing a football club in the East End of Glasgow had the noble goal of helping to alleviate the appalling suffering and degradation of the huddled masses crammed into the tiny disease-infested hovels of the Calton, Bridgeton and the other slums of Glasgow around St Mary's.

Andrew Kerins was born in 1840 in Ballymote in County Sligo, just a few years before the Great Hunger struck. As a young boy and youth he would have witnessed at first hand the dreadful suffering of many in his community, including members of his own family. He studied teaching and joined the Marist Brothers in 1864 before moving to Scotland in the 1870s, making the journey on a coal ship. In Glasgow Brother Walfrid (as he was now known) was assigned to the teaching of young children in some of the poorest quarters of Glasgow. This was in accordance with the Marist ethos which was (and remains) to teach the most neglected and marginalised children. He taught first at St Mary's School in the Calton and later the nearby Sacred Heart School where he became headmaster in 1874. The conditions he encountered in the East End of Glasgow would not have been dissimilar to those of the towns and villages that he would have witnessed being emptied of its people – his people – in the aftermath of the Great Hunger. Given the huge concentration of Irish migrants in these parts of Glasgow it is unsurprising that Andrew Kerins would have felt a high degree of empathy and compassion to his fellow countrymen and women. As a teacher in the East End of Glasgow he would have come into contact with many names which were only too familiar to him as most of the Irish refugees and migrants of the Famine and its aftermath came from the part of Ireland that he called 'home'. He may have looked down the school roll and saw familiar surnames such as Walsh, Brennan, Gallagher, O'Hara and other names that were commonplace in Sligo and may have pondered if these had some connection to those bearing the very same surnames back in the land that he had left behind when called to teach on the banks of the Clyde.

Of course, Andrew Kerins was no simple teacher who found himself among a community he recognised as his own and felt a natural duty to help. It was not mere idealism or sentiment that motivated the man from Ballymote to dedicate his life to those in need. He was also a member of a religious order and, as such, would have been deeply formed and shaped by a Christian vision of the world and would have viewed the world – and everyone he encountered – through these lenses. In particular, Brother Walfrid would have reflected on the inescapable and unconditional imperatives that lie at the very heart of the Christian world outlook and saw everyone as his brother and sister and would reach out to those in need. Little wonder that this man from Co. Sligo would look for opportunities to make life better for the children whom he taught and for their families. And if forming a football club in the East End of Glasgow would help these hungry children then Brother Walfrid from Ballymote would not be shy in doing just that.

'And then came Celtic Football and Athletic Club'

Celtic Football Club was established by Brother Walfrid and other leading members of the Irish community such as John Glass and Pat Welsh. The initial idea of founding of a football club that might to help to provide food and education for the poor children of Irish refugees who had fled Ireland during and in the wake of the Great Hunger. Charities dispensing soup and bread to the poor were widespread throughout Glasgow and many other cities and towns throughout Europe as the industrial revolution attracted many people from the countryside seeking work. Soon after his arrival in Glasgow Brother Walfrid organised the 'Poor Children's Dinner Table' charity in 1867 which fed up to 2,400 of the poorest children in Glasgow in 13 districts in the East End of Glasgow. So when an opportunity came up – quite unexpectedly – to help to support this charity work, it was of no surprise that Brother Walfrid did not let it pass.

While the purpose of Brother Walfrid's charity, and many other similar ventures, was to feed victims of poverty irrespective of creed, some groups used the plight these people found themselves in for other ends. According to Mark Burke:

> Some among the Protestant establishment who perceived an opportunity to thwart the spread of the Catholic threat opened soup kitchens to the swelling throng of starving Irish. A hot meal would be provided upon the simple act of renouncing their faith. Desperate and famished, many felt that they were left with little choice but to 'take the soup'.[4]

This misuse of the soup kitchen – of exchanging faith for food (or 'souperism') was viewed with great fear and loathing by many in the Catholic community as it preyed on the vulnerability of famine victims. It is not that all who offered food-aid at this time were of such a nature. Some leading Anglicans including the Archbishop of Dublin at that time, Richard Whatley, denounced and strongly condemned the practice. Many Anglicans set up soup kitchens that did not proselytise, as did the Quakers whose soup kitchens were concerned solely with charitable work and were never associated with the practice. Yet there were some evangelical Bible societies who did engage in such practices including serving meat soups on Fridays – which Catholics were forbidden by their faith from consuming,

---

4. M Burke, 'The Case for Brother Walfrid', in J Bradley (2004), p. 103.

and by the fact that they couldn't afford meat in the first place. This practice of proselytising spread to the United States of America, England and Scotland and anywhere where the dominant religious ethos viewed the newly arrived Irish with suspicion. Thus, in addition to responding to the needs of the poor in the East End of Glasgow, one of the motivations of Brother Walfrid (himself a Catholic religious brother) in helping to establish Celtic Football Club, would have been to stop 'his flock' effectively turning away from its religious faith in order to gain food. Yet there soon became much more to Celtic than just that.

As most Celtic fans know the club was formally constituted at a meeting in St Mary's Hall in East Rose Street – now Forbes Street – in the Calton district of Glasgow on 6 November 1887 with the purpose of helping to alleviate poverty through forming a football team that would raise much-needed funds for Brother Walfrid's 'Poor Children's Dinner Table'. The story of the founding of Celtic is well known and recorded and involved another club with a very distinctive Irish identity, Hibernians. The Edinburgh club was formed in 1875 in Leith by Irish émigrés from the Cowgate area of the city. It was self-consciously an Irish Catholic club and for the first 12 years of its existence you had to be a member of the Catholic Young Men's Society and have been to mass on the previous Sunday in order to be eligible for selection the following Saturday![5] Hibs was one of a number of football clubs associated with the Irish community around that time including Dumbarton Harp, Inverness Celtic and the short-lived but very interesting Dundee Harp. One remarkable footnote in Scottish football history associated with this now defunct club is that on the 18 September 1875 it secured a (recorded) 35–0 win over Aberdeen Rovers on the very same day that Arbroath thumped Bon Accord 36–0, a score that remains the highest victory in any senior football competition. Even more bizarrely, it seems that the referee in the Dundee Harp – Aberdeen Rovers game had actually made the score 37–0 but the Harp's secretary suggested a miscount must have occurred as he had recorded only 35! The match official, unable to give a precise number of goals scored, accepted the lower number and sent that figure to the Scottish football authorities, depriving Dundee Harps of a possible place in world football history!

It was, of course, the arrival in Glasgow in September of the newly (self) acclaimed 'World Champions of Association Football' (having defeated

5. See, for example, S Dobson and J Goddard, *The Economics of Football* (Cambridge: Cambridge University Press, 2001).

the English Champions, Preston North End), Hibernians of Edinburgh, for a charity match in support of Brother Walfrid's charity that caused quite a stir. It was not the first-string Hibs team that played but their 'star factor' meant that a large crowd of some 12,000 attended that charity match in Renton. Afterwards, and also after 'refreshments' in St Mary's Hall, it seems that the Secretary of Hibernians, John McFadden, challenged the assembled audience to consider doing in Glasgow what Hibs had done in Edinburgh and establish a team that would make the Irish proud! A number of weeks later, on 6 November 1887, Brother Walfrid, John Glass, Pat Welsh and a number of other leading members of the Irish community in Glasgow reassembled and decided to set up a football club in the East End of Glasgow in response to the challenge from the established 'Irish' team from Edinburgh. But what emerged in the East End of Glasgow was completely different from anything had existed before or has been created since. A quite remarkable entity grew among the poorest of the poor in Glasgow and quickly became the source of celebration and hope for the huddled masses in that area and far beyond. Brother Walfrid and his co-founders were always dreaming something else, something new, something beyond even their vision and imagination. Those who founded Celtic Football Club did it entirely differently from their co-religionists and fellow Irish who had been so successful in footballing terms in Edinburgh. Celtic was not simply (or at all) a west of Scotland mirror of their eastern compatriots. It was entirely different from anything that had been seen in Scotland or anywhere else in the world at that time.

Consciously, the founders decided that this new football club would not be confessional or insular. From its inception Celtic was open to all sections of society. While those such as Brother Walfrid, John Glass, Pat Welsh and the other founders of Celtic may have been motivated initially by the horrendous conditions suffered by the Irish emigrants in the East End of Glasgow to establish the club as a means of supporting the children of the impoverished Irish communities in places such as the Calton and Bridgeton, it was the need of the child and not his or her religious background that determined access to support and sustenance. The Glasgow-born historian and educationalist, Frank O'Hagan, points out that the notion of 'charity' is foundational to and a fundamental principle of Celtic Football Club. According to O'Hagan 'the roots and original rationale, mission and raison d'être of Celtic Football Club are inextricably linked to the concept of charity.'[6] O'Hagan goes on to highlight the inclusive and out-reaching nature and vision upon which Celtic was founded and concludes that 'Celtic Football Club, at the beginning of the 21st century, is true to its founder's vision and clearly recognises that it has a wider role in its responsibility of being a major social institution promoting health, well-being and social integration.'[7]

The founders also saw the importance of Celtic as something beyond the material. While the initial primary goal was to help to provide food and education for the poor children of Irish emigrants who had fled Ireland during and in the wake of the Famine, the founding fathers – and not least Brother Walfrid – had a vision beyond that. The beneficiaries of Celtic Football Club – the children, their families and community – were not simply to be pitied and helped: rather, they were to be affirmed and, indeed, celebrated. The leaders of the Irish community who were instrumental in establishing Celtic and driving it forward understood from the outset that they were dealing with something of much greater intrinsic value than a sporting club or a business. Celtic was to become – and remains today – the bearer of a collective identity and the hopes and dreams of a community that had been excluded, marginalised and shunned by sections of the society into which it had arrived. It gave a sense of pride to this community and all who share the love and romance of the triumph of spirit over economics, of dreams over reality. It is little wonder that Celtic is held by its community of supporters as something much more than a football club and most certainly not a brand to be bought, sold and merchandised in the global football market. In marked contradistinction to a simple profit ethic that drives much of modern football, Celtic is underpinned by a sense of history and heritage, a social dimension that includes charity, social outreach and the promotion of the common good, and a philosophy of how to play football with style, flair and passion – as well as a pride in the direct and close connection with its supporters and wider Celtic family. Brother Walfrid – like the religious missionary he was – moved on to other places and other marginalised communities who needed his gifts just as the people in the East End of Glasgow. In 1893, just five years after Celtic played its first competitive game, Brother Walfrid was sent to London by the Marist Order, where he continued his work, organising football matches for and showing great kindness to the

---

6. F. O'Hagan, 'Celtic and Charity' in J Bradley (2004), p. 93.
7. ibid., p. 99.

barefoot children in the districts of Bethnal Green and Bow irrespective of religious or ethnic background. His work in Glasgow was finished. The club he had been instrumental in starting was in good hands and was flourishing and giving great joy to those whom he served and many others took pride in its achievements. It was now becoming a part of life and identity for communities throughout the world. Many young boys like George McCluskey dreamed of pulling the green and white hoops on and running onto the famous Celtic Park in front of a packed Jungle. 'Roy of the Rovers' had nothing on Celtic.

2

'The Apple Does Not Fall Far from the Tree'

GEORGE MCKINLAY CASSIDY MCCLUSKEY was born on 19 September 1957 in Beckford Lodge in Hamilton. He was the third child of John and Teresa McCluskey and the first son of the McCluskey family. It is not known what his two elder sisters Pat (born in 1952) and Jeannette (born in 1954) might have made of this male intrusion into their home other than the arrival of a young brother but it was not long before George was joined by male reinforcements as his brother John was born the following year. The McCluskey family unit was complete with the birth of the youngest sibling, Teresa, in 1974. George was taken from the hospital to the family home which was a small flat in Wylie Street in Hamilton. It was modest enough but certainly a considerable improvement on the housing conditions which previous generations of George's forebears would have endured. George's maternal grandparents lived in one of the 'miners' rows' (or 'raws' as they were commonly referred to) in the town. These were sets of tenement buildings or cottages which, as the name suggests, were built in the late 19th century for miners who worked in the local coal mine. Such accommodation was typical of much of the industrial landscape that formed the backbone of the Scottish economy (especially in the west-central belt of Scotland) in the 19th and first half of the 20th centuries and which made fortunes for mine owners and just about survival for those who worked down the mines and their families. While there were other industries in Scotland during this time, including jute-making in Dundee, fishing in the north east and ship-building on the Clyde – and all of these produced extremely close-knit communities – it was above all coal mining that dominated and defined towns and villages in the west-central belt of Scotland and that shaped communities such as Hamilton. There is nothing uniquely Scottish about this. Mining – and especially coalmining – throughout the world is a special form of industrial enterprise that produced unique communities and individuals. Perhaps it is the back-breaking work and a common sense of mutual reliance on one another in extremely difficult and dangerous conditions; perhaps it is a shared poverty and common living experience. Whatever it was that made them, mining areas have almost universally produced extremely tight-knit communities that are built on and exhibit values such as solidarity, self-reliance, determination and compassion for those in need.

It was precisely into this type of community that George McCluskey was born and in which he grew up. George's father, John, had been a miner himself for a number of years and had been working in the mines in Fife when George was born. This was typical for many of the men in the Lanarkshire region and many of the towns and villages such as Glenboig, Carfin, Uddingston and Coatbridge – as well as Hamilton – owed their existence and development to the mining industry. Going down the mine was generally the only way for those who had no other way to earn a living for their families. Despite the large and – at that time – booming shipyard industry along the Clyde (of which the Govan Shipyard was the first and largest), securing the much more well-paid and safer jobs there was not really a realistic option for many who were descendants of the Irish diaspora that caused tens of thousands of Irish refugees fleeing poverty and famine to arrive in Scotland during the second part of the 19th century. Traditionally people from that community found it difficult to get jobs in the shipyards and tended to find employment in the mines or in road or canal building. Excluded from positions within the labour aristocracy by virtue of their background, many, like John McCluskey, became miners or labourers. It is highly possible that without his wonderful football talent and the institution of Celtic Football Club George McCluskey would have been forced to follow in the footsteps of many from his community. His very name would have revealed where he was from.

A name that contains a family history

George's full name itself contains a small family history which many especially in the west of Scotland can connect with. George was in fact the fourth George McKinlay Cassidy McCluskey. It is not that the boy growing up in Lanarkshire had inherited a royal title, rather he was the fourth person in his family to be called such. Interestingly he was not even the only George McCluskey in his family at that time. George tells a rather interesting story about a cousin of the same name (and approximately the same age) who was not shy in introducing himself to young women in bars and discos as, 'George McCluskey and I play for Glasgow Celtic.' George (the real Celtic footballer) wasn't affected by (or even aware) of his cousin's misuse of his reputation and fame until one day after a match at Celtic Park a young woman tried to get into the players' lounge at Celtic Park after a game claiming that she had met George McCluskey in a bar the night before and he had arranged to meet her after the match in the players' lounge (and 'sure I'll introduce you to all the players'). George (who had just finished playing the game) had to apologise to the young woman – whom he had never met – that she couldn't come in to meet the rest of the team as he didn't know her and then had to explain to his fiancée, Anne (whom he married), that he knew her not!

The name 'George' is one that had been passed on through several generations of the family. The other names are the original surnames of George's ancestors and tell a story of immigration and an escape from poverty and hunger. All three names – McKinlay, Cassidy and McCluskey – are common to the Donegal/north Sligo/south Derry triangle from which so many Irish fled during the 19th century and especially in the decades following the Great Hunger of the 1840s. The name 'McKinlay' is derived from the Gaelic name '*Mac Fhionnlaigh*' ('son of the fair-skinned warrior'). It was a name that was common in Tyrone until the mid-17th century and the arrival of Oliver Cromwell. Branches of the McKinlay clan are found throughout Sligo and Mayo (both counties in the rugged western fringe of Ireland) and may have been 'moved' there due to Cromwell's 'to Hell or to Connaught' ethnic cleansing policy during the 17th century. The name 'McCluskey' comes from the Gaelic '*Bloscaidhe*' which is a branch of the Ó *Catháin* clan which had ownership of large parts of Donegal and Derry up until the early 17th century. On George's mother's side the other surname that appears on the family tree is O'Hara. Again this is a surname prominent in Co. Sligo and Co. Donegal and is an Anglicised form of the Gaelic 'Ó *hEaghra*'. George's younger brother John has carried out extensive research into the McCluskey family background and confirms that all of the branches of the McCluskey family's antecedents fled Ireland in the aftermath of the Great Hunger and sought refuge in the villages and towns of the west of Scotland and in areas such as Calton and the Gorbals in Glasgow. They were most certainly part of that great wave of migration that arrived in Scotland from poverty-stricken Ireland during those traumatic decades. The Scotland they found was not quite the welcoming and open society these new migrants might have hoped to find. Their Gaelic language and Catholic religion did not endear this community to the host Scottish community.

It is difficult for us today to comprehend the degree of hostility and suspicion that this wave of outsiders encountered in their new homeland and the social exclusion that persisted for subsequent generations. At that time Scotland was not simply an overwhelmingly Protestant country, it was almost exclusively so. The Protestant Reformation had created a national Church, strongly Calvinistic and Presbyterian in outlook. By the start of the 19th century the Catholic population of Scotland had shrunk almost to the point of elimination. It made up around one per cent of the total population, concentrated in Banffshire region in the north east, a few remote and inaccessible glens and some of the Western Isles such as Barra and South Uist. According to the 1801 Census, Glasgow (a city with a population of more than 77,000 at the time) had only 28 Catholic residents – and 32 anti-Catholic organisations![8]

But, despite the hardship and suspicion that these first generations of Irish immigrants encountered, they had at least found an escape from starvation – and they set about building a new life in Scotland. They were enormously resourceful and hardworking. They possessed a very deep sense of solidarity and communal spirit. Every obstacle and challenge could be, and was, overcome. If access to social advancement was a barrier due to their ethnic identity and religious adherence then they would seek advancement through getting education for their children. If access to education was an issue then they would build their own schools and train their own teachers. The McKinlay, Cassidy and McCluskey families – like the tens of thousands of others who had made the journey to Scotland – arrived, found a place to live and then began to develop as a community in the villages and towns throughout the west-central belt of Scotland. In those early days they may have had little, but they also had much – a strong sense of self-help, sharing, solidarity, family and care for those in need. Their own experience certainly shaped them to create a special space where they settled and forged an identity that continues to reach out to others and especially the vulnerable members of society – a trait not lost on Celtic Football Club. It was in such a community that supported one another that the young McCluskey grew up.

---

8. Interviewed on *Celtic: the Irish* Connection, Joe Bradley points out that there were only two Catholics living in the entire county of Lanarkshire at this time.

'It takes a village to raise a child'

There is a wonderful ancient African proverb that tells us that 'it takes a village to raise a child'. This expresses the belief that all of us are formed, moulded and shaped by the community, people and social interactions around us – and especially the extended family. None of us are asocial individuals. What we grow up to be tends to be what we were encouraged to become.

Of course you do not need to hold a doctorate in social development or child psychology to grasp the underlying truth of this saying. Throughout the history of the world and in almost every single culture the importance of the extended family and community for the protection, development, education, nurturing and affirmation of the child has long been universally recognized and acclaimed. This is particularly true at times of crisis – be it within individual families when a member of the family needs to be supported, or on a much wider scale such as when entire groups of people face severe socio-economic challenge, exclusion, discrimination, marginalisation and threat. It is truly remarkable that throughout human history many have found hope and salvation in and through that single most supportive social institution – the extended family. So it was for the families that settled in tenements in areas in and around Glasgow, such as the Gorbals, the Garngad, Clydebank, Govan, Calton and Port Glasgow, as well as in numerous towns and villages throughout the west-central belt of Scotland including Coatbridge, Croy, Carfin, Hamilton, Birkenshaw, Viewpark and Uddingston. Circumstances may have been difficult in terms of material wealth but these communities possessed something much richer than simple material wealth. Friendship, mutual support, solidarity and, above all else, love became the core values for those extended families that formed the new communities which first of all survived and then began to thrive in their new home. Being part of a large and close family had many benefits, and George's mother could turn to any of her own siblings for help. There was one night in particular when her younger sister, Mary, did indeed provide crucial help as George's Aunt Mary recalls:

> It was a Friday night and I went to visit Teresa in Hamilton as I usually did. George was about a year old and a normal healthy baby. But this night he was a bit unsettled and disturbed in the cot. We checked George and he had a roaring temperature. Suddenly he went completely

limp and then into a severe fit and shaking all over with his eyes rolling
in his head, and a real fever. Teresa started to scream and cry and ran
out shouting for help. I don't know where I had got the idea from but I
ran into the kitchen and soaked a towel in cold water and applied it to
George's head. A nurse, Mrs Gribbin, lived in the flat above and must
have heard Teresa shouting for help. She came down and together we kept
placing cold towels on George's head and body until the ambulance came.

George was taken to the Strathclyde Hospital in Motherwell where he
spent the next couple of days. The seizure caused him to lose partial sight
in his right eye – which almost led him to fail the medical when he was
being transferred to Leeds United. But it could have been much more
serious than that. The doctor informed the family that had it not been
for the prompt action of George's Aunt Mary it is highly possible that the
infant McCluskey could have died before medical help arrived that night.

For the McCluskey family Hamilton had served well as a place of birth
and early years. However, it was not to become the permanent home for
this young family. A move down the old Edinburgh Road to the village of
Birkenshaw was undertaken. The move from Hamilton to Birkenshaw by
the McCluskey family may not appear to be a major one; after all, they
are two small and similar villages in the same region of western Scotland
only a couple of miles apart. The communities were very similar and
were, in fact, often linked through family ties. Indeed, this was the reason
that George gives for the move to Birkenshaw. Teresa (George's mother)
was a girl from that village and her family lived there. Many know and
understand that there is a common desire for a young mother to bring
up the new family in the company of her parents and siblings where the
children can be close to their grandparents and find instant friends in their
cousins. George's memories of growing up in Birkenshaw as a young child
are happy ones. His father was a hard-working provider for his family.
Like many other devoted husbands and fathers, John had to make difficult
sacrifices in life to provide for his family. Work was hard and (often) scarce
for people of his background and John was forced to take whatever work
was available. Yet he did so without complaint, avoiding passing on to any
of his children a sense of bitterness or regret. John and Teresa brought up
their children to respect everyone, to have concern for those in need and
to understand what was really important in life. These values are ones that
George and Anne and the rest of the extended McCluskey family have

sought to pass on to the next generation – and a love for Celtic Football Club and everything it stands for sits easy with that.

In today's materialist world in which parents are pressured and almost bullied by the advertising industry to buy the 'must have' latest consumer goods for their children, George tells a story about his own upbringing and how the (apparently) simplest things can contain profound truths and values. It was coming towards his fourth birthday. His mother had told him that he was special (as she did with all her children) and that they – just the two of them – would have a special day. George tells it as follows:

> I reckon that it was about a week before my fourth birthday – though at the time it seemed like an age for a wee boy to keep a secret. My mother showed me a big bottle of lemonade and some cakes and sweets that she had hidden behind the sofa and said, 'George, we'll have a great day when you're four... just don't tell your sisters.' I remember as a wee boy feeling special, looking at the sofa that hid my treat and knowing that I was indeed special. My mother brought me and my younger brother, John, who was just about walking at the time, to the local park and we had a wonderful day on the swings and roundabouts and drinking lemonade and eating sweets. The fact that I remember this still shows just how much this means to me. My parents weren't rich in terms of material wealth but they gave all of their children everything they ever needed.

'What do you think of my children, Aidan?'

The values that George McCluskey observed and experienced in his own growing up have not been lost on him. The understanding of the important things in life and how excessive material wealth contains hidden dangers was revealed to me in a late-night conversation that George and I had some years ago while washing dishes in his house! It was the night before a Celtic v Rangers game at Ibrox and we had just finished a beautiful meal (cooked by George's wife Anne). George and I were on 'dishes duty' and solving the problems of the world, Celtic and lots beside. The conversation came round to talking about George's career, his transfers and experiences playing for different clubs. I then asked him if he ever wished if he had been 10 years younger. 'Why would you ask that?', George responded. Well, I mused, George moved to Leeds from Celtic in 1983 and if he had have made that move 10 years later then he would have got serious money and probably would have been a rather wealthy man by now. The conversation between George and myself went around the idea that if he had have been playing at his peak in the 1990s instead of the 1980s then he would have been getting (say) £10,000 per week – which was not excessive for a top striker in England during the 1990s – and that he and his family would have been set for life. Tempting or what? George went quiet for a minute as he gathered a response. 'What do you think of my children, Aidan?' I was somewhat taken aback by this question and wondered what on earth this had to do with my original one. Well, I give my honest opinion and stated that the three girls, Leeanne, Natalie and Ashleigh, and his son Barry, struck me as very rounded and extremely friendly and polite young people who were (are) a credit to their parents. But what had this to do with being 10 years younger? George then gave me an insight into his own thinking on raising children and the values that he had tried to pass on to them – values that he had been handed down to him for his mother and father:

I love my children and hope that Anne and I have brought them up correctly and given them the right values to live their lives by. They worked hard at school and know the importance of education. They understand that to get on in life you need to work hard. They are close to the guys they grew up with and with their cousins and all the other relatives. I'd hope that if they see anyone in need that they'd help them. I wonder what values they might be living their lives by today if they had been brought up surrounded by wealth and opulence. Perhaps they may have grown up fine and have become the great young people they are today. But I think that the temptation to be materialistic, selfish and self-centred would have been there if they'd been growing up in that scenario. If they grew up like that they mightn't be Celtic supporters today! They certainly wouldn't have their pals, their view on life and so on. The money might have been nice but I can honestly say that there are certain values that Anne and I have passed on to our children that we learned from our own parents and I'm delighted for that. Money isn't everything. In fact it's not very important at all so long as you have enough to live.

The phrase 'the apple didn't fall far from the tree' certainly had a resonance that evening. The early days in Birkenshaw under the love and guidance of Teresa and John McCluskey were not lost on their first son.

3

School Days, Bus Protests and Celtic Win the European Cup!

IN 1961 THE happy life that George had experienced during his first years at home came to an inevitable end as his mother took him on another exciting journey and he took the first and tentative steps that almost every young boy and girl makes – his first day of school! George remembers it as an exciting time as he looked forward to joining up with his big sisters, Pat and Jeanette, who were already at St John the Baptist Primary School in Uddingston. Although it was almost two miles from Birkenshaw it was the nearest Catholic primary school in the area and most of George's cousins and friends went there. George had no difficulties settling in and was, by all accounts, a very well behaved, bright and sociable young boy, popular with teachers and his fellow pupils alike. If school life appears to have been going quite smoothly for the young boy from Birkenshaw there was one incident in particular that still stands out clearly in his memory – the bus protest of 1965.

Standing up for what is right – the mothers in Birkenshaw

On 1 December 1955 a certain Rosa Parks, a seamstress by profession and civil rights activist by vocation, boarded a bus in Montgomery, Alabama. She was sitting in the front-most row in which African Americans were permitted to sit. A white man got on the bus and the driver, James F Blake, instructed all those in the 'coloured section' of the bus to move back as in line with company segregation policy which dictated that when the section reserved for whites was full the driver could order those in the 'coloured section' to move back or stand to make room for any white passengers who had boarded the bus. All the African Americans on the bus complied with the instruction of the bus driver except one – Rosa Parks. James F Blake was not unknown to Rosa Parks. Some 12 years earlier Rosa had the misfortune of attempting to board the city bus driven by Blake who ordered her to board from the back door only to drive off leaving her at the bus stop. Rosa Parks swore never to suffer such humiliation and injustice again. And she was true to her promise and refused to move. She was promptly arrested, brought to the police station and convicted in court. This led to a campaign led by the civil rights activist, Martin Luther King, of the boycotting of public buses until the authorities declared an end to public transport segregation. After 381 days the civil authorities (prompted by the bus companies) caved in and declared an end to segregation in the public transportation sector. Rosa Parks' refusal to give up her seat proved to be a seminal event in the civil rights protest against the policy of racial segregation and discrimination in the southern States of America. Almost a decade after that dramatic action by Rosa Parks that sparked the 'Montgomery Bus Boycott', a group of women – mostly mothers – in a remote and little-known village called Birkenshaw did something quite similar and no less important. This most unlikely group of radicals decided that they had had enough and would no longer 'sit at the back of the bus' – even if there was no bus!

The Birkenshaw Bus Boycott

It may not have been quite the same world-breaking news of the Montgomery Bus Boycott, nevertheless the Birkenshaw version of peaceful protest was motivated by the same feeling of an injustice towards the children of St John the Baptist School (and, by extension) the wider community. The dispute arose at the start of the new school year in 1965 around the provision (or, more accurately, non-provision) of transport for the children of Birkenshaw who attended St John the Baptist in Uddingston. The distance between the two towns is approximately a mile and a half. This in itself might be considered as quite a daunting journey for children of primary school age, especially when the weather was bad and in the darkness of the winter months. Many of the mothers who had to bring their children to school also had younger children not of school age or babies in prams. The journey from Birkenshaw to St John the Baptist often took an hour each way by foot. In order to get to school three major roads – busy even then – had to be crossed and the numbers having to make the journey were increasing as the population of

Birkenshaw increased. Then, in the early 1960s, the authorities provided a school bus to bring children from Birkenshaw and the surrounding area to the non-Catholic primary school in Tannochside. The parents of the children at St John the Baptist school expected something similar. After all, Tannochside Primary School was much closer to Birkenshaw than St John the Baptist in Uddingston was and only one road had to be crossed. The Catholic school authorities wrote in requesting a similar arrangement for the children who had to travel to their school. So did the parents. The North Lanarkshire authorities simply ignored these requests. The conclusion that the authorities were treating the parents and children of St John the Baptist's differently from their peers at Tannochside as a result of their status as a Catholic school was, unsurprisingly, reached by many of the parents and in 1965 the mothers decided that they'd had enough and that the children would not attend school until the education authorities provided a bus.

George's mother, Teresa, was not a natural rebel or troublemaker. Nor was Teresa Toal. The two women had been best friends since childhood and this friendship had only deepened as they began to raise their own families. The McCluskeys and Toals lived side by side and the Toal children – Ellen, Teresa, Edward and Peter – were more like family members than friends for the McCluskey siblings. Teresa McCluskey and Teresa Toal – like all the rest of the parents of the children at St John the Baptist – just wanted to raise their families. They were most certainly not militant agitators. They were much too busy for that. Yet they were not to be walked all over and felt that the authorities were wrong in their treatment of their community and, especially, of their children. They simply would not stand for it. They had rights and if the authorities would not recognise these then the community would make them. The sense of extended family, common identity and solidarity on which the tight-knit community of Birkenshaw was built quickly came to the fore as the campaign to get a school bus began with Teresa McCluskey and Teresa Toal playing a leading role. According to George it was all quite simple and civilised; yet it also revealed an inner strength and determination of the women and mothers who were primarily in charge of the day-to-day raising of their children. Every morning the children would put on their school uniforms as usual. However, instead of making their way to Uddingston to school, they would go with their mothers to Birkenshaw Circle where the main bus stop was and wait for a bus which, of course, wouldn't come. Around 9.15 they'd all head off back home, change out of their uniforms and go out and play. This daily ritual was kept up for a number of days until the educational authorities gave in and provided transport for the children of St John the Baptist, much to the disappointment of George and his pals who were quite prepared to stay out on protest for longer. At the time and at the age of eight missing school didn't seem to be such a sacrifice provided that a football match could be organised among the 'protestors'. Looking back on it, the campaign by the women of Birkenshaw was quite remarkable indeed and no small victory of ordinary people motivated by a sense of justice for their children over seemingly more powerful authorities. For the young McCluskey growing up, this action became part of the folklore of a confident and self-reliant community that refused to see itself as second class. It also served as a reminder, if one was needed, that there were people who did think like that. Awareness of difference and belonging to a somewhat 'outside' community was a constant in growing up in the west of Scotland. Not that this in any way led to isolation or inferiority on the part of these communities in which George found himself. They possessed a shared sense of common identity that owed much to Ireland as the country of their forebears. It was an almost unconscious one at that, an awareness of their difference as a community with its own story to tell about where it came from, what shaped and influenced it and what values and views it had on life that it held dear and sought to pass on to subsequent generations. In addition to this it also possessed a quite unique and precious vehicle through which it could (and continues to) remember and celebrate its identity – Celtic Football Club.

School days and holidays

For George McCluskey and his pals the victory of the mothers and community of Birkenshaw meant that when they were once again brought to the bus stop at Birkenshaw Circle a bus would dutifully arrive and take the children to school where the 'real business' of learning would begin as normal. George enjoyed school and was a keen student who sought to do his best. Encouraged by his parents and in the company of his sisters, cousins and friends, the young McCluskey thrived in the close-knit atmosphere in the primary school. There was, of course, one school activity George lived for – football:

I know that it's a cliché and people often say that school days are the happiest time of your life, but for me, my days in St John the Baptist were full of very happy memories. I loved learning, meeting my friends and, above all, football matches at lunch time! It wasn't so much a game but a sort of *melee* when our class would play another class with the minimum of rules or regulations. Usual kids' stuff – the object of the game was to score more goals than the other team.

Yet, like many other wonderful footballers throughout the world, it was in a school yard like the one in St John the Baptist and the 'football field' like the one in Birkenshaw that George McCluskey began to develop the skills that would lead him to becoming a Celtic legend. Also, it seems, skills that are developed in youth academies and at special coaching courses today, were developed very much in the playground for those of George's generation and often through having to improvise to overcome some basic challenges such as trying to keep your shoe on when you had a shot at goal!

Every summer, just before we get ready to go back to school, my mother would take us into Glasgow to get our school uniforms and shoes which had to do you for the year. This was a big financial challenge for my parents (given that there were four of us at school at the time) and, like every other family from a working class background, my mother would have paid the bill 'on tick'. Your mother would have bought you a pair of black slip-on plimsolls or 'gutties' (as we called them) which were used during PE or for playing football at lunch-time. The shoes had a canvas upper, a rubber sole and an elasticated tongue which kept them on. For a young lad running around after a ball in the playground 'gutties' were perfect – except when the elasticated tongue began to suffer under the wear and tear of endless football games. I distinctly remember when it happened to me and that I ended up with a pair of 'gutties' in which both of the elasticated bits had more or less gone. Trying to get past a whole crowd of defenders was hard enough with your shoes falling off but having a crack at goal often ended up with the ball heading towards the target closely followed by your shoe! I put down my ability to dribble and keep close control of the ball in tight situations in my playing days to those lunch time games when I simply tried to keep the ball and not lose my shoe.

Whether or not it was a result of this unorthodox training method, the young George McCluskey was showing considerable promise and became a regular member of his school team. Normally it was comprised of the students in their final year at school (Primary Seven). George played for it for three years, making his debut while still only in Primary Five. The experience of playing against other boys who were all older, bigger and stronger than he certainly stood him in good stead as he developed as a player and gave him an appetite for what was to come.

Not that everything in those days was about school and football. There was also the serious matter of summer holidays and, like families everywhere, these couple of weeks were precious indeed. It gave the family (and relatives and friends) an opportunity to step outside of their busy lives and connect with each other away from the routine of everyday life. For hardworking parents like John and Teresa McCluskey, this was an opportunity for what is now called quality family time. Holidays for the McCluskey clan were important indeed and much looked forward to by the entire family and community. This was before the time of cheap air travel that has made foreign holidays possible for many people today. Yet it was a time for freedom, adventure, fun and excitement. Those two weeks in the summer in Rothesay on the Isle of Bute were really looked forward to by George, his family and friends. There may not have been any Mediterranean sun, water worlds or theme parks, but for young families from the places like Lanarkshire, Glasgow and the west of Scotland region generally, places like Rothesay had a special quality. It was a place where the McCluskey children and their friends and cousins could play all day long and parents could relax. It was also an opportunity for George's father and his pal, Eddie Toal (Teresa Toal's husband), to make some money from the unsuspecting visitors from Glasgow. George recalls those days:

> We all loved the annual visit to Rothesay in the summer. All the cousins, aunties, uncles, friends and neighbours seemed to descend upon the ferry for Rothesay for those two weeks and for our family it was ideal with loads of company and football and games all day long. They were called the 'Co (or Co-op) holidays' as they were booked through the Co-operative Company with your mother saving a certain amount every week or month in her Co-op account to pay for them. One of the highlights was the sports day which, as far as I can recall, was held

quite early on. I suppose it was a way of getting us all together at the start of the holiday. It also turned out to be a way of my father and his pal from Birkenshaw, Eddie Toal, making some money which our families would benefit from throughout the fortnight.

According to George, his father and Eddie Toal used the two McCluskey boys' athletic ability to good stead. They were exceptionally quick – the fastest runners in their respective age groups. The two men from Birkenshaw would make sure that everyone (and especially the unsuspecting Glaswegians) would hear just how good the two McCluskey boys were and that they were 'certs' to win their races. The boys would then be sent out in the heats with strict instructions to qualify for the final but not to look too impressive. This they did with ease and bets were placed which, on the basis of the evidence witnessed, led many from Glasgow to bet against the pair from Lanarkshire. Needless to say there were some astonished looks on the faces of some when the two lads romped home easy winners and smiles on the faces of John McCluskey (senior) and Eddie Toal as they collected their winnings! All that training and playing football hadn't gone to waste. There were, of course, other things happening around that time that also encouraged the young Lanarkshire lad's desire to play football at the highest level – including one unforgettable evening in May 1967.

'So where were you when Celtic won the European Cup?'

In every generation certain watershed moments occur that seem to define the era and remain etched in the memory of those who witnessed them. For some it might be when Neil Armstrong took those first steps on the moon, the collapse of the Berlin Wall or the release of Nelson Mandela from captivity on Robben Island. For people of a certain generation and from a certain background an event in Portugal on 25 May 1967 can certainly be seen as a watershed moment that left an indelible memory on those lucky enough to have witnessed it. Get a group of Celtic fans who were living during that time together and inevitably the question crops up, 'So, where were you when Celtic won the European Cup?'

For George and his family and many of his friends, supporting Celtic was not a choice between supporting one team or another. It was not even a sporting decision. To follow Celtic was part of everyday life and identity of the community in which George grew up. There was nothing unique about Birkenshaw or many of the other centres where the Irish had settled in the west of Scotland. It was, and remains, the same throughout so many countries in the world. Celtic supporters clubs and associations exist the length and breadth of Scotland, England and Wales. In Ireland it is almost inevitable that even for those who have been seduced by the incessant media fixation with the English Premier League, or who follow some other team due to family loyalty or simple curiosity or the desire to be different, supporting Celtic is a given. In the USA and Australia people get out of their beds at unearthly hours and drive huge distances to meet up with their fellow Celtic supporters to catch the games on television. Go to the remotest parts of the planet with a green and white hooped shirt on and pretty soon someone will come up to you and ask how Celtic are doing.

It is not just among those who can trace their roots back to Ireland that the love of this great club abides. Celtic has a romantic attraction about itself that is quite inexplicable and ineffable. Many people with no connection whatsoever with Scotland, Ireland or the Irish diaspora have fallen in love with the green and white hooped shirt and those who wear it. Part of it – and only a small part of it – may come from Celtic being the first club outside of Spain, Portugal or Italy to win the European Cup. More than that, it was how Celtic did it that both stunned and delighted many as it did so. That night in May 1967 is etched in the memory of many football fans of a certain age throughout the world as an (apparently) unfancied team from Scotland completely took apart what was considered to be one of Europe's finest teams – the formidable Inter Milan. What makes the achievement all the more remarkable is that the Celtic side that played that night had been assembled from within a 30-mile radius of Glasgow and had it not been for a certain Bobby Lennox from Saltcoats the distance would have been 10 miles! The Italian giants had won the European Cup twice in the previous three years and were widely expected to put the upstarts from Glasgow firmly in their place. This scenario was not in the minds or expectations of the thousands of Celtic fans who had travelled to Lisbon or the millions who, like the young George, were glued to the television to watch their heroes set about doing the impossible. Having fallen behind after seven minutes to a penalty Celtic set about trying to break down the famous *catenaccio* (literally 'door-bolt') that had served Inter so well during the 1960s. This was not a simple dull negative system that many teams of questionable ability use when they take a lead and then 'park the bus'. The *catenaccio* is a highly technical and skilful tactical system that relies on an organised and effective backline focused on nullifying opponents' attacks and preventing goal-scoring opportunities. At Inter it had been perfected by their Franco-Argentine trainer, Helenio Herrera, to sap the will of opponents by defending a lead and being ruthlessly effective when the opportunity came. In Herrera's version of this four man-marking defenders were tightly assigned to the opposing attackers while an extra sweeper would pick up any loose ball that escaped the coverage of the defenders. Leading 1–0 so early on meant that the famous defensive shield upon which so much success had been achieved could be employed – and this Inter Milan side was expert at this.

That was the theory, at least, and the hearts of many Celtic fans sank wherever they were watching the game. Yet it was at this point that the form book was ripped up and the received wisdom of so many football 'experts' went out the proverbial window. The Celtic team that Jock Stein had built was not overawed, intimidated or fazed in any way by the enormity of the task it faced. Going behind the pride of Italian football so early on meant that Celtic would just have to go at them and score at least two goals. And how Celtic set about dismantling and unpicking the meanest defence in European football! Wave after wave of Celtic attacks pushed Inter Milan back and quite soon their defending wasn't of the controlled 'master class' mode that one had come to expect from the Italian giants. Inter hung on to half time still a goal to the good but it was through a mixture of desperate defending, a quite inspired display of goalkeeping by the Inter stopper, Giuliano Sarti, who was by far the Italians' best player that night and sheer good luck on the part of the Italians. The one-sided nature of the game can be demonstrated by the statistics. Celtic had an incredible 42 attempts on goal (compared with Inter Milan's five) of which 24 were on target. There were 10 corners in the match – all to Celtic. And the one statistic that really mattered was secured by a thunderbolt of a shot from 25 yards by Tommy Gemmell on the hour mark that not even Sarti in such inspired form could get near and then, with five minutes to go, Bobby Murdoch's shot was deftly turned into the Inter net by Stevie Chalmers making the result Celtic 2 – Inter Milan 1 and turning the football world upside down. Indeed, on that night in May 1967 Celtic had become the first Scottish, British, and northern European team to win European football's greatest trophy. Such was the enormity of the achievement that it moved another great footballing legend from Scotland, Bill Shankly, to tell Jock Stein shortly after the victory, 'John, you're immortal now!'

For the young McCluskey growing up in Lanarkshire the *catenaccio* defensive system of Inter Milan and the tactics that Jock Stein had used on that evening in Lisbon to take the aristocrats of European football to pieces were of no consequence or part of his consciousness or memory. What sticks out in his and the minds of Celtic supporters throughout the world who watched that incredible match that evening was that Celtic had done the impossible. They had gone to the European Cup Final and in front of the tens of thousands of Celtic fans who had gone to Lisbon had destroyed the pride of Italy in the most comprehensive fashion. Like the fans who poured onto the pitch in joyous celebration at the final whistle, George remembers clearly how he, his family, cousins, friends and everyone (it seems) in Birkenshaw ran up and down the streets and into each other's homes celebrating what Celtic had achieved that evening; what they – the Celtic family – had achieved. Then George went with his young brother John to the waste ground where they played football every day and recreated the incredible match that had just taken place in Lisbon until their mother called them in for bed.

Everything had changed – and changed utterly. Nothing would ever be the same. Going to school the next day was full of excitement as everyone recalled the events that had happened the previous evening. For George and his pals at St John the Baptist and in the village of Birkenshaw the very persona of those playing a game of football had been transformed as each sought to be identified with (or more importantly to identify himself with) the legends who had won the European Cup. If you raced down the wing and 'skinned' a couple of opponents then you were indeed just like wee Jinky Johnstone! A thunderous pile driver of a shot made you Tommy Gemmell. If you were a tough competitive wee guy who wasn't afraid of getting stuck in you were no longer regarded as a 'dirty' player: you were Bertie Auld. The tall boy was no longer a big lanky 'drip': he was Billy McNeill. Even the goalkeeper – never the favoured position for kids of that age who all want to run after the ball and score goals – gained status as he was transformed into Ronnie Simpson! And if it transformed how the young boys of St John the Baptist saw themselves playing football in the school yard, the big win had a huge impact on the community that Celtic grew out of and represented. Looking back on that magical night in Lisbon almost 50 years ago still stirs vivid and powerful memories in George and a deep appreciation of what it did to his family, his community and the entire Celtic family:

I suppose as a community we understood that we were different. We would go to school together and to mass in St John the Baptist on Sundays. But we also knew that we had something else that made us special – Celtic. It was part of our identity and how we loved that connection with Celtic. They were us and we were them. What happened in 1967 with Celtic winning the European Cup was unbelievable and gave us such a lift and sense of pride. There was incredible excitement around all our houses and even at such an early age I was aware that Celtic was doing something huge and doing it for us. It was the talk of the whole school and you could literally touch the pride that swept through the community. We could (and did) hold our heads high. We had achieved something that had never been achieved in Scotland or anywhere else in Europe outside of Spain and Italy. And it was achieved by a wonderful group of players who we could go and see on a Saturday, whose names we knew, would sing songs about and, crucially, we could identify with. And all from the Glasgow area! The word 'legend' is overused now days, but the 'Lisbon Lions' are legends and what Jock Stein did was truly remarkable.

Yet this quite incredible achievement by Celtic in 1967 cannot, in itself, explain why so many people around the world who have no Irish or Scottish roots have come to love Celtic. After all, many unfancied sides have created similar upsets in Europe yet have not attracted anything like the same following outside of their respective natural fan base as Celtic have. Twenty-two clubs have won the European Cup/Champions League since the beginning of this competition in 1955–56 and it is fair to say that those with great financial clout have dominated the competition. It is only reasonable to presume that those who can attract the best players (usually with the lure of money) make the greatest progress. Hence the success of teams such as Real Madrid, Barcelona, Manchester United, Bayern Munich, AC Milan etc. Yet, from time to time (and especially before the arrival of the totally obscene money in recent years), an unfancied team (like Celtic during the late 1960s and 1970s) emerged to challenge the seemingly natural order of the world of football. Teams like Feyenoord (1970), Steau Bucuresti (1986) and PSV Eindhoven (1988) can all lay claim to having won the top competition in European club football against general expectation. Yet, wonderful as these achievements were, none of these clubs have been taken to the hearts of supporters throughout the world as Celtic have. George has his own thoughts on the appeal of Celtic to so many football supporters from entirely diverse communities:

Of course that triumph of the Celtic against the odds was almost 50 years ago but it does point to something deeper than just one match or cup victory. Everyone loves the underdog and seeing the form book ripped up. Yet there is far more to Celtic's victory than that. Yes, Celtic do have a certain way of playing football and that night in Lisbon the team certainly did play 'the Celtic way'. The reaction of the fans at the end of the match was incredible and still sends shivers up my spine when I look at the DVD of the game. The joy on the faces of the Celtic fans on the TV that night was the same joy and celebration that I remember on the faces all of my family, aunts, uncles, cousins, and friends that evening. Our supporters are indeed wonderful ambassadors for our club and travel everywhere with pride, dignity and respect for themselves and for others. The idea of Celtic as 'one big family' is something that cannot be emphasised enough and is so valuable. I think that when people meet Celtic fans they very quickly understand that they are not just another group of football fans who are simply passionate about their team. Celtic fans have something different. They have an identity, a way of looking at the world that goes beyond football, a shared sense of history and a great joy in celebrating life – even of the result doesn't go Celtic's way. The Celtic story is an absolutely wonderful and inspiring story and I think that many people can see their own hopes and dreams in this most romantic of clubs with its wonderful supporters. I guess that's why Celtic can reach out to so many beyond its fans base and why the green and white hoops of Celtic is one of the most recognised football shirts in the world today.

These school days in Lanarkshire were indeed happy ones for George McCluskey. Celtic had just won the European Cup and he could dream that he someday would also play in Celtic Park in front of the Jungle against Rangers or 'in the heat of Lisbon' as he played in the school playground of St John the Baptist's or on the 'pitch' in Birkenshaw. The 11 plus qualifications exam was looming and, with it, an end to his primary school days. George was about to move on to the next stage of his life.

4

Moving on, Changing School and Keeping your Appendix

THE LAST YEAR of primary school for most children is dominated by the thoughts of moving on to the 'big' school. This is usually a time of great excitement mixed with uncertainty as one prepares to step into the unknown of the post-primary school and leaving the familiar territory of the primary school (and, often, many friends) behind. At that time this process of transfer from primary to post-primary was facilitated by the results of a rather intimidating public examination which most children sat during their final year at primary school – the dreaded 11 plus qualification exam!

This exam was, in many respects, the most important and, for many, the scariest exam that a young person would sit. It was designed, apparently, to decide if a candidate had academic potential and should be admitted to a grammar school or secondary senior, which offered the chance of sitting Highers and advancing to university, or was of a less academic bent and of a more 'practical' disposition (although there was no test for that) and destined for a place in a junior secondary and then to a trade or unskilled job. And all of this at the age of 11! In addition to the injustice of effectively setting out career paths at such an early age, the pressure that such an exam puts young children under, dividing children from one another and labelling some as 'failures', a further criticism of the 11 plus was that it favoured not so much the brighter children but rather those from more affluent backgrounds. Indeed, throughout their history grammar schools have been very much the preserve of the middle and upper classes. For the children of St John the Baptist Primary School, however, the idea of going to Our Lady's High School or St Joseph's High School in Motherwell, was simply not a realistic choice – for most of them anyway. The vast majority would move together to the junior secondary school, St Catherine's Junior High School in Viewpark, where they would complete their education before entering the world of work. For some, however, this would not be the case and the ambitious and dedicated teachers at St John the Baptist pushed and encouraged their students with the goal of getting some of them, at least, on the road to a possible university education. Every year a small number of the brightest pupils at St John the Baptist's did just that despite all the social disadvantage faced by communities such as Birkenshaw. The 11 plus results were delivered on a Saturday morning in the assembly halls in schools throughout Scotland to anxious pupils who gathered to await to be told in which post-primary school they were being offered a place. On that day George McKinlay Cassidy McCluskey was informed that he had been awarded a place in St Joseph's High School in Motherwell. There was great excitement indeed in the McCluskey home that morning as George recalls:

> I remember the day of the 11 plus results very clearly. I suppose it was a very big day in the life of a wee boy who was about to leave primary school and find out which school he was going to go to for the rest of his school life. I wasn't worried about it at all as my big sister Jeanette and loads of my cousins and friends were already at St Catherine's. We all went home from St John the Baptist on the Friday and wished each other 'Good luck!' but I think that most of us felt that we would come back the next day to get the news that we had 'failed' and would be going to St Catherine's. I suppose that this expectation came from the previous experiences of big brothers and sisters so there was quite a bit of excitement when it was announced that I was going to St Joseph's. Naturally my parents were delighted and proud as were my sisters and brother. Aunts and uncles and neighbours were also thrilled to hear that 'our George' had passed the 11 plus and would be going to St Joseph's in Motherwell next year. I didn't know what to feel – really chuffed... but also a little bit worried about having to go to a school where I wouldn't know everyone. Suddenly coming from a very close family and tight-knit community had become a disadvantage!

Yet getting a child into a 'higher' school also involved considerable costs. The school uniform was more expensive than the junior secondary one, there were additional costs including the school's PE uniform and books to be bought for additional subjects which were not studied at the junior secondary schools. There were also transport costs to Motherwell to be considered but financial concerns were not going to stop this young lad from getting the best chance of an education. Teresa and John McCluskey were not wealthy in material terms but they were certainly determined to help all of their children to achieve their very best and avail of every life-changing opportunity that came their way. As always, a modest family budget was stretched to ensure that the McCluskey children would have the chance to advance in life. George and the rest of the McCluskey children often marvel at how their mother and father managed to meet so many needs, doing so without any apparent fuss or problem. If the children needed something then John and Teresa McCluskey somehow made it possible. And so George McCluskey entered first year at St Joseph's High School in Motherwell at the age of 11.

George's time in the High School was short-lived. Like many young people he found the transition for primary to post-primary very difficult and, unlike in schools today where there are induction programmes and pastoral care support to help young children adjust to their new surroundings, George was very much in a 'sink or swim' culture of all schools in that era – and George was very much sinking. Coming from a school community in which he knew everybody, now he knew only a few. Even the journey to school now was difficult. Whereas on the bus that the mothers had 'won' that took him from Birkenshaw to primary school and on which he knew everyone, he now took a bus to Motherwell on which he knew practically no one. Even break times and lunch times were different. There was no running out into the playground with all your pals and dreaming you were playing for Celtic! Out of his comfort zone and away from his pals, George very quickly went from being the happiest boy in St John the Baptist to becoming a very sad and upset young lad. He describes these days as follows:

I went from being a happy wee lad who knew everyone in his school to a very sad and lonely young boy. It was not that I was bullied or anything like that. I just felt really lonely and missed everyone I had grown up with and who had gone to St Catherine's. Instead of knowing practically everyone in the school (like I did at primary school) I only knew one or two guys in my year group in St Joseph's. My health began to suffer, I had a sore stomach all the time, I felt sick, anxious and depressed and would have cried at the thought of going to school. I guess I was just a wee boy lost.

One of George's closest pals made it from St John the Baptist to St Joseph's High School with him. Paul Brannan confirms George's account of not settling into the new school:

There were about half a dozen of us from St John the Baptist who went to St Joseph's. When our first day came round we naturally kept close to each other. I remember going into Motherwell for lunch on our first day and for almost all of us, this was a big adventure. I recall that even on this first day George seemed very unhappy and didn't want to be there. It was a difficult time for all of us (like all kids making that transition) but George really was struggling. As far as I recall George only spent a couple of days at St Joseph's and then just didn't appear at the bus stop. Soon after we heard that he had transferred to St Catherine's. I also recall some of the teachers at St Joseph's being disappointed that he hadn't stayed as they were looking at having a better football team. Even then the word about George McCluskey being a great player had reached the ears of the teachers there before he even got to St Joseph's.

The move from a close-knit school to the 'big school' hadn't gone well for George but the 11-year-old had a cunning plan. He would feign appendicitis so he wouldn't have to go to school! George laughs about it now but back then it was no laughing matter. This was a very serious and well-thought-out plan (at least in the mind of that 11-year-old boy) to get out of going to school. 'Roger the Dodger' of *The Beano* couldn't have come up with a better plan.[9]

I must have been really desperate to avoid going to school and I guess that in my young mind I had to think of something that would not let my mother and father down. They were so pleased that I had got to the High School and I thought that I would be a failure to them if I couldn't make a go of it. I also knew that they had spent a lot of money on me with the school uniform, books and all that so I didn't want to tell them that they had wasted all this on me. I should have gone straight to my mother and told her how upset and unhappy I was but I was only 11 and wanted to make them so proud of me. Of course

9. 'Roger the Dodger' was a fictional character in the comic *The Beano* whose basic remit was to avoid doing chores and homework which usually involves him concocting complex and ultimately disastrous plans. Like Roger, George's 'cunning plan' was doomed to fail.

they already were and a school uniform didn't matter one bit to them. All they wanted was for their children to be happy. I came up with a plan that would solve my problem and get me out of school without 'letting them down'.

In George's primary school there had been a girl in his class who had appendicitis and she had to go to hospital to get her appendix out. She returned to school some weeks later as right as rain and everyone became experts on appendicitis, its symptoms and its cure. So George took on the symptoms of appendicitis in the hope (!) that he would be able to skip school for some weeks. When he showed all the signs of serious stomach pains his mother took him to the doctor for an examination. George described the 'pain' perfectly and the doctor naturally concluded that he did indeed have acute appendicitis and recommended that it had to be removed as soon as possible. The young lad was most pleased at this and within a couple of days he was lying in a hospital bed to have his appendix removed the following day. The doctor in the hospital told George and his mother what the operation entailed and then he started to have second thoughts. George had to spend the night in hospital on his own contemplating the operation to be carried out the next day and the pain he would be in during his recovery. By the time Teresa McCluskey came the next morning he decided that he didn't have appendicitis after all!

Looking back on it I am sure that my mother didn't think that I really had appendicitis at all. She certainly knew that her 'wee boy' wasn't well and that this episode was a cry for help. A mother knows her children much better than any doctor. So when she came to the hospital and asked me how I was I did what any 11-year-old son would do when he turned to his mother for help. I broke down and told her the truth. There was no scolding, annoyance or embarrassment. She simply smiled at me, gave me a hug and told me that everything would be fine and that 'this wee problem would be sorted out very easily' and that I had nothing to worry about. So I found myself back home again with my appendix still attached and getting ready to go back to school.

This time there was not going to be an unhappy boy going to a strange school. George's parents had decided that his happiness and well-being were much more important than having a son going to a high school.

So they took him out of the school in Motherwell and sent him to St Catherine's where he would be among his former school friends, cousins and neighbours. His older sister Jeannette was there and every lunchtime she would come round to the boys' playground just to keep an eye on him and see if he was settling in ok.

Life has a funny way of repeating itself and years later George and his wife, Anne, faced a similar situation with one of their own children, Natalie. Natalie is their third child and very bright. An extremely talented student Natalie achieved excellent grades in her Highers and secured a place at university in Glasgow. Everyone in the extended McCluskey family was, naturally delighted – not least the proud parents, George and Anne. They understood the importance of education and the opportunities that a university education brings. So their 'wee girl' headed off to start her university education with a spring in her step and a smile on the faces of her mother and father. She was embarking on a journey in life that previous generations wouldn't have dreamed of. Yet it was no plain sailing. Not at all. Natalie was only into her university education a couple of weeks when both George and Anne noticed that things were not right with their daughter:

Natalie wasn't the same girl at all. You'd imagine that when she went to university everything would be exciting and that she'd be coming home with stories about what university life was like and all the things that were happening at college. Yet when you'd come back from work Natalie would be in bed. She was a naturally lively and young lassie who was always the life and soul of any social gathering. You would have thought that Natalie would have been 'tailor made' for university life. Yet this was not the case and Anne and I were very concerned. Natalie would complain about being tired, having a sore stomach and would be profoundly 'down' all the time. Looking at Natalie and how sad she was brought my own memories of my days in the High School back to me and I instantly recognised that she was simply depressed (like I had been all those years ago). The decision was easy and didn't take much agonising or soul-searching. Anne – like my own mother when I was in that same situation – took the lead and simply asked Natalie what *she* wanted to do. It was very much a case of 'forget about what people will think', not 'try to give it another shot'. All we cared about was our daughter and, after a series of long conversations with Natalie about how she was feeling, Anne announced the solution to this young woman's worries just like my own mother had done with me at another time. Natalie left university and once again became the happy young woman she had been. She moved on in life and found her own way back to third-level education becoming a graduate of the Central College of Commerce in Glasgow specialising in information management. Today Natalie is a civil servant. I guess my own experience as a young boy stuck with me and helped myself, Anne and Natalie make the right decision. The happiness and wellbeing of your children should always be your primary concern. I learned that from my own parents and hope I've passed than on to my children too.

For a bright student like George, going to St Catherine's may have been a 'step down' in terms of academic demands and potential future life choices. But for George it was exactly the right move. He was now among his pals, friends and family. And he could resume dominating the boys' playground at lunch-time when the football appeared and a school yard in Viewpark (where Celtic legends like the great Jinky Johnstone was from) was transformed into 'Paradise' indeed. Moving from primary school to post-primary school had been eventful to say the least. Now it was about to get even more eventful.

Early Playing Days and Signing for Celtic

5

Starting on the Road to Paradise

School Football, the Red Rockets, Orange Towels and the Celtic Boys Club

THE RECONNECTION OF George McCluskey with his pals in St Catherine's following his weeks in St Joseph's and his brush with appendicitis was both easy and welcome. He was back with most of those who he had been at primary school with and not among strangers. Indeed, George knew many at St Catherine's from the outset since he had had a 'three year football career' on the school team at primary school. Academically he had no problems and was most certainly one of the brightest students in his year group. Yet the normal pathway to the world of work via an apprenticeship or technical college was not on the radar of the young lad from Birkenshaw who was, by now, lighting up the playground and football pitch at St Catherine's. Although football was being played 24/7 by many of the young lads in the school, St Catherine's didn't have a school football team and so George had to look elsewhere to start his football career at junior level.

George didn't start as a 'Red Rocket'. The Blantyre Red Rockets (to give them their full title) was a junior football club set up by George's father. John McCluskey had been working in the steelworks in Ravenscraig at that time and, shortly before he set up the 'Red Rockets' he was approached by one of the coaches from Coltness United who was keen on signing young George for the club. Coltness was a very successful junior boys football club that could boast the legendary Tommy Gemmell, fellow Celt Bobby Jeffery and Motherwell player Sandy Jones as players who were graduates of the Lanarkshire team's youth team system. This is what grassroots football was all about and John McCluskey had no reservations whatsoever in placing his young lad in the hands of this well organised and prominent club. The first step on the ladder. The fact that most of the team was Protestant – due to the religious breakdown of that part of Scotland – was never an issue to George or his father who attended as many matches as possible and watched his son blossom into one of the most promising footballers of his age group. Not long after George had started playing for Coltness John started his own boys' team in the nearby town of Blantyre and, sure enough, the inevitable happened. Much to John McCluskey's delight his team, the Blantyre Red Rockets made the final of the Lanarkshire and District under-12 competition in their first year... but only to face Coltness under-12s – a very powerful and successful team with a lethal weapon that no other under-12 team had been able to stop, one George McCluskey.

I remember the final well. It was 1969 and we had a really good team then and I was pretty much the target to get the ball to. My experience playing for the school team at St John the Baptist while under-age meant that I was never going to be intimidated by some big lad who was assigned to mark me. We were well coached and playing at a level much above everyone else in our age-group. One thing I always remember about my father at that time was that even though he had started his own boys' team and obviously knew that I would be a really good asset for his club he never once tried to get me to switch teams and join the Rockets. The longer I have been training young teams at Celtic the more I have come to appreciate just how my father put my own football development first and above his own team's interests. Often coaches of under-age teams can get completely fixated on their own team or club. My father and a couple of his pals had set up this club for young guys in our own area of Lanarkshire and invested countless evenings and weekends training, coaching and looking after these kids. The easiest and most natural thing he could have done was to say to me 'Look son. You're doing well and playing some great football. You can join the Red Rockets and be a star here too.' And, of course, I would have joined at a heartbeat. The Red Rocket boys were mostly from my own area and many of them were my pals from school. And as for my father, sure he had been the first person who showed me to kick a ball, my first coach, mentor and was, after all, my own father. Yet he never thought of doing that for one second. As far as he was concerned his young boy was being well looked after, developing as a footballer and was, above all else, happy. He looked forward to all my games and took great pride in all my goals, even at that level, and wished me all the best every time I played... except once. It was the night before the match and my father and I were speaking about the game the next day. It's not that my father was looking for me not to give it my best shot but I guess that he knew that none of his boys could cope with me. He just smiled at me and said, 'OK, George, I hope you've a great game tomorrow... just hope you're not too hard on my boys'.

The next day Coltness beat the Blantyre Red Rockets 4–1 with George McCluskey scoring a hat-trick. Lucky that the young lad wasn't too hard on his father's team! One thing, however, did put a bit of a sour taste into George's first experience of 'real football' in Scotland – even at under-age level. George distinctly remembers the excitement of going into the team's dressing rooms and seeing them laid out for the first time with shirts and shorts on pegs and beside each boy's space on the bench was an orange towel. The choice of colour would scarcely have been an accident or an oversight. The Coltness side that day was predominantly Protestant while the Red Rockets were drawn from a more Catholic (but not exclusively) Catholic part of Lanarkshire. To place orange towels on the benches of an under-12 team as they prepared to play a football match reveals much about how some adults viewed the game. George remains philosophical if, perhaps, somewhat disappointed about that detail:

We were only kids going to play what for us was the biggest game in our lives. For someone to decide that a new set of towels should be provided should have been great and given us young lads a sense of importance of the occasion and what it meant to us as footballers setting out on our journey in this great game. Someone, somewhere in the club decided on the colour and I am certain that they would have known exactly what this meant. The fact that a young Catholic called McCluskey was running riot through every opposition defence wouldn't have factored into their thinking at all. But it speaks so much more about the adults who chose that than the young boys I was playing with. As for my father? After he got over the disappointment of the defeat and the mixed emotions of his son scoring a hat-trick against his team, he scarcely mentioned the orange towel incident. I suppose he thought like me (or like what he and my mother had taught me) and not to make something as petty as selecting a certain of towel annoy you. The guys I was playing with were great lads and the coaches were great in making us work hard, develop our skills and keep looking at the chance of moving forward to the next level. I'm pretty sure that that was the last time when I was in a dressing room decked out with orange towels.

It was indeed the last time for George's time playing for Coltness had come to an end. He switched straight away to the 'Rockets' with similar effect. Shortly after scoring that hat-trick against the Red Rockets George hit another one – this time for the Blayntyre Red Rockets and against Celtic Boys Club. The very next day the manager of the Celtic Boys Club called round to see John McCluskey and the young lad from Birkenshaw promptly moved to the club that was always going to get him anyway. He joined Celtic Boys.

Celtic Boys: the next rung on the ladder

The club was established in 1966 and initially based in the Maryhill district of Glasgow and for a short time was independent of Celtic Football Club. Former Celtic player and chief scout at Celtic, John Higgins, recognised the potential of such a club and established a relationship between the two, principally through convincing the authorities at Celtic to allow the boys club to avail of Celtic's training facilities at Barrowfield. Soon Celtic Boys Club became a 'feeder club' or junior football 'academy' which would attract and develop young talent and identify and pass on some of the best young talent in Scotland to the club from which it got its name. It soon became a conveyor belt for talented (mostly) Celtic minded youngsters and many successfully 'graduated' from this junior club to wear the green and white hoops at Celtic Park with distinction. These include Roy Aitken, Charlie Nicholas, Gerry Crainey, Paul and Willie McStay, Peter Grant, Joe Miller, Derek White, Tosh McKinlay, John Kennedy, Gary Caldwell, Stephen McManus and many more too numerous to list. It was a big step up for George both in terms of competition for a place on the first team but also in terms of expectation and profile. George was very much in the eye of those who were on the lookout for new and exciting talent and all the more so as he had already developed a reputation for being special indeed.

George relished the new challenge of playing at a higher level. It was something that was second nature for him from primary school football to Coltness. Moving up to new levels didn't seem to faze him even at this early stage. He was used to 'stretching himself' from primary school. But his seemingly almost nonchalant and modest attitude was accompanied by a determination to push himself as far as he could go and an abundance of talent and ability. One of his best pals, John Burns, was also playing for Celtic Boys at that time. They lived only a couple of doors apart in Birkenshaw and were ideal training partners for each other – 'Burnsie' being a goalkeeper and George a striker. The two 13-year-old boys became part of life in Birkenshaw at that time as people walked home from work or the shops passing two young boys practicing football every evening together. One was developing his shooting skills and the other his diving and saving – and both dreaming of playing for Celtic.

John Kirkwood was also a member of the same Celtic Boys Club team as George and an extremely talented footballer himself. John came from Viewpark – about a mile from Birkenshaw and a celebrated small (originally) mining town that produced the legendary Jinky Johnstone. Football and Celtic was the life-blood of every young lad in Viewpark and John was staring for St Columba's Boys' Guild which had won the league and cup the previous season. Standing at the bus stop on the way back from school, John overheard a conversation between some of his school and teammates. It was his close friend, Tam Brannan, who, accidentally, introduced John Kirkwood to the name 'George McCluskey'.

We all think that Kirky's good, but I watched St Catherine's playing. They have a guy, George McCluskey from Birkenshaw and I tell you – what a player – even better than Kirky! I'm telling you, this guy is something special.

The natural disappointment of the now crestfallen Kirkwood who had just been put down by his peers was soon replaced by a curiosity of who this upstart was and just how good he really was. John didn't have long to wait. In 1972 he trialled for Celtic Boys and was placed on the right-side of midfield in a forward line led by the (by then) established first striker, George McCluskey. John's own account of that trial is modest and self-effacing and he no doubt must have made a very good impression on the coaches as he was selected to play for Celtic Boys in a semi-final against the Spurs Boys Club on the following Wednesday evening. John just records in his thoughts of his trial for Celtic Boys that 'I can't remember much about George on that first day except that he scored a couple of goals, an occurrence to which I would become accustomed.' The next time he would meet up with George would be on the bus to the game against Spurs Boys Club the following week. Travelling as a member of Celtic Boys would not be without a bit of concern or even a cost though.

Wearing the green and white with pride – and pain

Viewpark bus stop is two stops the other side of Glasgow from Birkenshaw Circle. John Kirkwood would have been worried that evening that he would be on time and was on the correct bus for Barrowfield. He was both delighted and relieved to see two guys he recognised looking out for him as the bus pulled up at the bus stop at Birkenshaw. It was George and the Celtic Boys' goalkeeper, John Burns. They were not hard to spot. John Kirkwood was in normal, non-descript clothes like any other young teenage lad and carrying a standard sports bag. George and John Burns, on the other hand, stood out in the full Celtic Boys regalia – white shirt, green blazer, grey trousers, Celtic tie and (just in case there was any doubt) Celtic kit bag. John Kirkwood was totally awe-struck. For the young lad from Viewpark this was a realisation of the enormity of what he was getting into. This was real Celtic and there was no mistaking that these were young men who were marked out as potential future players for the great Glasgow Celtic. The game that evening was a success for Celtic (winning 2 -1) and for young Kirkwood. He had passed the test on a cold, wind-swept pitch at Tory Glen (near Hampden) and could now wear the Celtic Boys uniform with pride over the next few years as he travelled to training and games with his new friend from Birkenshaw who had, indeed, proved the assessment of his pal from St Columba's, Tam Brannan, right. The friendship established on the bus that night from Viewpark and on the football pitches with Celtic Boys Club has continued to this day and George McCluskey and John Kirkwood remain firm friends living only a couple of houses apart in Uddingston. But travelling together and dreaming of playing for Celtic was not always without challenges. Not everyone you met were 'Celtic minded' and being a young lad dressed in Celtic gear did not always attract the reaction that one might have wanted. John describes the typical experiences of a member of the Celtic Boy Club:

The journey to training and games was a mixed experience. You felt a pride in yourself, family and community since the uniform obviously identified us as possible Celtic players. Being dressed in the shirt, tie and blazer had the effect of making you feel professional and proud. However as you crossed into unknown territory, things could become a little more daunting. Burnsie (John Burns) was not always present on our journeys since his place as first-choice keeper in the team was being contested by a couple of other goalies at the time. So, sometimes Burnsie would be with George and sometimes not. But I remember always feeling relieved at the sight of George (and Burnsie) as the bus approached their bus stop. I did not like travelling alone, bedecked in the full Celtic regalia.

John goes on to reveal that frequently the lads would have to run a bit of a gauntlet of shouts and insults from people who were (as John points out) 'not Celtic minded'. Going to training wasn't a problem as they would have used the 'Green' Edinburgh bus which would have gone down the London Road and dropped them at a stop just past the gate of the training ground at Barrowfield. Coming back was a different matter, however. Due to the infrequency of the 'Green' bus, the boys had to opt for the 'Red' bus which they caught at the Bowler's Rest Pub near Parkhead Cross. This entailed them walking through the Carntyne area which was considered by many to be quite a 'tough' housing scheme and not particularly 'Celtic minded.' Walking through such territory with your uniform and kit bag proudly proclaiming your footballing allegiance and (presumed) religious affiliation certainly made the return journey from training a bit exciting if not down-right dangerous! Although the boys themselves were never seriously physically attacked they were continually harassed – and not just by local youths. Sometimes adults also joined in the taunting and John vividly remembers that nasty aspect of being associated with Celtic. Not everyone in the Celtic Boys Club was fortunate to escape physically unharmed coming and going from training. John Kirkwood tells of one shocking but not unique or solitary incident that occurred during his days at Celtic Boys which served as a reminder about what wearing the green and white of Celtic meant to some other people:

A teammate of ours, James McCafferty, turned up at a mid-week game with his face in a helluva mess. The result of an encounter with Rangers fans on his trip home form Barrowfield, the previous Saturday. Two black eyes, a broken nose and covered in lacerations. Quite a going-over for 14 or 15-year-old. A very frightening reminder for us all.

During the more 'scarier' times of being followed and taunted John took great comfort from his pal and team-mate from Birkenshaw who simply refused to back down to the threats and faced down those who were intent on intimidating these young lads whose sole crime was publically appearing as potential Celtic players of the future. And in George McCluskey a real gem for the future was most certainly emerging. For his teammates and all who were following Celtic Boys Club to identify the next generation who would light up Celtic Park, the name George McCluskey was coming more and more to the fore. For his fellow team-mate who played alongside him and who supplied the ball from the middle of the park which, more than often, George seemed to put into the net with consummate ease and incessant regularity, it seemed obvious that the young lad who got on the 'Green' bus two stops after 'Kirky' was destined for greatness. John Kirkwood's assessment of George McCluskey is revealing, reflective and accurate:

George was by miles the best player of our group at Celtic Boys and all of us knew it. In fact, George probably was, and still is, the best 15-year-old I, personally, have ever seen. Obviously I am biased, as I played at close range with him and benefitted from his brilliance. I think I could count in one hand, how many games in two and half years, that George didn't score. He scored with ease, from anywhere within a 30 yard radius of the goals. He hit the ball as hard as Peter Lorimer[10] – only George was just 14 and could hit the ball as hard! He was very well balanced, had a beautiful touch and seemed to glide effortlessly past opponents. He was a joy to play with – and Tam Brannan was right – he was better than me. By the way, Davie Provan said that George was the most gifted player he had ever played with – and that's at professional level.

High recommendation indeed. George's own memories of playing for

10. Peter Lorimer was the legendary Leeds United and Scottish international footballer at that time. An attacking midfielder, he was generally credited as having one of the hardest shots in football.

Celtic Boys are, as is typical of the man, extremely modest and humble. Unlike many others who would recall numerous stories and accounts about goal-scoring feats and honours won, George focuses on two particular memories that stand out of playing for Celtic Boys Club. The first reflects the pride George has in the sacrifices made by his parents for their children in order to give them a chance in life. In 1970 both George and his younger brother, John, were playing for Celtic Boys – a source of great joy and pride for George's parents, his family, his relatives and the community to which he belonged. Celtic Boys were going on a tour and both George and John were selected and needed suits for the tournament. The suits duly appeared and the two McCluskey boys went off and did themselves, their families and Celtic Boys proud. It was only a few years ago – and after the death of Teresa and John McCluskey (senior) – that George came to find out about how the money for the suits came about. George and John were at a family evening and talking about Celtic Boys and having to get suits to go on tour. George pondered on how their parents were able to afford one suit never mind two when John explained how this had actually come about:

> Did our mum never tell you, George? Remember her gold bracelet went missing for a month or two at that time.[11] She told me a couple of years before she died that she pawned it so that she could get us the suits so that we could go on tour. Our father had to work every hour of overtime that God gave him at Ravenscraig to get it back.

It is a story that George tells with great pride of just how much his parents did for him and John to give them that opportunity to follow their dream. The other story of playing for Celtic Boys Club is a much less happy one. George was so full of pride when his younger brother, John, followed him into the ranks of Celtic Boys. John was – like George – an outrageously talented footballer from the first time, it seems, he was able to kick a football. A wonderfully gifted and skilful player, John McCluskey looked set to follow in the footsteps of his big brother. Both of them dreamed of playing together for Celtic and for a time that seemed inevitable. Unfortunately events proved otherwise and the younger McCluskey didn't (through no fault of his own) make the breakthrough into the senior team. Celtic fans can only look back on the outrageous talent of George's

---

11. This bracelet was the only piece of valuable jewellery that Teresa McCluskey possessed.

younger brother and imagine what might have been if both McCluskey boys had played together at the highest level. Glimpses of what might have been did appear at youth level as John seemed destined to follow in his older brother's footsteps. During those days both George and John were playing absolute perfect and lethal football. The next couple of seasons would see George gain international school-boy recognition and score some wonderful goals in competitions at the highest-level that would set the young lad from Lanarkshire on the road to realising the dream that he and 'Burnsie' had as they practiced together every evening on the local football pitch in Birkenshaw. The journey from Celtic Boys Club to Celtic Football Club was beginning and now for real. Dreams were about to come true.

6

Scoring against Bellshill Academy and England
as Well

FOR ANY CELTIC-MINDED youngster, George was definitely 'living the dream.' Playing for the Celtic Boys Club, wearing the uniform going to training and playing in the hoops during matches, George McCluskey was a very fortunate and privileged boy indeed. And he was only too aware of it. George took nothing for granted and was simply delighted to be playing football for Celtic Boys and kept training as hard as he could and to become the best he could become. During his formative years at Celtic Boys he continued to develop as a player and was getting attention from those in charge of spotting potential players for the Scottish school-boys international panel. You would certainly not need to have been the most incisive coach to have identified George McCluskey as one to watch for the future. He was, after all, a very special talent who was banging in goals with such regularity and terrorising opponents that it was only a matter of time before the Scottish under-15 coaches contacted Celtic Boys about the young lad from Birkenshaw. He most certainly ticked every box for any coach of an under-15 team. He was strong and brave, could lead the line, had great vision, could strike a ball with tremendous power with either foot, had pace and agility and had loads of experience as well. He was, it seemed, an obvious choice for international selection. There was one thing lacking: George's school – St Catherine's – didn't have a football team. George puts this down to the school being quite small (less than 300 students) and co-ed also which meant that the potential squad for selection was effectively halved. So John Higgins, the chief Celtic scout, had to approach the Principal at St Catherine's to request that the school would have to establish a football team and compete in inter-school competitions if George was to be considered for Scottish honours.

They need not have worried for the Principal was only too keen to help in this regard. After all, it would be quite a boost for the local school to be able to boast an international footballer in its ranks and provide a most positive role model for the rest of the students to look up to and be inspired by. John then went to the PE teacher, Tommy Cassidy, to get him to start up a school team. Tommy himself had worked with Celtic Boys over a number of years and had been responsible for bringing one James Connolly Johnstone to the attention of Celtic and was only too aware of the ability of young George. He had one reservation, however: the lads at St Catherine's were simply not good enough to enter a league and would find the experience too difficult. John Higgins assured him that St Catherine's didn't need to enter a league competition to meet the criteria set by the authorities. All they needed to do was to enter a cup competition which they duly did. There was no expectation of winning anything as they weren't exactly blessed with the best young players in Lanarkshire, nor did they have any experience as playing together as a team. And, sure, the whole point of the exercise was to enable George McCluskey to be considered for selection for the Scottish schoolboys team – wasn't it?

Perhaps so, but life has a certain way of ripping up the form book and making the unlikely come true. And so it did when Tommy Cassidy entered St Catherine's into its first football tournament. It was a modest enough competition with around six to eight schools playing each other for a trophy that inevitably ended up in Bellshill Academy. Bellshill was a school with in excess of 1,000 students and a long tradition of football success. Not for one minute did Tommy Cassidy expect that the creation of a football team in the school to allow one of its best to get a chance to play for Scotland would have led to a final against Bellshill Academy. But, having won all of its previous games, St Catherine's made it through to the semi-final to play the 'Galacticos' of Bellshill Academy who won the cup every year. This was a mismatch on a 'David v Goliath' scale with surely no hope at all for the wee school from Viewpark. Yet St Catherine's had a 'secret weapon' and a 'secret system' which Tommy Cassidy unleashed at half-time. This is how George recalls the campaign:

The PE teacher, Mr Cassidy, called basically all of the boys of our year group together to announce that we were going to form an under-15 football team and play in a cup tournament that was starting in a couple of weeks' time. Since there were only about 30 boys in our year (and half of them didn't play football) it didn't take the coach too long

73

to select his squad. It more or less comprised of anyone who wanted to play and who could kick a ball! I guess that it was a bit like when a new coach comes onto the training pitch at the first training session and looks at what he's got to work with and, to be honest, I don't think that Tommy was looking at an Ajax or Barcelona-type youth academy! So he decided to pick the biggest and toughest boys who might make up for what we may have lacked in class and skill with hard work and physical strength. It worked as to our (and everyone else's) shock we made the semi-final and were over the moon for that. As for hoping to go the final step and winning the cup, well, that looked nigh impossible. Our opponents in the semi-final were Bellshill Academy who were the overwhelming favourites to win the competition outright. They had a far bigger pool to draw from – being almost four times the size of St Catherine's – and had a tradition of winning. We had only played two or three games together as a team and no one held out much hope for us. At half-time we trudged off the pitch 5–0 in arrears. The underdogs from St Catherine's certainly looked out of their league against the self-assured Bellshill team. But our manager was about to give a half-time talk that Big Jock or Alex Ferguson would have been proud of.

Tommy Cassidy kind of emphasised that we were being humiliated on the pitch by a bunch of rather wealthy and pampered spoiled brats who were laughing at us and now was the time to go out and get stuck in. Oh, and one special tactical instruction was given by Tommy, 'Just get the ball up the pitch to George and he will do the rest.' Well, the guys took their coach at his word and set about the Bellshill team with a physical intensity that would have put the fear of God into anyone. It was basically 'route one football' the whole of the second half as we ran riot and came out winners by six goals to five, with me scoring all six of our goals. And we won the final 3–0 with me scoring twice. I'm pretty sure that our opponents must have heard of our 'tactics' against Bellshill Academy and stayed out of the way! It was a great achievement for our school to win against all the odds and gave our families and our community a great deal of pride. Looking back on my football career over the years this was an achievement that does stick in my mind.

Roy of the Rovers stuff indeed. Now George was eligible for selection for Scotland and two games would come to define McCluskey's ability to play on the big stage. One would be for Scotland and the other for Celtic Boys.

The respective opponents would be England and Manchester United.

Special games and special goals

It was little wonder that John Higgins and Tommy Cassidy had worked so hard to get George in a position to be available to be selected for Scotland schoolboys. He was a quite unique talent – one of those footballers whom a coach comes across very rarely. It was not that they were overly interested in the Scottish schoolboy set-up. The only club of final destination that these two fine football coaches were remotely interested in was Celtic Football Club. Getting an international cap at that level would be good for George's prospects as he approached the age at which he would either sign apprenticeship or 'S' forms and begin a football career or to look for something else. Playing for Celtic Boys guaranteed you nothing in terms of a future career in football as John Kirkwood bluntly stated:

> In our group at Celtic Boys there were approximately 50 very talented young lads who played or trailed for the team, and remember, this was only for our age group. I guess that we all knew that George was the 'stand-out player' by miles and if anyone was going to make it onto Celtic's books, it would be George. And he did. And he was the only one of our group.

The 'attrition rate' of young promising footballers is still as high today as it was then and for every young footballer who realises his dream and gets to move to the next step and is signed by a top team many others are 'let go'. Playing for Celtic Boys certainly put you in 'the shop window' and basically gave Celtic first pick when it came to the end of your tenure at Celtic Boys before you turned 16 years of age, but you did have to take your chance. George McCluskey most certainly did just that in one particularly high profile game in his final season for Celtic Boys.

The game that John Higgins was so keen on to get George to be eligible for was an under-15 match between England and Scotland at Wembley Stadium on 9 June 1973. Unlike today, there were few live televised games at that time but ITV decided to show this game that would reveal the talent for the future, including a young Alan Curbishly who went on to play for West Ham, Birmingham, Aston Villa and Charlton. The Scotland captain that day, George Boyd, was signed that very evening by the

Middlesbrough manager, Jackie Charlton, who had been commentating at the match! Other players were picked up by various clubs on the strength of their performance and the exposure that the game had given, as it was the first time that a schoolboy fixture was shown on British television. It also unveiled the talent of George McCluskey to a wide audience as well to his fellow Celtic Boys' teammates with whom he had been playing in an invitation European youth tournament the week before. Indeed, Celtic Boys had made the final that same weekend but had to play without their talismanic striker who was off to Wembley for even more serious business. No matter, the Celtic Boys beat Eastercraigs – a junior club affiliated to Rangers – at Celtic Park on the Sunday, having watched a quite inspired George McCluskey score two goals in a famous 4–2 victory over England the day before. George was by miles the standout player on the pitch that day and his second goal in particular emphasised his quality. Those who were there or who watched it on television concur on the wonderful individual goal that McCluskey scored. George took the ball, ghosted past a couple of defenders and unleashed an unstoppable shot into the top corner of the net from some 25 yards from the goal. Those who were at Wembley that afternoon were indeed privileged to see such a goal from a young lad of just 15. John Kirkwood and the rest of the Celtic Boys were jumping around various houses having seen their teammate score against England just one day after they had celebrated winning their own tournament. The McCluskey household was going crazy too, as all the family, relatives and friends saw 'our George' scoring on national television. George's younger brother, John, had already joined him at Celtic Boys and was making quite a name for himself. And George was now the hottest young prospect in football in Scotland and beyond. It seemed only a matter of time until he would fulfil his dream and sign for Celtic Football Club.

7

Signing for Celtic

GEORGE'S EXPLOITS AT junior and schools level were indeed the stuff of football legend. He could take a game by the scruff of the neck and completely turn it around. It seemed that no matter the opposition, or indeed, even how good or bad his own team was, the decisive factor in the outcome of the game was very often George McCluskey. Both in junior and schools competitions the instruction from the side-lines was 'get the ball to McCluskey'. George would then do the rest. This, of course, might seem a bit trite and simplistic, but it was something that became a trademark of the young lad from Birkenshaw throughout his football career. Never afraid to show himself and certainly not shy of getting cut down by perhaps less talented opponents, George was a godsend to any coach or manager. Even at this young age he had an incredibly powerful strike, was wonderful at laying the ball off to fellow players and then moving into space. He could head well and had the most sublime of touches which he used to devastating effect, especially in making defenders look cumbersome and flatfooted. He was also deceptively quick in running into space, especially when his own team were on the attack. As soon as his team had the ball and were going forward, the young McCluskey was heading towards the danger area with one eye on where the ball was and the other on where there was space in the box. Above all else, George had an uncanny ability, even at an early age, to anticipate where the ball might arrive and be there just in case!

'To play football the Glasgow Celtic way!'

George puts much of this down to the early coaching of his father and people like Tom Cassidy. George's father, John, drilled into him from when he first started to play football that it was a simple game and that the clue was in the name. It was not basketball or rugby. Lumping the ball up the pitch and into the opponents' penalty box at the first opportunity was not only bad for the spectator; it also was bad football as it always gave the defender the advantage as every ball coming up the pitch could be attacked by the defender. John McCluskey also saw this style of football as being suited to physically big lads whose advantage would be overcome as boys grew up. It didn't help to develop the basic skills of pass and movement, retaining possession and playing the ball into space – and it certainly didn't suit the young George McCluskey's game. George recalls his formation and development and the lessons he learnt through the coaching his father provided in those early days:

I think my father realised very early on that the 'long-ball game' was not for me. I was tall and strong enough but I was never going to be one of those old-fashioned 'Number 9' 'battering-ram' types who thrived in the 'route one' world of football. I have to give my father a lot of credit for my early development. Lots of underage team coaches in those days simply picked the two biggest players they had in the squad and made one of them centre-forward and the other centre-half. That dictated the type of football the team would play – physical and direct. As a coach of underage teams at Celtic now myself, I hate to see this type of coaching. It does the young player no good at all in the long run as their physical height and strength tends to mean less and less as the other boys grow up. It also can stunt the football development of the big lad himself as he becomes forced at an early age into playing in a certain sort of way – simply as a target man who can hold the ball up or try to outmuscle the defenders or, alternatively, as a centre-half who can try to hold up and neutralise the forwards. Once the ball gets past him he's lost. Reading the game, anticipation, being comfortable on the ball, passing the ball, playing the ball into space, retaining possession, bringing other people into play – all of the basics skills that you need to become a successful footballer – are lacking in someone whose main attributes are nothing but height and strength. So from a very early age I was encouraged to play a certain way. My game from being a youngster has always been about anticipation, movement, drifting in, arriving at the right time and trusting that your teammates will create enough opportunities. All I had to do was to try to take them.

George also had another major influence that shaped how he approached football. Like everyone in his family and many in his community, George had been brought up to play football 'the Celtic way'. From going to see games at Celtic Park, talking with his pals in school and in Birkenshaw, listening to his father, his uncles (and aunts) and all around him as they recreated games past and compared players from different decades, the young McCluskey's early football formation would have been shaped by those around him and the footballing philosophy that had always been intrinsic to the team from the East End of Glasgow. Indeed, Celtic always prided themselves with how they played the game. From Willie Maley's earliest teams right through to the present day, Celtic have always valued players with flair and promoted a style of football that is based on pace and movement, moving the ball from side to side, attacking down the flanks, having midfielders who can pass the ball, pick out the forwards as they move into space and get up to support the attack as well as defenders who are comfortable on the ball. Every generation of Celtic teams throws up such players who excite the faithful. Players like Jimmy Quinn from Croy, the 'Mighty Atom' Patsy Gallagher who was born in a work-house in Ramelton in Donegal, the all-time leading goalscorer in British football Jimmy McCrory, the inspirational winger Jimmy Delaney, the miraculous and bewildering Charlie Tully and a host of others whose feats were the stuff of legend, whose names and famous games were part of the folklore of the community and family that George grew up in. Even the goalkeepers who played for Celtic had a romance about them and none more so than the 'Prince of Goalkeepers', the legendary Johnny Thompson. And of course you had the Lisbon Lions at that time with players such as Billy McNeill, Bobby Lennox, Bobby Murdoch and the majestic Jimmy 'Jinky' Johnstone who were all still at Celtic Park when the young lad from Birkenshaw arrived. And 'playing the Celtic way' was not something of previous eras. Celtic continue to produce wonderful, skilful and attacking players to this day with the likes of the brilliant Henrik Larsson and the sublime Shunsuke Nakamura typifying Celtic's football philosophy in modern times.

Growing up in Lanarkshire in a family and community that was (and remains to this day) 'Celtic minded', it seems only natural that this way of play would have rubbed off on the young McCluskey. Like every young footballer, he would have modelled himself on his sporting heroes who he watched as often as he could and whose exploits he would have followed with a keen interest. At that time in the late 1960s and early 1970s there were many wonderful players in the Hoops who the young footballer from Birkenshaw would have as role models. This included some of those whom George had watched in awe on television on that magical evening in Lisbon in 1967. Others, included Tommy Callaghan, Dixie Deans, Harry Hood, Davy Hay, Kenny Dalglish and many other inspirational players were at Celtic around that heady time. Since George had been playing for the Celtic Boys Club for several years, it only seemed a matter of time before he would move from what was essentially a 'nursery club' for possible future players and fulfil his dream of joining his boyhood heroes at Celtic Park. But other teams were also aware of the potential of the young striker from Birkenshaw, including a very famous team from the north west of England that had a tradition of taking players of great flair from Scotland including Denis Law and Pat Crerand (who was signed from Celtic in 1965) – Manchester United. George McCluskey was firmly on the radar of the Manchester United Manager, Tommy Docherty, himself a Scot and former Celtic player. McCluskey's recent destruction of England at Wembley had not been missed by Docherty (or a host of other football managers) so it was very much a matter of moving on from Celtic Boys. But to which club? Joining Celtic was not quite the done deal that many of the Celtic tradition may presume.

Sharing stories about homemade soup and signing a precious talent

Given the history of the community that George and his family belonged to and the foundation of Celtic Football Club itself, it might be somewhat ironic that a conversation about the best way to make soup took on a certain life of its own as the young lad from Birkenshaw's footballing future was taking place. After all, the term 'taking the soup' was one that many in the Irish community throughout the world would be aware of. During the worst year of the Great Hunger (often referred to as 'Black '47') some of the starving Irish survived by receiving a daily meal of soup provided by the local relief authorities. Some religious denominations set up their own soup kitchens where people could receive a life-line – providing that they renounced their Catholic faith and adopted the religion of the provider. 'Taking the soup' was synonymous among the Irish diaspora with turning your back on your community and religion and was (and still remains) a term of scorn and rebuke. By a peculiar quirk of circumstances a discussion on the subject of cooking soup took place as George's potential signing for Celtic was being talked about!

'Mammy, there's two men at the door'

George tells of the evening that two rather well-known men came to the McCluskey household and introduced themselves to George's mother and father: 'Good evening and sorry to bother you. My name is Jock Stein, the manager of Celtic, and this is my assistant, Sean Fallon. Would it be possible to come in and have a word with you? We'd like to talk to you about your son, George.' Naturally the arrival of these visitors caused quite a stir in the house and the girls promptly fled the scene for their bedrooms or round to their friends' houses. George was 'allowed' to stay as he might want to know what was going on! The initial conversation in the house was largely led by Fallon and George's father with the assistant manager, supported by Big Jock, saying that they had watched George's development over the past few years and were very keen to sign him for Celtic. Sean Fallon was Jock Stein's right-hand man and assistant manager at Celtic. The former Celtic full-back, however, was no mere assistant to Stein. Sean Fallon had been Bob Kelly's preferred candidate for manager to Stein (who Kelly wished to become the assistant manager until Stein refused and threatened to take a managerial position in England). To his credit Fallon became an able and supportive assistant to Stein and often undertook the securing of promising young players who went on to become Celtic greats, including legends such as Davy Hay, Danny McGrain, Kenny Dalglish and Packy Bonner. It seemed that, once the young talent had been identified, the 'immortal' Jock Stein would arrive and let the persuasive powers of his powerful assistant from Co. Sligo do the rest.

If they had have thought that a simple invite to sign on the dotted line would suffice in such a Celtic minded household then they were to be disappointed – for an hour or so at least. George was stunned by his father's initial reluctance to sign. He assumed that his father would have snapped the hand off Fallon and put his name to whatever contract was offered. But John McCluskey, despite being a Celtic fanatic, was first and foremost George's father and wanted to act in the very best interests of his son. A massive decision on his son's future was to be made that evening and John wanted to be certain that it would be the best one for George. He was also well aware of the interest being shown by Manchester United and other teams 'down south' and that perhaps more money might be offered by these teams – although it was never about money for John McCluskey. As someone who had been involved in coaching under-age teams for years and developing young talent, John was only too well aware of how many a promising young lad's football career had failed to blossom due to making the wrong move. While it certainly was a great honour to be asked by Stein and Fallon to sign your son up for Celtic – and their very presence in the McCluskey home showed just how much they valued him as a future player – John would have to take into account many considerations before making his mind up as to whether or not his young lad would sign for the club he and his family adored. Sean Fallon read the situation very well and realised that the signing of young McCluskey was not a 'done deal'. Far from it. He suggested to Jock Stein that it might be better if he went with John McCluskey somewhere else where they could discuss the business of the evening over a quiet pint in a more relaxed atmosphere. This might be more conducive to coming to a decision. The two retired to a nearby bar leaving Jock Stein, Teresa McCluskey and a nervous George McCluskey to await whatever decision the Celtic assistant manager and John McCluskey would come up with. The next hour would decide the following stage of the young McCluskey's football career.

While the two men were off discussing the future of young George, Teresa McCluskey was continuing with the domestic duties in the kitchen. Jock Stein stood between the door of the living room, where George was sitting trying to look interested in watching the television, and the kitchen where George's mother was preparing a pot of soup for the next day. The conversation between the two adults went back and forwards about George's future and the best way to make soup! George's recollection of that discussion is very clear:

Big Jock made it very clear that he would love to see me playing for Celtic – 'as I'm sure the whole family would love to see that, Mrs McCluskey. Just imagine how you'd all feel going to Celtic Park and seeing your George playing in the Hoops'. My mother answered that she was sure that he was right but that depended on what was best for George and that there was talk that Manchester United were looking for him. Jock Stein then went on to say that he was sure that Manchester United were a great club and that George would do well anywhere but 'Manchester is quite a bit away', and life was different there. And he would miss home, his brothers and sister and pals – 'and your soup Mrs McCluskey'! and, 'By the way, when my wife makes soup she swears that you should always put pepper in with the salt. What do you think?'. The conversation went on with both talking about my future, how they had nothing to do with the decision (which the two men in the bar were no doubt coming to any minute now!) and the best way to cook soup. My mother was a very wise woman and understood exactly what was going on. Jock Stein was not there as a driver to mark time and take Sean Fallon home after he discussed my future with my father. The two were a double act and my mother was well aware of that. She knew that Celtic must have been very keen to sign me and that Jock Stein and Sean Fallon had decided to come to our home to make sure that both my mother and father were for this. Looking back on it now I feel incredibly privileged that Jock Stein and Sean Fallon must have felt that I was good enough for both of them to come to our house in Birkenshaw to sign me. My mother kept coming back to say to Stein that she certainly wanted me to sign for Celtic and that would be the best thing for me. 'After all', she said, 'George has done brilliantly so far and who knows what he might do if he gets the chance to play for Celtic? Oh, and Mr Stein, I think that your wife is right in putting pepper in with the salt'.

After an hour and rather more than a bit, my father and Sean Fallon came in the door announcing to all and sundry that George McCluskey was going to sign for Celtic. The 'S' [schoolboy] forms were duly produced and signed by Sean Fallon and my father. In truth, the deal was agreed not in a bar in Birkenshaw but in the kitchen in my home over a pot of soup.

Little did anyone know that evening when George McCluskey at the age of 15 signed for Celtic that he would be followed by his young brother, John, who signed 'S' forms in October that year becoming the youngest ever 'S' signing until one Paul McStay signed for Celtic some years later. George's comment was priceless:

I was told by everyone that I was the greatest young footballer in Britain. Then my young brother comes along at the age of 13, signs for Celtic and I wonder am I the best player in my own house!

Tommy Docherty's failed attempt to catch the signature of George

McCluskey came back to hurt Manchester United not once but twice over the next couple of years. The first was in 1974 when the Celtic under-17s played the English side in a European Youth tournament at Celtic Park where George scored the only goal of the game. Two years later the two clubs met again in a game that lives long in the memory of at least one witness, George's life-long friend and former team mate, John Kirkwood. Interestingly the game wasn't part of any tournament. In fact it was the result of a challenge by a rather boastful Tommy Docherty who claimed that he had assembled the best youth team in Britain for Manchester United and dared Celtic to take them on. Celtic duly agreed, and another English team arrived at Celtic Park brimming with confidence. George by now was playing in the Celtic reserves and led the line for Celtic that evening. John had also left Celtic Boys and was playing junior football. He recalls that he watched the game from behind the dugout, sporting a pair of crutches as he had a broken leg at the time and remembers the cameo appearance made by the youngest player on the pitch that evening – John McCluskey – who revealed tantalising glimpses of the player he could have become had life been different:

> John made a virtuoso appearance late in the second half. He was two years younger than most of the other players and he was just on when the ball switched from the right side of the pitch to the left which was John's natural side. Right in front of the main stand John, with his first touch, spun round and controlled the ball with his backside (á la Lubo). He then nutmegged the first defender, flew past a second and crossed the ball into the box. That brought the crowd to its feet! What cheek, what confidence, what brilliance!

George, however, was not to be upstaged and not by his younger brother. He gave a master class of centre-forward play and ran the Manchester United defence ragged as he scored a hat-trick in a 6–2 demolition of Tommy Docherty's much-vaunted wonder-kids. It was very much boys against men and the absolute standout player on view was indeed the brightest young prospect in British football at that time – George McCluskey.

Playing in the Green and White Hoops of Celtic

8

Moving through the Ranks

MANY FOOTBALL SUPPORTERS of a certain age will fondly remember the days of their childhood when they played football on the streets with gable walls, lamp posts, fire hydrants, street signs, gate posts and whatever else couldn't move and was deemed suitable being pressed into service for the goals. If a decent piece of waste ground or parkland could be found then a few coats or jumpers would be placed on the ground and the goals carefully paced out. Teams would be picked and matches of epic proportion, deadly intent and of vital importance would ensue. These games would continue almost endlessly, and were only brought to conclusion by a kid brother or sister bringing a message from a mother that so-and-so 'has to come home because his dinner is ready.' Often if a game was still going on when it was getting too dark to play the shout 'next goal the winner' would go up – which seemed unfair to the team that was winning by a cricket score! And it was generally adhered to. The following day would always bring another chance for glory and redemption of honour. These were indeed serious games and not to be dismissed as a lot of young lads 'kicking a ball about'. We all had our heroes in those days and we sought to imitate and emulate them. And when we played on it, that piece of parkland or street crossroads was transformed into something quite different, something remarkable, when one team centred the ball. Skipping past a couple of people made you feel just like Jinky Johnstone or George Best. Someone who might run onto the ball to hit a blistering shot past a helpless keeper might smile to himself when his teammates told him that he hit that ball like Tommy Gemmell. Because inside he knew he was just like the big left-back who did indeed have a thunderous shot that on many occasions was unleashed with great effect, none more than on that wonderful evening in Lisbon in May 1967 when the man from Motherwell scored 'that goal'. For most of us who used jumpers for goal posts, running out onto the

86

pitch in the green and white hoops of Celtic in front of a packed Jungle (or playing for any other top class team) would always remain a dream. For George McCluskey such feats were about to become reality. He had signed for the club that he, his family and his community adored. Now there was only the small matter of getting onto the team!

George left school as soon as he could and joined the Celtic ground staff. He went straight into the reserves which was unusual because Celtic normally farmed out under-age signings to junior teams for a year of experience at 'man's level' which tended to be pretty physical. Junior clubs tended to be made up of good players who hadn't quite made the grade yet, those who were 'on the way down' or those who were trying to impress scouts from professional teams. Quite a number of these players would show little sympathy or concern for young lads who had been farmed out for experience. The young signees would be signed by Celtic on a 'provisional' form and then sign one for the junior club. That year at junior level could make or break a player's career in the unforgiving game of football. Indeed, John Kirkwood told me that a player as wonderfully gifted as Tommy Burns just made the grade in his year only after playing junior football for Maryhill. George did in fact sign junior forms for Thorniewood Juniors who were based in Viewpark but never actually played for them. Jock Stein had already seen, heard about and read enough of the young lad from Birkenshaw and had decided to move him onto the next level.

Training at Barrowfield and being tortured by Tommy Burns

Although the training grounds at Barrowfield and Celtic Park were familiar to him as a member of Celtic Boys, this would be an entirely new, different and daunting experience. George was no longer the young star who had led the line with such distinction for Celtic Boys over the past few years. Now, going onto the training pitch or walking through the main door into Celtic Park was for real. He was now the newest Celtic player, entering a world in which he would see at close hand those whom he had only previously watched as a supporter from the Jungle. Celtic Park was awash with stars and this could – and often did – intimidate the most confident and self-assured of aspiring young footballers. Of the Lisbon Lions, Billy McNeill, Bobby Lennox, Bobby Murdoch and Jimmy Johnstone were still playing for Celtic. Added to that were other outstanding players including Danny

McGrain, George Connelly, Jim Brogan, Harry Hood, 'Dixie' Deans and Kenny Dalglish. For a young lad like George this must have seemed like a dream – or a nightmare. Here he was, at the age of 16 going into training every day and seeing his boyhood heroes, trying to imagine how he would ever break through onto the Celtic team in such illustrious company. And if that wasn't a challenge in itself, the young lads he was joining with were no mean squad themselves. Quite a few of the Celtic Boys team that had won the European Youth Cup in 1973 graduated into the ranks of the senior club around that time including Robert (Rab) Hannah, Jim Casey and Duncan (Dunky) Martin. There was one other young lad from Celtic Boys who had emerged at Celtic Park around that time and who would become George's best friend during his career there and throughout the next decades until his untimely death in 2008 – a young red-headed lad from the Calton, Tommy Burns.

Going to train with the reserves at Celtic Park as a young aspiring player was not easy. First of all you could not be intimidated by the whole experience or who you met every day and who you were playing with in the reserves. After all there were some serious players in the reserve side at that time including some who had been dropped from the first-team squad and were seeking to prove themselves. There were others who were coming back from injury, and young guys like George himself who were striving to impress and move to the ultimate level to be on the official team-sheet, playing for Celtic on Saturday at 3.00 pm. This was not a place to be shy or reticent. Above all else you had to show that you were eager. This was no easy feat as Jock Stein took very much a 'hands on' approach to management and seemed to be everywhere. You walked past his office on the way into Celtic Park and he always seemed to notice you as you arrived. He also appeared at Barrowfield to see how the training was going on and always speaking to the coaches about no one else but you! At least that's what it seemed to George, and this gave a mischievous young lad with a wicked sense of humour endless opportunities to wind him up.

Even though it's only 10 miles from Birkenshaw to Glasgow there is a world of difference between the two places and their people. I had been going to see Celtic from I was a boy and had been up and down to Barrowfield and Celtic Park and numerous other grounds playing for Celtic Boys and the likes, but we were still seen as almost 'country bumpkins' by some of the city lads and Tommy Burns was the worst of them! Tommy was a 'street-wise' lad from Calton and he always seemed to be looking to wind some of us up and he was pure genius at it – I usually fell for it.

George recalls one particular episode in which he was the victim of Tommy's wicked sense of humour. It was in 1974 when Celtic were playing at Aberdeen. Neither of the lads had made their debut yet but they accompanied the team as 'kit boys'. Willie Fernie was in charge of the 'S-formers' and, on occasion, would have picked two of the under-age players to travel with the team with the responsibility of sorting the kit out before the match. This was a great opportunity for young lads trying to get onto the next level to get a bit of insight and inspiration. For George and Tommy this was their first experience of travelling on the team bus and staying in a hotel with the side as they prepared for a match. At that time 'S-formers' were on £10 per week which was worth a lot more then than now. George would have given his mother £5 on the Tuesday (when he received it). This was a valuable boost to the McCluskey household and helped to bridge the gap until John McCluskey got paid on the Friday. The other fiver was used by George to travel to and from training on the bus and other small expenses. Armed with this crisp £5 note, George set off with his pal on the team bus on the Friday as Celtic prepared to take on Aberdeen the following day.

I remember being very excited as we headed up the road for Aberdeen. We were on the coach with the likes of Danny McGrain, Kenny Dalglish, and the rest of the other first team players and you did get a sense that this was the only thing in the world you wanted to do in life – play for Celtic. I suppose also that staying in a classy hotel was also very novel for both me and Tommy and it all was part of the excitement. We were rooming together – something that we did many times afterwards. We ate with the team at 7.00 in the evening and went to our room at half past eight. About an hour later we thought that we were still hungry and being young lads from ordinary working-class backgrounds staying in a top-class hotel, we decided to call room service and ordered sandwiches and soft drinks. When the waiter arrived with our order (which cost £1.40 in total) I was in the bathroom. I decided to be the 'big lad' and shouted out to Tommy that I'd get it and that there was a fiver in my jacket pocket. Tommy took the note, gave it to the waiter and told him to keep the change! I came out to find Tommy falling about the room in hysterical laughter. I called him every name under the sun and protested that that £5 had to do me until the following Tuesday and to get me to training and everything else but that only made him laugh all the more. But Tommy Burns was also a great friend and gave me whatever he had so that I did survive until the next pay day. I imagine the waiter was thinking, 'I can't wait to get room service for the players. If the kit boys tip like this what will I make from those guys!'

Of course the practical jokes played by Tommy Burns was only one aspect of the relationship between George McCluskey and the lad from Calton who loved Celtic as much as his team-mate from Lanarkshire. A very close bond of friendship and mutual respect grew quickly between the two and they became almost inseparable both on and off the pitch. As they moved through the reserves towards the first-team an almost telepathic understanding was established between the red-headed midfielder and the tall striker. Indeed, it seemed for many Celtic fans that McCluskey was at his best when Burns was at his best. The two fed off each other and developed an almost unconscious, uncanny understanding of where one of them would be and where the other would be delivering the ball to. Jim Mervyn, one of the most prominent Celtic supporters from Belfast, observes:

I've been going to see Celtic all my life and you do get to notice partnerships that can't simply be taught on the training pitch or by coaching or practice. They are intuitive and so natural that you would think that the players could read each others' minds. Burns and McCluskey were just like that. Tommy would move through the midfield – usually down the left or through the middle – and hit a ball into space almost anticipating that McCluskey would arrive just at the right moment. Which, more often than not, he did! It is my firm opinion that Tommy Burns saw something in George McCluskey that others didn't. Some saw him primarily as an out and out striker. But he was much more than that and Tommy Burns recognised that in him both as a player and later as a manager when he signed him for Kilmarnock in 1992. Indeed, Tommy always said, when talking about George McCluskey, that he almost single-handedly got Kilmarnock promoted to the SPL in the 1992/93 season and kept them there the following year.

Invited to a party by Ronnie Wood, pizza, dropped from a final and winning player of the tournament

During George's time playing in the reserve team at Celtic he was also in the Scotland under-age teams. In April, 1976 Andy Roxburgh took the under-17 Scotland team to the International Youth Tournament in Cannes. This was a highly prestigious competition which featured the top European sides as well as Brazil. On their way to the final Scotland beat Finland 5–1, drew 0–0 with Brazil and beat Italy 2–1. That took them to the final where they would face the tournament favourites and hosts, France. George had had an outstanding competition up to then and most observers (and teammates) saw Scotland's hopes as resting on the shoulders of the young lad from Birkenshaw. The young Scotland squad had got to the final of the tournament under the careful eye of Andy Roxburgh, who would later become the manager of the Scottish international team. The former professional footballer, school teacher and coach was eminently qualified and experienced enough to take this young squad and get the very best out of them. Working with guys of the youth team's age was second nature to Roxburgh. He had great tactical awareness and motivational skill and was a strict disciplinarian – something that was required when taking a group of teenagers away for an extended period to a very important tournament. Everything was going so well up to the final. Little did he know that a rebellion of sorts was brewing.

It actually wasn't really a rebellion at all. In fact it was pretty much down to food (or lack of) and an attempt by George and some of the squad to bring some pizzas back to the rest of the team. The Scotland squad were staying in pretty basic accommodation that most certainly couldn't be described as a luxury hotel. Perhaps it was due to the Cannes Film Festival which was taking place at the same time, or maybe the SFA had decided to go for the cheapest accommodation available. Whatever the reason, George and the under-17s squad were not a happy bunch at receiving their final meal of the day at six o'clock in the evening. The night before the final someone suggested that some of them should sneak out and bring back some pizzas and soft drinks. An 'escape committee' was instantly set up and soon George, his great mate from the Celtic Boys

Club, Rab Hannah, and three or four others found themselves climbing out a window and setting out on their mission. The group soon found a pizzeria and began ordering whatever they could vaguely recognise on the menu – remembering that for most of these young lads this was going to be the first real pizza they would ever have had. Just as they were about to leave a car pulled up and a couple of rather famous celebrities (along with the biggest personal security personnel they had ever seen) got out and one of them approached the group from Scotland for a conversation. It was none other than the Rolling Stones guitarist, Ronnie Wood! Perhaps it's the innocence or fearlessness of youth, but the young lads awaiting their pizza order found themselves talking with a member of one of the biggest rock groups of all time as another member of the group, Mick Jagger, stood looking at the menu.

> It probably was one of the most bizarre, surreal and unbelievable incidents in my life. Here we were, a bunch of kids from Scotland, about to play in a major international football final, and we'd sneaked out to buy pizza when a yellow Citroën pulls up with some of the biggest rock stars in the world and we end up talking to them. Ronnie Wood asked us what we were doing and our response was a mixture of 'buying pizzas' and 'playing football'! He was absolutely dead-on and just loved a bit of conversation. I asked him if Rod Stewart was over in Cannes but he told me that he was in New York. I then told him that I preferred him when he played with the Faces and asked him would he not join that group again. He turned to me and asked me my name. I told him. Ronnie Wood then looked me straight in the eye and said, 'Listen, George, I have just joined the greatest rock and roll band in the world but you want me to go back and join the Faces! I love what you're saying but I don't think so.' We had great fun and Ronnie wanted to bring us to a party up in their chateau but all we wanted to do was to get back to the hotel with the pizzas and not get caught.

The adventure was not over, despite having just met Ronnie Wood and knocked-back his invitation to a Rolling Stones party. The lads, now laden with pizzas, had to get back in without their absence being noticed. That should have been easy as the only people who knew what was going on was the entire under-18 squad and the only ones who 'weren't in the know' were the management team. How could this cunning plan fail?

Well fail it did. George was first up to the window that the guys had been lowered from an hour beforehand and as the whistles/signals/secret signs were given, supporting hands did come out the window (about two metres above the ground). George got a lift up and then heard a scattering below him as the others ran for cover and he was yanked up into the room by one very angry Andy Roxburgh. The inquest began, with George and the only other person 'captured' – his Celtic Boys Club pal, Rab Hannah – being accused of going out to try to buy alcohol. There was absolutely not a chance of that (George never touched a drink until his mid-20s, and then only socially), but he (and Rab) were dropped for the final the following day. George was not one bit pleased and felt that he had been used as a scapegoat for a decision that the whole squad had signed-up for. For a lad of his age it seemed extremely harsh to be dropped from an international final for trying to get your pals some food.

I sat on the bench absolutely fuming. I never looked at Andy Roxburgh and he never cast a glance at me. The score was 0–0 for most of the match but France were all over us and there only looked to be one winner and it was not Scotland. With about 20 minutes to go he turned to me and told me to get warmed up. I almost told him to 'get stuffed' and that I should have been on from the start. But, thankfully, I didn't. I went on the park and the game changed. I picked the ball in the middle of the park (I was playing midfield throughout the tournament), beat three or four players, got to the bye-line and cut the ball back for Gordon Boyd to score from close-range. We won 1–0 to become the first (and only) Scottish international team to win a tournament. I was awarded the 'Player of the Tournament'. I am not sure how Andy Roxburgh took it but I certainly know that Rab Hannah was pleased. Rab had been benched like me over 'pizza-gate' and never played in the final. That didn't stop him running around shouting at the manager, 'Andy, if you had played the thorough-bred from the start instead of those three cart-horses we'd have won 3–0!' All the time I was telling him to shut-up or we'd never get picked to play for Scotland again.

From the reserves to the first team – mind the gap

George McCluskey didn't stay too many seasons in the reserves. Within a couple of years he was to show that youth was no major barrier to getting on the first team and that if you were good enough then you would get your chance. After that, it really depended what you did when your chance came around. By the start of the 1975/76 season changes were beginning to happen at Celtic and opportunities started to emerge. That season was seen by many to be the end of an era for the club, and the beginning of a new period. The wonderful and unprecedented record breaking run of winning nine League titles in a row had to come to an end at some stage, and this was the case in May 1975 when, for the first time in almost a decade, the Scottish League Championship trophy didn't reside in the trophy room at Celtic Park.

Billy McNeill and Jimmy Johnstone called it a day after McNeill lifted the Scottish Cup on the last day of the 1974/75 season, leaving the incomparable Bobby Lennox as the sole Lisbon Lion still gracing the green and white hoops as the 1975/76 season started. He had been ever-present during that incredible trophy-filled decade, having joined Celtic in 1962, and was still terrorising defenders down the left with his blistering speed, commitment, anticipation and phenomenal goal-scoring ability – which left him bested only by Jimmy McGrory as all-time Celtic goal-scorer. He would continue to grace the Hoops for another five years. Tommy Callaghan, a veteran of seven campaigns of the nine-in-a-row, was still playing in the Hoops – although the following season would be his last for Celtic. Celtic were not a spent force. Far from it. There is a misconception among many Celtic supporters that the Lisbon Lions were, by and large, the 'nine-in-a-row team'. This was not the case. Football teams always change and no set of players will all hit their peak at the same time. Those glory years of Celtic, when they dominated Scottish football and were a massive presence in Europe, were a result of top class players repeatedly replacing top class players. The team that played in the European Cup Final on that most disappointing of nights in Milan in 1970 against Feyenoord had seven of the Lisbon Lions in its starting 11. It could well have been eight had Jim Craig not been injured. A year later only McNeill, Craig, Johnstone and Lennox were on the pitch when Celtic beat Rangers 2–1 at Hampden in the Scottish Cup Final. Players were leaving, moving on or retiring, but they were being replaced by players of similar quality and ability as the revolution that Jock Stein had put into place continued.

There was a seamlessness, a flawlessness, about Celtic in those days. Standards were not being lowered nor was there any compromise of the flamboyant style that has always characterised the 'Celtic way'. This instinctive and exciting approach to football was summed up in Jock Stein's immortal words in 1967 immediately after Celtic won the European Cup that, 'We did it by playing football. Pure, beautiful, inventive football.' It was this approach to the game that characterised Celtic during those years. There was also a hunger to continue their dominance in the domestic game and to push Celtic to remain a major force in Europe. One European Cup victory in 1967, runner-up in 1970, a semi-final defeat to Inter Milan after extra time in 1972 and another semi-final defeat in 1974 by a shameful Athletico Madrid side that (literally) kicked Celtic off the park and (as Jimmy Johnstone found out) in the tunnel, had only served notice to European football that this club from the East End of Glasgow was a club to be reckoned with and not some flash in the pan. The 'pure, beautiful, inventive football' was not going away any time soon – and new players were being brought in to deliver this message to the opposition. The green and white hoops with their panache for attacking football, their imagination and, above all else, pure passion for the game, seemed to be on the point of writing another magnificent chapter in Celtic's proud history. It would not be easy for anyone, and certainly not a young 18-year-old from just outside Glasgow, to break into a team in which ambition, talent, experience, competition for places and reputation existed in abundance.

As the season 1975/76 approached there was much for Celtic fans to consider with a degree of optimism. Harry Hood and Dixie Deans were scoring with ease, Paul Wilson had established himself in the front line and players like Ronnie Glavin, who was more than capable of scoring from midfield, made competition for the first-team squad fierce indeed. The 'Quality Street Gang', that prodigious Celtic reserve team of young players in the late 1960s and early 1970s which Stein had nurtured and developed to replace the Lisbon Lions, were showing just how good they really were. Players like George Connelly, Danny McGrain, Pat McCluskey (no relation) and the incomparable Kenny Dalglish, were playing a leading role in a Celtic team that promised much. In addition a new breed of youngsters were coming through and were not to be denied. Prominent among these were Johnny Doyle, Tommy Burns, Roy Aitken and our young man from Birkenshaw – George McCluskey. To break through onto the first team would be no mean feat, as George himself recalls:

> I guess that when you look back to that time I don't think any of us
> really understood just how much of an achievement it was to make the

Celtic team. Even though we had lost the league and the nine-in-a-row had come to an end, there was no sense that the Celtic team was in any way finished or over the top. Indeed, there was quality all over the pitch and competition for places was fierce. Big Jock had been building a team for the future and many of the previously established team had moved on. From my point of view as a goal scorer, competition was particularly strong. You had Kenny Dalglish who could score from anywhere by simply arriving at the exact moment and literally passing the ball into the net. Bobby Lennox – a particular inspiration of mine – looked every bit as fast and sharp as ever. Also, Celtic had a certain style of playing football that didn't rely solely on their main strikers. The 'Celtic way' of playing football meant that goals came from everywhere and we had plenty of players at that time who could do that. I suppose as one of the young boys coming through you always thought you had a chance but you also understood that there were some great footballers on the team and that there were other young lads like yourself waiting for their chance.

Looking back on that time, with the wealth of talent that was already at Celtic Park, it is a testament to George's ability and attitude that he was not overwhelmed by the challenge as many others in his youth cohort were. Indeed, George's great friend and fellow youth team member, John Kirkwood, pointed out that George was the only one from that youth team who actually made the breakthrough onto the first team. According to John:

Certainly George was the most talented of our youth group and it should be of no surprise that he would have been the one who made it onto the first team if anybody were to do it. There were a lot of wonderfully talented footballers at Celtic at that time so anyone who was going to break into the team would have to be exceptional. And George certainly possessed that special 'something else'. He had loads of ability and a wonderful temperament and attitude. He never seemed to worry about [whether] he would make the grade. He just got on with it. And he had a great appetite for learning and was always adding things to his game and picking up advice from the established players. George was an exceptionally intelligent footballer even as a youth player. His game was all about arriving at the right time, anticipation, wonderful control, a subtle touch and a shot like a mule in both feet. He was not the fastest of players and certainly didn't run around the pitch aimlessly for 90 minutes. He had, however, a rangy running style that was deceptively quick and the wonderful habit of feinting past defenders and being able to turn in the tightest of spaces. He was also an incredibly brave player of considerable courage and despite taking severe abuse from some pretty physical defenders in those days he was never one to hide and would always come looking for the ball. That's what probably made him stand out from the rest of us.

The young lad from Birkenshaw had now completed his apprenticeship in football that had started off using jumpers for goalposts on the parklands and waste grounds of Lanarkshire and had finished playing in the reserves for Celtic. He was now about to step onto Celtic Park and in front of his family and friends in the Jungle – and this time it was for real.

9

Making a Debut, Starring against Rangers then Catching a Bus Home

'Right George – get the tracksuit off and get ready to go on'

IN FRONT OF 16,000 fans, George was coming on as a substitute for Paul Wilson in the second half in Celtic's home leg of the European Cup Winners' Cup game against the Icelandic team, Valur FC. Celtic had won the first leg in Reykjavik 2–0 two weeks previously and were big favourites to complete the job at Celtic Park. They certainly did that, thumping the Icelanders 7–0, with Harry Hood scoring twice and one each from big Johannes 'Shuggie' Edvaldsson, Kenny Dalglish, Pat McCluskey, John 'Dixie' Deans and Tommy Callaghan. For the 18-year-old youngster making his debut in front of the fans he had stood his entire life with, this should have been an occasion never to be forgotten. Surprisingly, George remembers little of it:

> Trying to remember individual games and what happened during the match is funny. Some matches – particularly the important ones – remain firmly etched in the memory and you seem to be able to recall every incident and kick of the ball. You'd think that I should be able to remember my debut for Celtic but strangely I remember very little about it. Maybe, because it was such an important milestone for me, it just kind of passed me by. Or maybe I was simply too young (being 18 at the time) to take it all in. I really thought that I made my debut against Rangers which was a couple of weeks later. Dixie Deans, who was playing that night, keeps reminding me that I came on against Valur in the second-half but, to be honest, I can't recall anything about it.

Be that as it may, it is recorded that halfway through the second half

with the game securely in the bag, George was given the 'nod' by Sean
Fallon (acting manager at that time in the absence of Jock Stein who was
recovering in hospital after a near-fatal car crash). The team that evening
included the likes of Danny McGrain and up front Kenny Dalglish, Dixie
Deans, Tommy Callaghan and Harry Hood – all of whom had scored. At
half time everything was well in control and Sean Fallon decided to give
the young lad a first appearance in the first-team.

And so George McCluskey ran onto the ground that he would grace for
the next eight years and on which he would give Celtic fans such joy on
numerous occasions as they cheered on one of their own. There wasn't
enough time or need for the young lad from Birkenshaw to make a name
for himself that night. But he had made a huge mark in his career by
running over the line and onto the pitch to replace Paul Wilson. Talking to
Celtic fans of a certain age it seems that half of Glasgow and Lanarkshire
must have been at the game as numerous people from Birkenshaw,
Hamilton, Uddingston, Coatbridge, Viewpark, Motherwell and every part
of that region absolutely swear that they were there on the night that 'our
George played his first match'. George keeps reminding them that this
was not the 1972 Scottish Cup Final at Hampden when Celtic thumped
Hibs 6–1 watched by a crowd of over 100,000, including a young George
McCluskey who watched and dreamt of playing in the green and white
hoops some day and scoring the winning goal (though that was to wait for
some more years). In any case, those who claim that they were at Celtic
Park to see George run on to make his debut against Valur FC on a cold
night in October 1975 were not entirely telling lies. After all, the young
man from Birkenshaw played for all of those who followed Celtic in his
community. So they were there, in a very real sense. And George did not
take this new milestone for granted. The young lad, coming from a family
and a community that was truly Celtic minded, had just fulfilled his every
ambition – even if he couldn't recall much about it after. He had indeed run
across towards the Jungle where he had stood from a boy and watched his
heroes. He was now on his way to becoming one of them. But for now it
was back to training as normal with the reserves for the next few weeks.
He had made his first appearance in the green and white hoops by coming
off the bench when the tie was well won. He knew that meant Celtic rated
him as a player for the future and he was prepared to work even harder to
claim a place on the first team. Little did he know that, it seems, Jock Stein
(while still in hospital) would pick the league game against Rangers to give

the 18-year-old lad his first start.

'Sean, I can't speak but I can still bloody hear you!'

Stein had almost been killed in a car crash; a collision with another car being driven down the wrong way on a dual carriageway just before the start of the 1975/76 season. The steering wheel had crushed his chest (in the days before airbags) and as a result of his injuries he was in hospital for several months, unable to speak. Officially replaced by his able assistant, Sean Fallon, Stein had to step back from managing Celtic for most of that season. Yet, such was the measure and drive of the man, he continued to keep a very direct interest in and influence on what was happening at Celtic, even when he was recovering in hospital. Sean Fallon visited him almost daily and, as Stein grew stronger, these visits effectively became management meetings at which Fallon would report everything back to Stein including how players were doing in training, match reports and team selection and strategy for forthcoming games. Since Stein could not speak he communicated with Fallon on a notepad which he kept by his bedside. One of these visits by Fallon to Stein in the final days of October had an enormous impact on the career of George. Celtic had lost the League Cup Final on the 24 October, going down 1–0 to Rangers in an ill-tempered and untidy affair at Hampden with Alex MacDonald scoring the only goal. Not for the first nor the last time was an exciting, talented and attacking Celtic side thwarted by their more physical and more defensive-minded rivals. Having lost the first league game to Rangers 2–1 at Ibrox at the beginning of the season, Rangers were going for their third straight victory on the bounce. The team from Govan seemed to think that they had a way of nullifying the Celtic threat. No matter which combination of Dalglish, Hood, Lennox or Callaghan presented itself, Rangers had found a way to stop them playing. Stein was also aware that, this being the first season in which the new format of teams playing each other four times rather than twice as previously, there was a distinct danger that the Rangers' system, left unchecked, might just steamroller its way to a position of dominance. Something different had to be done. But what?

It must have been a fascinating management meeting for Fallon and Stein between the defeat in the League Cup Final and the forthcoming league game at Celtic Park. Fallon would have given a detailed and accurate description of the defeat at the hands of Rangers the week before and both he and Stein would have searched for a solution, for something different that might change things for the better. Celtic Reserves had played Dundee on the Wednesday night, winning 4–0 with George scoring twice. Legend has it that Jock Stein took up his pen and inquired about the game and, in particular, how George McCluskey had played. It must have been in Stein's mind to consider playing George against Rangers. Fallon took up the notepad and read Stein's queries. He then picked up the pen and jotted down that George had had a great game and scored two goals. He then handed the notepad back for Jock Stein to read. Stein studied the reply and then took the pen and wrote the classic line that became legendary among the team at that time: 'Sean, I can't speak but I can still bloody hear you!' And, 'Play him on the right – number seven' was the next line that Stein wrote and it turned out to be a master-stroke. It also was quite an innovative and bold decision as the young lad would not be playing in his favourite and best position of striker. Harry Hood, Dixie Deans and Kenny Dalglish would provide enough striking options. McCluskey was to play out on the right with the option to come inside when the opportunity presented itself. The young lad of 18 years with only a second-half appearance from the bench against Valur FC to his name, was to be thrown into a game against Rangers that Celtic couldn't afford to lose if they were to have any chance of stopping a super-confident rival outfit.

George arrived at Celtic Park early that morning for what was in those days a novel early kick-off time. Fans today are used to games being played at all sorts of ridiculous times and on all days of the week. The weekend game, which traditionally kicked off at 3.00 pm on a Saturday, has long since been sacrificed on the altar of satellite television. Indeed, today the weekend schedule often starts on a Friday evening and continues right through to the Monday or even Tuesday of the next week. Such is the power of those who possess and wield the television rights of planet football. In 1975 that scenario was unheard of. Football meant 3.00 pm on a Saturday, or a Wednesday evening kick-off for European games, League Cup games (until the semi-final stage), Scottish Cup replays and the occasional league match that had to be rescheduled due to fixture congestion. However, around this time, the Scottish football authorities (in conjunction with the police and local authorities) had decided to experiment with a lunch-time kick-off at Celtic Park in the hope that an early start would reduce the possibility of alcohol fuelled crowd problems. This was a pressure match for several teams in terms of the league campaign. Celtic were a solitary point in front of Rangers, with Motherwell, Hibs and Hearts just behind them. Yet for young McCluskey the real pressure was just about to hit.

'George, were you not listening when the team was read out? You're playing today!'

George had made the 14 man pool for the game but hadn't got over excited about that. Sure, he was delighted to be on the squad, as that meant that he would be able to watch the game from the dug-out as the number 14. Introduced in the late 1960s, substitutions (or replacements) were still extremely limited and in 1975 teams were only permitted to make a maximum of two in any game. Just getting into the 14 man squad didn't mean with any certainty that you'd be playing that game as there were generally two more seasoned and better regarded players on the bench who would be called upon if needed. The role of the number 14 was usually assigned to a promising young player on the cusp of breaking into the first team – someone just like George. The experience would be invaluable and it was an indication that you were definitely on the manager's radar. It also gave the established players an indication of where the potential threat to their position was coming from.

The up and coming young aspirant from Birkenshaw knew his job well. He had done it on a number of occasions before and, indeed, the previous week had played this role against the very same opposition at the League Cup Final at Hampden. There'd be no difference at this game. You go in with the team, get changed, sit down, the manager reads out the team-sheet and then you go and get the boots for the rest of the team and sort out the towels etc for after the game while the manager gave the team-talk to the players who'll be directly involved in the game. So just after Sean Fallon read out the team who were playing that day, George got up and was about to set about his role as the 'number 14', when Kenny Dalglish asked him, 'Where are you going, George?'

'I'm off to get the boots for you guys,' was George's reply.

Dalglish retorted, 'Were you not listening, George? You're on the team. You're starting at number seven.'

This was somewhat of a surprise to McCluskey to say the least. He was absolutely speechless. Getting his first start for Celtic! Against Rangers! Wearing the famous number seven on the shorts – the same number that Jinky Johnstone had worn with such distinction! My Lord! Sharp intake of breath required and then getting the boots and shorts on to get ready to face Rangers at Celtic Park. George's own recollection of that goes as follows:

> I suppose that it was no bad thing that I didn't know until just before the game that I would be actually starting. There was no time for nerves or to think about it for days before the game. I was only an 18-year-old lad and, like many other guys at that age, I didn't fully appreciate the importance of the occasion. I just lined up behind Kenny Dalglish and the rest of the team and ran out onto the pitch to the roar of the Jungle and got ready for the start of 90 minutes of a Celtic v Rangers match.

It was as well that George fully understood how such games were to be played. Often a young man making his first full debut, and against his club's greatest rivals, can be overawed by the magnitude of the occasion and the game can simply pass him by. Certainly the decision to play young McCluskey was the talk of the crowd as the team was announced over the tannoy, with George's admirers delighted to see the young lad from Birkenshaw getting his chance to show just how good he was and others perhaps a little more anxious about what the next 90 minutes might reveal for this most gifted but still very young talent. All knew that if McCluskey was to play on the right then one man would be assigned the task of marking him: John Greig.

John Greig was no ordinary defender. It was not for nothing that this Rangers stalwart was awarded with the honour of 'the greatest Rangers player ever' by Rangers fans in 1999 defeating the likes of Jim Baxter, Sandy Jardine, Graeme Souness, Davy Cooper, Ally McCoist and a host of other contenders. He was both his club's and country's captain and a Rangers-man to the core. No doubt the Rangers fans that day would have been supremely confident that this 'giant of Scottish football' would not be bested by an 18-year-old upstart making his full debut. One word of warning to the aspiring striker from a tough uncompromising Rangers legend should suffice in quieting any threat from that source.

The game had just started and the players moved into position with George moving onto the right. John Greig followed him as he had been tasked to do. 'You might think you're good, kid, but if I were you I wouldn't be too keen on wanting to see too much of the ball today. I will kick you up and down this pitch every chance I get.' George just laughed at Greig. He was well used to coming up against defenders who would try to intimidate. After all, he had been facing that type since he was playing at school level. As someone who had been the key forward for every team he had played for, getting such attention came with the territory. Playing at this new level would be no different. George McCluskey was a brave footballer who never hid or backed down from any opponent – no matter how hard that person thought he was. 'Listen,' he said, 'you're an old man and you're going to have to catch me first.' He took a couple of hard tackles early on but he simply got up and got on with it. As the game progressed the Celtic crowd were increasingly delighted with the impact the young lad was making. His wing play gave Rangers (and the 'greatest Rangers player ever') a major headache as George had a great game that day, cutting inside and outside, making himself available, laying the ball off and giving what was generally agreed by the press and football pundits as an extremely promising display in his first Glasgow derby.

The game was not without controversy, with Rangers taking a lead early in the second half through a goal from Derek Parlane. The Rangers centre-forward certainly put the ball past Peter Latchford in the Celtic goal but it didn't strike the referee or linesmen that standing in a position that was at least five yards off-side was against the rules of the game. The Celtic players restarted the game in total disbelief and with a considerable sense of injustice. Heads didn't drop, however, and the lad having a stormer up the right wing set about his work with even more determination. It was little wonder that the Celtic equaliser came from a move down that side. George collected the ball wide on the right, moved about 10 yards along that side before cutting in and drilling a powerful shot towards the far post. It was going in alright and George McCluskey would have ended a perfect 90-minute debut against Rangers as goal scorer and man of the match, except Paul Wilson was standing almost on the line at the back post and allowed the ball to canon off his abdomen and into the net. Whether or not Wilson was just making sure that the ball went into the Rangers goal or simply that it was hit was such force that he couldn't get out of the way was completely irrelevant for George McCluskey. All that mattered was the result (which kept Celtic at the top of the league) and that he had acquitted himself well. And he had indeed. With 10 minutes to go the young lad had given his all and was, naturally, beginning to tire as he was replaced by the legendary Harry Hood, going off to a rousing ovation from the Celtic fans. A new star had just arrived. After the game John Greig – who had promised him at the start of the match a torrid time if he went near the ball – sought him out in the changing rooms, shook his hand and congratulated George for an outstanding performance: 'Fair play to you, boy, you had a great game. And I was only kidding on about what I'd do to you at the start of the game. You'll do well if you keep it up.' George was pretty chuffed. Congratulated by a Rangers legend was one thing. Being cheered off by the Jungle was another. All he had to do was to get a shower, take it all in and get home to Birkenshaw. That proved an adventure in itself.

Catching a bus from Celtic Park to Birkenshaw Circle

When you think of how professional footballers today – with their vast salaries and matching lifestyles – travel to and from games in their top of the range luxury cars and how the players' car park at every top football stadium looks like a show room for the rich and famous, you have to pinch yourself when you hear how young George made his way back home after the game that day. He had just played the game of his life so far against Rangers and had probably been the difference between Celtic getting a point and their being defeated for a second time in the space of a week by their great rivals. George didn't get into his car because, well, he didn't have one. In fact he didn't even have a driving licence. Such was life in those days. Most of the other guys did have cars and headed off back home, but the young lad from Birkenshaw never bothered to think of asking for a lift. He was too modest and shy for that and, besides, he knew his way from Celtic Park to Birkenshaw Circle. Hadn't he spent the past five years going up and down that road on the 'Green Bus' along the Old Edinburgh Road? So George, in his Celtic suit, walked out of the ground and down to the bus stop at Parkhead Cross. However, what he hadn't thought about was that the bus stop on days such as this was Rangers territory and that there were around 20 supporters there who had been at the game that day and who might not have been delighted to have witnessed the great display young George had given an hour or two beforehand! George's recollection of the episode is precious:

> I must have been on such a high that I didn't even think about how I was getting home. I just walked round from Celtic Park to the bus stop as normal... only to see a crowd of Rangers supporters already waiting there. For some reason they didn't notice me but I can tell you

in the short time/seeming eternity that I was at the bus stop my mind did empty itself of what had happened on the pitch that afternoon and focused more on thoughts about getting on the bus, the bus journey itself and how to get off the bus!

Fortunately for George, a bus pulled up and it was not one that he would have to share with the opposition fans on his journey back to Birkenshaw.

I was standing there wondering what [was] going to happen next and then a bus was passing by. I just heard a screech of brakes and the bus came to a sudden stop. It wasn't a public bus but one full of Celtic supporters. The doors of the bus opened and the Rangers fans took a step back expecting a confrontation. Suddenly a couple of guys jumped off the bus, grabbed me and manhandled me onto the bus saying, 'What in God's name are you standing there for?' Someone on the bus must have recognised me and shouted for the bus to stop. Unbelievably it was the Bellshill Celtic Supporters Club, run by Mrs McSherry who was sitting at the front of the bus. The bus went stony silent for a second or two and I asked them did they enjoy the game and did I do alright and then the whole bus started to chant my name and cheer. We had a sing song the whole way back and they dropped me right at my own house. I think it was just in case I ended up trying to catch a bus from Bellshill to Birkenshaw with another group of Rangers supporters!

That was not the last of the drama for that day. Being the modest guy that he was then and remains today, George had just sort of left Celtic Park after the game without hanging around too long. He just presumed that he would go home and come back to training on Monday morning with the reserves as normal. He hadn't thought about the fact that Celtic were playing Boavista in the European Cup Winners Cup at Celtic Park the following Wednesday night or that this game might involve him! Of course this was before mobile phones had been invented so communication was somewhat different. George's parents had recently got a phone for the house but the girls generally monopolised it talking with their friends. Eventually someone had to drive from Celtic Park to the McCluskey home in Birkenshaw to inform the latest Celtic sensation that he was in the team to play against Boavista and would have to report for training at Seamill the next day and bring his kit.

Another great game, getting dropped and meeting Tommy Gemmell

In so many ways this busy and exciting day in November tells much about the type of person George McCluskey was – and is. It started with a young lad of 18 going to play in his first full debut against their bitterest rivals, Rangers. He had an outstanding game despite the close attention of a genuine Rangers legend. He made it back home safely thanks to Mrs McSherry and the Bellshill Celtic Supporters Club. And to make this fairy tale day complete he had to pack his bag for training at Seamill to prepare for European football. He certainly had 'arrived on the scene' but George McCluskey took nothing for granted that day. In a 12-hour period he exhibited the characteristics that would define both his footballing career and his life off the pitch. Brave, calm and unflappable, but also trusting and, above all else, humble. Many young (and not so young) players then and, especially, today would have had an entirely different attitude after playing like McCluskey did. After all, he had made quite an impression in his debut against Rangers and had massively enhanced his standing in the eyes of the management, his peers and the fans. The very least that most footballers would have done after such a performance would have been to expect and even demand a starting place in the next game or it would have been all over the press the next day. For a young lad like George to have put in such a performance it would have been the case of the football agent phoning the club and looking to negotiate new contract. Of course things were different then, but so was George McCluskey. There was no arrogance or expectation about the young lad who had just delivered an outstanding performance in an important game against Celtic's bitterest rivals:

To be perfectly honest I never thought about the Boavista game for one second. I was just delighted that I had played well and made my mum and dad and family proud, all my pals and the people I'd meet every day. I regard that game as the start of my Celtic career and one that I cherish. But I never took anything for granted. After all, when you look at the Celtic team at that time it was full of players who had achieved so much including league titles, cups, international caps – and that's without looking at the guys who had won the European Cup – the Lisbon Lions – and the other players who had been part of the nine-in-a-Row who were still playing that time! When you look around the dressing-room and see the likes of Kenny Dalglish, Bobby Lennox,

Harry Hood, Dixie Deans and a host of others you can't expect to walk onto the team on the basis of a good game against Rangers. So it was a big surprise when I was told to get my bag packed and get ready to go to Seamill. It was great excitement for me but the one I felt sorry for was my mother. The house was pandemonium with all the relatives and neighbours calling in and analysing the game and then she has to start getting my clothes and training gear together for the next morning. But that was never a problem for her. She had been doing that for years for me and John. Just took everything in her stride and made sure that I'd be fine for the next morning.

Celtic had drawn 0–0 in Portugal in the first leg and were favourites to complete the job at Celtic Park. This they duly did with a 3–1 win with goals from Dalglish, Edvaldsson and Deans. Again McCluskey was moved onto the right where he had, by all accounts, an outstanding game and was for many man of the match that evening. There was little time for that to go to his head. A glowing report from Sean Fallon was not enough to convince Jock Stein that young George was quite ready for an extended run out in the team and he found himself on the bench for the next game in Dundee on the Saturday. George puts that down to Stein's way of keeping you in your place. Celtic were getting beaten 1–0 and the Celtic fans were getting restless. Many were shouting for the Celtic manager to 'bring on McCluskey' which, with half an hour to go, the manager did.

When George took up his place on the right he was greeted by a Celtic legend – but not wearing the green and white hoops by which Celtic fans remembered him so fondly. The great Celtic full back Tommy Gemmell, whose thunderous equalising goal in Lisbon in 1967 is etched in the mind of every single Celtic fan in the world, had moved from Celtic to Nottingham Forest in 1971 and then to Dundee in 1973. Now playing at left-back against the club for whom he had played with distinction for a decade, what would be the advice that he would give the up and coming young lad who he would be marking?

Well, if George had expected words of encouragement and kind wishes from the veteran full-back, he would have been disappointed. Big Tommy Gemmell was not that sort of a romantic footballer. No doubt he would have read some of the glowing reports in the papers about the latest 'bright young thing' and would relish putting him in his place. After all, the left-back had seen off some of the greatest forwards in European football during those glory years at Celtic. Here was a wee lad who deserved to be kicked! George tells it as follows:

> There was about 30 minutes to go and we were getting beaten 1–0. I was told to get on and move onto the right as I had done in the previous two games. I wasn't on the pitch 10 seconds when Tommy came up behind me and said in my ear, 'I am going to kick you up and down this pitch every chance I get young lad.' I just thought, 'Jesus, here's me being told for the second time in a week by two of the greatest full-backs in the game that I'm going to be kicked all over the park. Maybe there's a full-backs' union that I have never heard of and that's out to get me!'
>
> Well, I was 18 and afraid of no one so I just gave Tommy the very same answer I gave to John Grieg the week before and said, 'Listen Tommy. You're just like John Grieg. You're an old man. Before you try to kick me you'll have to catch me first.' Sure enough, just like John Greig, the first man to come up to me at the end and put his arm around me was big Tommy who said, 'You're going to get a lot of that, George, and you'll have to take it. You've done well and took it all. Keep that attitude and you'll do well son.'

Unfortunately this did not end up another 'Roy of the Rovers' match for George. Dundee held on to their one goal lead and Celtic lost their top spot in the Scottish League to Rangers. George played one more game that month against St Johnstone at Celtic Park which Celtic won 3–2. He then didn't see first team action again that season until being brought on as late substitute at an away 2–0 defeat at Hibs in April 1976. The 1975/76 race for the Scottish League title see-sawed between Celtic and Rangers throughout the rest of the winter and spring with a disastrous month of April in which Celtic played five games (losing three and drawing two) and effectively handing the title to Rangers. Many fans still question why Jock Stein didn't give his young up and coming talent more game time. Some of those who had followed McCluskey's progress over the years wondered how Celtic might have done had the young lad from Birkenshaw – who had made such an impact when he made his debut at the start of November, but not seen in first team action since 22nd of that month – been used more often. George's explanation for this apparent 'fall out of favour' is less dramatic and very much in line with Stein's style of management:

Jock Stein was very much a 'hands on' type of manager who trusted what he saw with his own eyes. Sure, he would take advice from others but he would not make that decide what he thought. He also was playing a background role season, naturally, with being in hospital and would have given Sean Fallon his place. Sean would have been very prominent in the day-to-day running of the team during Jock's absence, but we all got the sense that Stein was working behind the scenes and was still a huge influence even from his hospital bed. I think that Jock must have thought that I might not be ready just yet and that I needed to be brought along slowly and carefully. I also think that what people forget is that I was only a young lad of 18 at the time and that Celtic had some wonderful strikers and forwards in the side who it was almost impossible to choose between. Kenny Dalglish was only coming to his prime and was, by miles, the best footballer in Britain and one of the best in Europe. Bobby Lennox was still destroying defences with his pace and scoring with ease. You also had the likes of Harry Hood and Paul Wilson – and there was also some fantastic talent coming through and pushing for places on the team. Also I think that Jock Stein regarded me as a talent for the future; someone he had signed, given a first taste of playing for Celtic at the highest level and who he would develop in good time. I was playing well in the reserves and establishing myself as one of the first team squad. Like all players who had tasted first team football I was anxious to get back onto the pitch and this added an edge to my training. The whole squad – not to mention the supporters – was devastated by losing a league title that we should have won. But this made us more determined for the following season. I was sure that if I kept the same attitude and kept working hard my time would come sooner rather than later.

Most fans thought the same. Young McCluskey was now beginning to look the finished article. Players moved on in the closed season – notably Harry Hood who went to play in the United States for San Antonio Thunder, opening up opportunities for a striker like George McCluskey. As the beginning of the 1976/77 season loomed, it seemed that George was about to make a real name for himself. Little did he or his many admirers know, this coming season was going to be his greatest challenge to date.

10

'Whatever Happened to that Young Boy McCluskey?'

THE SEASON OF 1976/77 couldn't have started more brightly for George McCluskey. Jock Stein had recovered from his horrific road accident and was fully focussed on re-establishing Celtic's domination in Scotland and plotting more success in Europe. The Scottish League was the number one priority since Celtic had not won it in the previous two years and Stein believed that Celtic now had the players to restore them to the very top again. George McCluskey had led the way for the new generation of quite outrageously talented young lads who were breaking into the first team, with Roy Aitken and Tommy Burns (from the reserves) and Johnny Doyle (who Celtic signed from Ayr United) all seizing their opportunity to stake a claim to a place in the starting 11 towards the end of the previous season. Some noted that, at a time when older players were losing their heads as Celtic threw away the league, these young lads promised a brighter future for the club. Many – including Jock Stein, one suspects – looked at McCluskey as a key player in the new campaign.

Certainly Stein must have rated the lad from Birkenshaw to whose home he had driven with Fallon a couple of years beforehand to ensure that this noted talent wore the green and white hoops of Celtic and not the red of Manchester United. Harry Hood had moved on but Celtic didn't make any sudden move on the transfer market to replace the proven striker. What they possessed already in George McCluskey was more than enough. Stein was now firmly back at the helm and had no hesitation in starting McCluskey as number nine in his very first game back as manager. The first match was a glamour friendly at Celtic Park on 7 August against Uruguayan champions, Penarol. Although billed as a 'friendly' it was, in many ways, a game in which Jock Stein laid down a marker on how he saw the future for Celtic and an opportunity for a new generation of players to stake a claim on a first team place. In particular the forward line had a new and exciting look about it with McCluskey leading the line with an eager Johnny Dolye and Kenny Dalglish running through from just behind him, with much of the passing being directed towards McCluskey by his 'soul-mate' Tommy Burns. The movement that night between Danny McGrain, Tommy Burns, Ronnie Glavin, Andy Lynch and Kenny Dalglish was by all accounts wonderful, with everything being directed towards George and Johnny Doyle, both of whom tortured a typically physical South American side. Late in the opening half Doyle was chopped down inside the box and a penalty was awarded to Celtic. Jock Stein had given the responsibility of taking penalties to George and, after some minutes of protests and theatricals from the Uruguayans, the young Celtic centre-forward buried the ball with considerable force into the corner of the Penarol net. The rout of an excellent Latin American team continued in the second half as Celtic ran out 3–0 winners. The crowd was delighted with what it saw and Stein, normally not noted for giving his assessment of his team at the start of a season (and especially not after a friendly), announced that Celtic were indeed making progress, singling out George McCluskey for special mention and praise. Perhaps the previous two seasons of frustration were finally over and Celtic fans would get to see just what new talent was emerging at Celtic Park.

The domestic season got off to a feisty start on 10 August with George McCluskey lining out in the number nine shorts in the Glasgow Cup Final against Rangers in front of 55,000 at Hampden Stadium alongside Kenny Dalglish and Johnny Doyle. This looked to be the beginning of a new and exciting young strike force that would lead Celtic to future glory – even if the result that day didn't go in Celtic's favour with Rangers running out 3–1 winners and big 'Shuggy' Edvaldson netting the sole Celtic score. George started the next two games of the season (both in the Scottish League Cup) and for those who had been predicting the emergence of this new talent for the previous couple of years it seemed that their judgement was being proved sound. A new talent had emerged and was about to blossom. That is how it seemed to the faithful at Celtic Park and to George himself.

Yet there was something not quite right about his game that revealed itself as the season begun. For a striker like George who relied on that crucial ability to simply be there when the ball arrived, fractions are vital. In the first three games he didn't score and seemed to be just a little bit 'off the pace'. He was dropped to the bench with the return of Bobby Lennox from injury and then missed the next few weeks with what seemed like a minor injury before coming off the bench at Tynecastle to score his first goal for Celtic in a 2–2 draw against Hearts. It was, unusually for George, a header, but it was his first goal for the Hoops in league football and would be, surely, the first of many that season and many seasons to come. Unfortunately the injury that George had picked up at the start of the season was much more serious than was first thought. George reclaimed the number nine position four days later in the midweek League Cup game at Albion Rovers. That was the last seen of him during the rest of that season and, indeed, for the opening months of the next. Little wonder that Celtic fans began to wonder what on earth had happened to the young Birkenshaw lad. George was off the scene so long that some even wondered if they would ever see him in the green and white hoops again. George must have had that same thought himself as he faced the most difficult challenge to his football career so far.

> After the first couple of games at the start of the season I felt a pain in my left knee that gradually got worse. It was a kind of nagging pain at the start but very quickly I realised that it was a serious problem. Then my knee just buckled when I hit the ball and I was in the most incredible pain. Yet when the club doctor examined me there was no sign of injury or, indeed, pain. Then when I went to training the next day the injury came back as soon as I hit the ball or made a quick turn. It was the most frustrating and worrying time in my football life. I was just 19 years of age, had made my debut the year before and just scored my first goal for Celtic. I was the first-choice striker and everything seemed to be happening for me. Then everything just seemed to fall apart. Suddenly, instead of getting ready to lead the line for Celtic and playing alongside Kenny Dalglish, Tommy Burns, Bobby Lennox and all the rest of guys, I was on the treatment table, getting back to training, beginning to feel like I was making progress, thinking that I was back to normal and then, one kick of the ball, and it was back to the treatment table.

What made it all the more frustrating for George was that every time he hobbled off the training pitch and came to the treatment table the club doctor couldn't find anything wrong with him. Even more problematic and bewildering was that George himself, having come off the training ground in agony, often couldn't actually feel any pain or pinpoint any obvious injury. It was almost as if it had gone as quickly as it came. Some people wondered if it was all in his head.

If things were rather bleak for the young lad from Birkenshaw they were certainly pretty bright for the new Celtic side that Stein had unleashed onto Scottish football that season after his own time in hospital. It almost looked like he had decided to make up for lost time – and how his team responded. Celtic were on fire and won the league from Rangers by 9 points. During an era when 2 points were awarded for a win this was a huge margin. May saw Celtic add the Scottish Cup with a 1–0 win over Rangers and, but for a most unfortunate 2–1 extra time defeat by Aberdeen in the League Cup Final in November of 1976, that season would have been even more satisfying for Stein as his rebuilding programme proved successful after a sluggish start. Kenny Dalglish was in outstanding form throughout the year and scored 54 goals that season (including 35 in the league) as a Celtic team ran rampant. Joe Craig, Ronnie Glavin and Johnny Doyle were also part of a Celtic attacking unit that more than made up for the disappointments of the previous couple of seasons. Little did Celtic supporters know what was just ahead of them as Dalglish lifted the Scottish Cup (and temporarily lost his winner's medal) on 7 May 1977. George McCluskey's absence seemed to go unnoticed except by those who knew just how good he could be. George was back to being a fan again. But this time round he wasn't a fan who was playing his way through the squads towards the dream of playing for Celtic. He had got to where he always wanted to be and now was limping around Celtic Park and visiting a medical team who couldn't treat him because they couldn't diagnose an injury that wasn't, apparently, there. During that season of triumph with Jock Stein back at the helm George McCluskey was listed as 'injured'. Some began to question whether the young lad who had shone so spectacularly throughout his junior days and promised so much in his first games in a Celtic shirt would return and fulfil his promise. During those dark times George himself must have wondered if he would ever hear the Celtic fans sing his name as they did at Dundee at the start of the previous season while sitting on the bench or on the Bellshill supporters bus after his debut against Rangers the year before.

Dalglish moves to Liverpool while George's nightmare continues

The injury that put paid to the 1976/77 season for young McCluskey was no better at the start of the next and his only involvement in the first part of the 1977/78 season was a couple of substitute appearances. What made it all the more difficult for both the player and club was that his presence was seriously missed at this time, following the unexpected departure of Kenny Dalglish at the end of the 1976 season. It is no exaggeration to state that on 9 August 1977 Celtic fans were devastated and shocked to learn that one of the finest players of his generation had been allowed to leave Celtic and go to play in front of the Kop at Anfield. Dalglish had graced the green and white hoops for nine seasons. He was the complete, almost perfect player, that any fan would dearly want on their team. He was creative, scored many fabulous goals, had great stamina and anticipation and was, in addition to all that, a marvellous team player who could and did bring the best out in his teammates. Jock Stein tried everything in his power to keep Dalglish at Celtic but it seems that 'King Kenny' was set on moving and there was nothing the club could do to stop him. It seems that Dalglish had decided long before the end of the season that he was on his way no matter what was on offer at Celtic Park.

Stein (not for the first time) rocked the Scottish football world by signing Alfie Conn, the former Rangers favourite, from Spurs in March 1977. Not that this was out of the ordinary for Celtic Football Club as it had always been welcoming to people of all faiths, backgrounds and creeds. Conn was an exceptionally talented and creative midfielder who, on his day, could be simply exhilarating and unplayable. What many fans do not know is that Alfie Conn took a massive pay cut to come to play for Celtic. When asked (as he frequently is) why he signed for Celtic, Conn's answer is always the same – 'Jock Stein'. The signing of Alfie Conn at the time seemed unusual, even baffling, given that Celtic already had the best midfielder in the British game and (arguably) in Europe in Kenny Dalglish. Some see this as an indication that Stein was already resigned to losing his talismanic striker and was looking for someone who would go some way towards replacing the quite simply irreplaceable. To this day many supporters still suspect that the board must also have been aware of this, was less determined than Stein on this matter and may not have been too unhappy to receive a record transfer fee of £440,000 from Liverpool to relinquish the services of this truly world-class footballer. Some suspect that the board felt that the Celtic youth system which was producing some of the best footballing talent in Britain at that time would fill the gap made by Dalglish's departure. Someone like George McCluskey perhaps? The problem for George (and Celtic) was that, while a wonderful opportunity to become a key member of the Celtic team was there, he wasn't. Struggling with an injury that came and went, George was back on the fringes of the Celtic side he so wished to play for. For a young lad who had just broken through onto the first team squad these were very dark days indeed. George recalls this difficult time:

> I suppose that at the start of the injury problem I didn't really comprehend just how serious an injury could be. At 18 or 19 you don't really think about things like that. I'd just made the first team and all I could think about was getting over the injury, getting stuck back into training again and back into the first team squad. It wasn't like I had broken my leg or anything like that. But as time went on and I wasn't getting any nearer to getting back to playing any sort of football things did start to creep into my mind. Training was no longer fun as I couldn't train seriously with any of my teammates. I couldn't really play practice matches with conviction or try to impress in the drills to show the manager that I was ready for selection. Even the discussions about the coming games, who might be playing and what the tactics might be just didn't seem to involve me. I was trying my best to be positive and optimistic in the circumstances and trying to convince myself that give it another couple of weeks I'd be fine again. But nothing seemed to change and the injury dragged on. And all I could do was watch the rest of the boys go onto the pitch on a Saturday and do what I was dying to do – play football.

As the weeks grew into months and the new season progressed with still no sign of a return to the team some may have been forgiven in giving up hope of seeing the young lad from Birkenshaw fulfil his promise. One man however did not give up hope in George McCluskey and was prepared to give him as much personal attention and support as he could. Jock Stein trusted in George's ability and character. He was not for giving up on him.

'Right George, just hit that ball as hard as you can and put Latchford in the back of the net!'

The 'mystery' injury that had put George out of action for almost a season and a half and which threatened his career was, in fact, damage to the cartilage in the left knee. The cartilage is a tough, rubbery tissue that functions as a cushion for bones at joints. They are effectively the 'shock absorbers' of the body. Footballers are constantly at risk to knee cartilage injuries due to twisting and turning, wear and tear and impact such as, well, getting kicked a lot by other players. Cartilage damage makes up around 12 per cent of footballing injuries and forwards, given that their movement has to be explosive and that they tend to be on the receiving end of some pretty serious tackling, are at particular risk of this type of injury. George had been receiving the knocks of a forward since he was in primary school so it was almost inevitable that it would take its toll. A cartilage injury is painful and certainly puts playing out of the question – but it is normally treatable by surgery. George had the classic symptoms of a tear to the meniscus cartilage: extreme pain (especially after playing) and a distinct lack of mobility. Some cartilage damage can finish a footballer's career. Our own John Kennedy, thought by many destined to become the 'new Billy McNeill', is one example of misfortune and a cynical tackle that resulted in a most promising football talent being stopped in its tracks. The young man from Bellshill gave a peerless display of defending at its best against Barcelona in the Nou Camp in March 2004 at the age of 19. This assured performance earned him a call up to the Scotland team to play Romania in a friendly at Hampden the next week where an appalling two-footed lunge from a certain Ionet Ganea did dreadful and, ultimately, career ending damage to the Celtic defender's knee. Despite several operations by one of the greatest knee surgeons in the world, Richard Steadman, John Kennedy was eventually forced to retire from playing football on medical grounds at the age of 26. All of those fortunate enough to have seen him play must agree that this was indeed a most tragic and untimely end to what surely would have been an illustrious career. A generation of Celtic fans were deprived of a most gifted and assured player who would have surely captained Celtic to many triumphs and glories.

George's cartilage injury was not as serious as the one that put John Kennedy out of football at such an early stage in his career or the even more dreaded cruciate ligament injury that has finished the careers of many sportspeople. The problem with George's injury was that it couldn't be detected by the medical staff at Celtic because the knee simply 'locked back' into its normal position when not moving in certain ways. So when George showed up for medical examination he had no pain and no obvious signs of displaced or damaged cartilages or tendons. Yet what escaped the attention of some of the best medical professionals in Scotland did not get past the wisdom of the manager at Celtic Park. Perhaps this is one difference between football then and now and how managers in a different era responded to situations such as the one that young McCluskey was in. In today's modern game the club's medical team would have almost total control over the player's treatment. And rightly so. After all, they are the experts and it is the individual footballer's career and health (including life post-football) that is at stake and not simply the club's interests. So much medical science and research has been carried out in the past few decades that there is much greater understanding of the human body today, meaning that injuries can be much better analysed and treated. Today's managers would most certainly stay out of that aspect of the football player. In the modern game if a player is injured the manager will seek to find out from the medical team how the player is progressing and when he may be able to train/play again. He would not for one second even think of involving himself in diagnosing an injury to a player. Things were different back then. At that time Celtic did have the best medical back-up and support you could wish for. After all, your prime assets in any football team are your best players and George certainly got the very best treatment. The problem was that since the injury didn't manifest itself off the pitch, the doctors were baffled and couldn't treat it because they couldn't see it. The solution came from a manager who was indeed quite remarkable and one who was not afraid to involve himself in this part of the player's problem. After all, Jock Stein had identified McCluskey as a wonderful talent as a boy, drove Sean Fallon to Birkenshaw to sign him, watched him develop and move through the ranks, told Fallon to play him against Rangers from his hospital bed and knew that this young man was courageous and brave and that the injury was not 'in his head'. George had been out of the team with this injury for almost a full season and without any sign of progress. Stein decided to take the 'medical law' into his own hands. A shoot-out with the then Celtic keeper, Peter Latchford, was about to decide the future of young McCluskey.

I was still at training at the time but the knee was continually giving me problems and there was no chance of me playing. One minute I was fine and the next I felt that jarring pain and then it was gone. It seemed that no one was believing me about this injury. Then, one day, when we were in the dressing room getting ready to go out to train, Big Jock came in and told me to come with him onto the park to have a look at this injury. He then turned to Peter Latchford and said, 'Peter, I need you as well.' So we both went out onto the training ground and Jock naturally told Peter to go into nets. No surprise there. He then put the ball somewhere inside the penalty box and said to me, 'Now listen George, I want you to hit that ball as hard as you can with your left foot straight at Peter and put him into the back of the net. And no holding back!' So I did what I was told. I took a run-up, swung my left leg, hit the ball as hard as I could at Peter and instantly fell on the ground in agony! Big Jock came running over to me shouting 'Don't move! Stay perfectly still!' I wasn't going anywhere, to be honest, even if I had wanted to. Jock Stein was right in my face and scared the hell out of me anyway! He then shouted to Peter to come up and together they carried me back to the dressing room and lay me on the treatment table. Jock then said, 'Don't you move one inch, George, and Peter, you make sure he doesn't!' He then vanished to the office where he phoned the club doctor, Dr Fitzsimmons who came down from his surgery right away to examine me. Initially he couldn't find anything wrong but all of a sudden he shouted out, 'There it is! I've got it now. It's a bucket handle injury, George.' My reply was to the effect that I had been trying to tell everyone that for almost a year and no one would believe me! Anyway, it was off to the *Bon Secours* Hospital two days later to get the cartilage out.

'And get that hedge cut, son'

George was relieved now that the injury mystery had been solved and he could look forward to going under the surgeon's knife. There was no hanging about. As soon as Celtic got the surgeon they wanted, the appointment was booked for the *Bon Secours* Hospital. Jock Stein – as typical of the man – insisted on bringing George there himself. When he got to the McCluskey house in Birkenshaw that morning there was quite a scene there. All of George's aunts had assembled at the house and George's mother, Teresa, was in quite a state as she prepared to watch her 'wee son' going to hospital. George's recollection was that 'You'd have thought I was going to get my leg amputated or that I was going to Lourdes.' Yet Stein defused the situation by assuring George's mother that he'd be out in a day or so and not to worry one bit and then he stopped and looked at the hedge outside the McCluskey house. He shook his head and looked very serious. Then he looked at Teresa McCluskey and said:

I knew when I came into the street that there was something not quite right here. All the other hedges in the street are trim and tidy but this hedge needs cut. Don't worry, Mrs McCluskey, George will do that as soon as he gets out of hospital and is on his feet again. George, get that hedge cut as soon as you're able. I don't want people talking.

According to George this was in keeping with the character of the great Celtic manager. Despite his toughness (and he was as hard as they come) he had a genuine concern for all of his charges and their families. So when he saw a mother naturally upset at the thought of her young son going for an operation he transformed the atmosphere as only he could. And he did make sure that George did cut the hedge when he got out of hospital! So now it was off to the *Bon Secours* Hospital for an important operation upon which George's entire future depended.

There was none of your key-hole surgery back in those days but Celtic got the top surgeon in the country, Dr George O'Brammy, to perform the operation which was a complete success. I was just delighted that after all the doubt that hung around me at this time, with some people thinking that it was all in my head or that I was feigning an injury because I just wasn't up to it, that there was an injury there the whole time and that the problem had been sorted out. For me it was an incredible relief and now I was more determined than ever to get back on the team and prove all the sceptics wrong.

George made his first appearance of that season on the last day of December 1977 coming off the bench at Ayr and featured in almost all of the games until the end of the season. He scored 10 times in the 'back half' of the season, notably hitting a hat-trick in a 7–1 thumping of Dundee in the Scottish Cup and both goals in the 2–1 victory over Hibs in the league in April. Unfortunately for Celtic the league was already a lost cause by the time young McCluskey got back to fitness, Kilmarnock put them out of the Cup at Rugby Park and the only hope of silverware was dashed at Hampden on 18 March as Rangers won the final of the League Cup 2–1 after extra time against a Celtic team that dominated the match but never got the result that it deserved. The season of 1978/79 had been a truly horrible one for Celtic in so many respects. The club that came so close to winning the treble the previous season fell far short of the expectations of the fans and most within Scottish football. Certainly the sudden and quite dramatic departure of Dalglish from the scene before the season begun was a blow from which Celtic didn't recover. Injuries to crucial players also played their part with both Pat Stanton and Danny McGrain missing almost the entire season while Bobby Lennox was absent for much of it. If there was a silver lining in a dismal season it was the re-emergence of George McCluskey. George's almost two-season period in the footballing wilderness was now over. One question that those who had followed George since his earliest days of playing football were asking was how he would respond to the challenge of leading the forward line now he was fully fit. The young man from Birkenshaw was about to answer that question.

'Ten Men Won the League Tralalalala!'

LIKE LISBON IN 1967 or the 'road to Seville' in 2003, the season of 1978/79 will always be remembered as one of those special seasons in the minds of Celtic fans who were fortunate enough to be around for it. Ask any Celtic fan worth their salt and they will tell you of the magic evening in May 1979 when Celtic won the League in the most dramatic fashion at Celtic Park. Even Celtic supporters who hadn't been born at that time will talk you through the pulsating excitement and nail-biting drama of the night when Celtic defeated their bitterest rivals in the final game of the season. Sure, Celtic have won the League on the final day of the Championship on quite a few occasions and occasionally in quite extraordinary circumstances. Such magical and heart-stopping performances include the 1986 triumph when Celtic had to beat St Mirren at Love Street by at least three goals and hope that Hearts would drop points at Dundee. That day, Celtic fans, already assured by the team fulfilling its part of the equation by being 5–0 up early in the second half, listened to the closing stages of the game in Dundee on their radios with a mixture of hope and anxiety as the score there remained at 0–0. That was until Albert Kidd, a self-confessed Celtic fan, broke Hearts fans' hearts by scoring two goals in the closing minutes and driving the Celtic fans (and players) into joyful celebration. Many remember the quite unforgettable and at times agonising last day of the 1998 season at Celtic Park when Celtic had to beat St Johnstone, otherwise a win for Rangers at Tannadice would win the League title for Rangers for the 10th year in a row, beating the record established by Celtic during the Jock Stein era. Larsson scored a wonderful goal in the second minute but it wasn't until Harald Brattbakk scored the second in the 74th minute that Celtic fans throughout the world could relax and celebrate sure in the knowledge that the precious record of nine Championships in a row was not to be bested. And, of course, who could forget the drama of the

'Helicopter Thursday' of 22 May 2008 when a Celtic side, in a seemingly hopeless position six weeks before the end of the season, won their final seven matches to become champions on that last day against Dundee United with a winning goal from Jan Vennegoor of Hesselink sealing the title for Celtic. The 2008 triumph was indeed remarkable in itself and is also a wonderful example of just how much Celtic is a club apart. The whole Celtic family were in mourning at the untimely death of a true Celtic boy, Tommy Burns. Tommy, Celtic player, captain, manager, legend and supporter who famously stated that 'when you pull on that jersey you're not just playing for a football club, you're playing for a people and a cause', had passed away just eight days before the match. His illness and death had an incredibly galvanising effect on the whole club in those sad weeks in April and May of 2008 and Celtic's triumph on that final day can rightly be put down to the effect that this great man had on the club that he loved and that loved him. Celtic won the League title that year – and they won it for Tommy Burns.

These dramatic last day victories, as well as many others, do indeed live in the memories and imagination of all Celtic fans who were lucky enough to witness them. It is difficult, in fact downright impossible, to place one cliff-hanging triumph above another but for many Celtic supporters – including many who were not even born yet – the culmination of the 1978/79 season is one that surely ranks with the greatest of them all. It was the season when 'ten men won the League'!

The departure of a football genius as a new season looms

If the loss of Kenny Dalglish the season before had left a gap that effectively derailed the 1977/78 campaign, then the decision by Jock Stein to stand down as manager of the club after 13 years of unparalleled success that had made him a name throughout European and world football was considered by almost everyone who had the slightest interest in the game as an even greater loss. After all, Jock Stein was not simply a great football manager, he was one of the greatest football managers ever. Looking back with the knowledge of today it is almost impossible to exaggerate what the Stein revolution did for Celtic. A simple listing of trophies and titles won by Celtic under Stein's management is, in itself, quite staggering: 10 League titles, eight Scottish Cup and six League Cup triumphs and, of course, becoming the first northern European team to win the European

Cup. Yet even these incredible achievements do not reveal the full extent of what Stein did at Celtic. What Jock Stein achieved was remarkable and, perhaps, unrepeatable. He took a team – albeit a team with a fantastic history and fan base – from a position of domestic weakness and made it into a formidable European force. And he did this with limited resources and a board that was notorious for its policy of financial conservatism.

Unlike the departure of Dalglish, Stein's decision to stand down at Celtic wasn't sudden or unexpected. Jock Stein had decided to step down at the end of the 1977/78 season and had an agreement with the board to appoint his successor, his choice being Billy McNeill. Whether Stein decided on his own volition to step aside or was 'persuaded' is a matter of conjecture and dispute. The journalist Archie McPherson is quite certain that Stein was encouraged to resign with an understanding that he would be given a place on the board. As it turned out all he was offered was a management position in the Celtic Pools company. By all accounts Stein was incensed by this offer and turned it down feeling a sense of betrayal by the Celtic board. Yet one basic question still remains unanswered: why did Jock Stein decide to stand down from managing a club that he had led to so many triumphs, a club that had just the season before come within a whisker of winning a treble – something which he achieved only once in his 13 years as Celtic manager and which has only been repeated once since?

This is a question that continues to create heated discussion among Celtic fans to this very day. Some suggest that he simply wasn't the same manager after the near fatal car crash and that he didn't have the appetite for continuing to try to move a team that he had managed for so many years to even greater glory. His signings at the time were questioned as were his team selections and tactics. Others maintain that Stein was disillusioned by the apparent willingness of the board to sell some of the wonderful talent that he had identified, nurtured, worked with, developed over the years and brought through onto the first team. Others suggest that Celtic's greatest ever manager, like other managers of Celtic since, recognised as signs of the times. The financial gap between English and Scottish football was now beginning to grow and perhaps Stein also recognised that. In simple terms winning the European Cup in 1967, lifting the League Championship nine times in a row and accumulating silverware beyond imagination was as good as it got – as good as it ever would get. And so, for some, Jock Stein did the logical thing and moved to England to manage Leeds United. For others, however, this simply didn't add up. Why would the great Jock Stein who had achieved so much at Celtic and who had now got the basis of yet another great team which would achieve so much in the future have decided to go to Leeds and manage a team that, quite frankly, had left their glory days firmly behind them? Besides, prior to his move to Leeds Stein had expressed little desire to manage in England. As it turned out he wouldn't be there for long. Stein's tenure at Leeds lasted only 44 days – exactly the same length of time Brian Clough had managed some four years previously. There the similarity stops. Clough, it seems, began his new job by alienating almost the entire Leeds squad, famously berating them at one of the first training sessions, reportedly saying, 'You can chuck all your medals and all your caps and all your pots and pans into the biggest bin you can because you've never won any of them fairly. You've done it all by bloody cheating!'[12] Hardly the way to get the dressing room on your side! According to Hugh Keevin's this was most certainly not the case with Jock Stein. Keevin's maintains that Jock Stein made an immediate and extremely favourable impression on the entire Leeds squad as he emphasised that he had come to return this once great team back to its glory days. Unfortunately for the Yorkshire team and its supporters Stein returned to Scotland just 44 days after taking the reins at Leeds to become Scotland's manager. Some, including Eddie Gray who was at Leeds at the time, feel that Stein's heart was never in the job for the long-run and that he was simply marking time until the position in Scotland became available.[13] Irrespective of the reason this colossus left Celtic, the club was faced with a huge challenge: how would the new manager fare in the shadow of the greatest manager that Celtic ever had?

The return of 'Cesar'

Billy McNeill had one huge advantage that no other potential successor could ever aspire to. He was 'Cesar', the greatest captain of Celtic ever, the man who led them during the 'nine-in-a-row' run and beyond and, above all else, the man who lifted the European Cup above his head on that incredible night in Lisbon in 1967. At the time Stein made the move to Leeds, McNeill was manager of Aberdeen. If anyone could take over the reins from Jock Stein and command the support of the fans it was

12. H Keevins, 'Jock Stein's 44 days in charge of Leeds United that led to the Scotland job' (*The Daily Record* 28th March 2009).
13. ibid.

Billy McNeill. No one could possibly doubt his leadership qualities, commitment to the Celtic cause or his status. The greatest manager in Celtic's history would be replaced by its greatest captain. The first season of his reign was to give Celtic fans something to remember.

With the new manager in place there was considerable optimism among the Celtic supporters that this season would be different. Tom McAdam, who had been signed as a striker from Dundee United the previous season following the departure of Dalglish, was tasked to lead the line for the new campaign. It was hoped that Alfie Conn, now back from injury, would now play a pivotal role in an attacking midfield that included Johnny Doyle and Tommy Burns. 'Shuggie' Edvaldsson would be ever-present that season. Regarded as a 'defender/midfielder/striker' (and used by Stein in all those positions), McNeill put the big Icelandic player in the heart of the defence where he established a very effective understanding with Roddy MacDonald. The new manager was also keen to get a freshness into the Celtic side, especially in the forward line and midfield. As the season progressed McNeill unloaded established players like Ronnie Glavin and Conn, and increasingly turned to younger players including Mick Conroy (signed from Port Glasgow Juniors by Stein in April 1978) and George himself. It should be remembered that as the 1978/79 season kicked off in August, George McCluskey was still only 21 years of age. McNeill also showed considerable astuteness and, indeed, courage during this first season in management by going into the transfer market and strengthening his team as the season progressed. The season was scarcely a month old when Celtic signed Davy Provan from Kilmarnock in September 1977 and followed that up two months later by signing a midfielder with a thunderous shot, Murdo McLeod, from Dumbarton. The team that triumphed in such dramatic circumstances in the final game at Celtic Park that season did indeed contain some changes from the opening games of the campaign and some of the players who played throughout the season ended up adapting to a new style of play and system and even ended up playing in a different position altogether. Tom McAdam who started the 1978/79 season as the classic 'number nine centre-forward' ended the season playing the classic 'number five centre-half' with George McCluskey wearing the shorts with number nine on them!

Anticipating a truly exciting season

Anyone who fancied placing a bet on who would emerge as league champions at the end of the season would have many factors to consider. Although Rangers would play all their home games at Hampden as Ibrox was being rebuilt, the Govan side was regarded by many as strong favourites for the title. They had greater experience than the youthful Celtic side and included in their squad established players such as Tom Forsyth, Derek Parlane, Alex MacDonald and Derek Johnstone as well as the emerging star Davie Cooper. They had won the treble the year before and as the season unfolded a second successful treble began to seem a distinct possibility. They won the League Cup and the Scottish Cup would follow, Celtic having exited from that competition at the hands of Aberdeen in March. Additional spice was added to this season with the appointment of a new manager by Rangers during the close season – the former Rangers captain and fans' favourite John Greig. Both sets of supporters looked forward to what would prove to be a titanic struggle between two teams led by two 'rookie' managers, both of whom had spent their entire football careers at their respective clubs and both of whom had captained their clubs to their greatest respective triumphs – Billy McNeill lifting European Cup in 1967 before the adoring faithful Celtic fans in Lisbon and John Greig being presented with the European Cup Winners' Cup in Barcelona in 1972. In many ways the season of 1978/79 was a clash of football philosophies and style – of attacking football and 'playing the Celtic way' versus the more defensive system that Rangers traditionally employed. It was very much a youthful Celtic side going against a more established Rangers outfit. It was about two fresh managers facing each other in their new roles. It also was about individual players and performances, and how they might affect things. And then there was the winter weather. In this great mix and contest the outcome would be decided.

The season started off with Celtic hitting the ground running. The first eight matches were won and nerves among Celtic fans following the departure of Jock Stein were settled as a Celtic team under its new manager looked confident and assured. George McCluskey didn't start in the first seven games but did in the next match – against Rangers at Celtic Park. Rangers had also made an impressive start and even at this early stage most football commentators were predicting a league championship that would come down to the wire; that it would come down to results against each other for the Glasgow rivals, as indeed it did. George's brother John always says that, 'George scored goals that really mattered... that hurt the opposition when it counted.' George was already getting a reputation for being a striker who didn't score the fifth goal in a rout of a 'minor' team. His goals tended to be against bigger clubs and on major occasions. In this first start of the season George opened his account for 1978/79 by scoring in a 3–1 win over Rangers at Celtic Park. That win put Celtic clear on top of the league but after a first defeat of the season against Hibs the following week points began to slip and then the very strong Rangers challenge emerged.

It was not that Celtic and Rangers had it all their own way during the early months of the league campaign. Hibs, Hearts, Aberdeen, Dundee United and (surprisingly) St Mirren were all making their own challenges at the top of the league. After their great start Celtic's form was, at best, inconsistent. During a potential 'campaign-implosion' period between the end of October and Christmas Celtic played eight games in the league and won only once – against Partick at Celtic Park, by a single goal scored by Tom McAdam. The young lad from Birkenshaw played in only two of those games. Celtic's league challenge was faltering and looked like it was heading for the rocks. Then came what many consider a stroke of good fortune for a forlorn looking Celtic – winter.

The winter of the end of 1978 and the first months of 1979 was one of the worst in recorded history and is still regarded as a 'landmark winter' in terms of severity. Heavy snow showers and sub-zero temperatures prevailed for many weeks, resulting in an unprecedented interruption of the Scottish football season. In those days undersoil heating was still very much in its experimental stage in England and had not yet reached Scotland. A fixture pile-up was inevitably created as a 'white-out' caused week after week of football matches to be called off. There was effectively a winter break in the Scottish football season that shut down the whole of Scottish football throughout January and February. The scale and duration of the disruption caused by the weather was quite breath-taking. Celtic, for example, didn't play a single league match between the 23 December 1978 and 3 March 1979. Incidentally, Celtic were able to play one game during this 'mini ice-age' when a short thaw for a couple of days – allied to some serious work from the ground-staff – allowed a League Cup game to go ahead at Celtic Park. The match against Montrose ended in a 4–2 win for the hosts with George scoring a hat-trick. One game that was postponed

Left: A very young George McCluskey at home in Hamilton c.1958.
Right: The Blantyre Red Rockets Under-12 team in 1969 with George in the middle of the front row. George's father, John McCluskey, formed and coached this underage team.

Teresa McCluskey with children Jeanette, Patricia, George and John on holiday in Rothesay.

Celtic Boys U-15 team with George in the back row, second from right.

A proud Teresa McCluskey looks at her son wearing his international cap.

Left: A young George McCluskey looking across at the Jungle where he used to stand as a Celtic supporter.
Right: Receiving the Celtic Young Player of the Year Award from Jock Stein in 1975.

Above: George McCluskey with wife Anne,
daughter Leeanne and the Scottish Cup (1980).
Right: With Anne, Leeanne and son, Barry (1982).

George McCluskey steers the ball past a despairing Peter McCloy into the net to win the 1980 Scottish Cup Final. (SNS Group / Alamy)

Scoring against St Mirren at Celtic Park in May 1982 to win the Scottish Premiership on the final day of the season. (SNS Group / Alamy)

Charlie Nicholas congratulates George McCluskey on scoring against Hibs in the 4-1 victory at Celtic Park in 1983. (SNS Group / Alamy)

George McCluskey (with blood streaming down his leg following a shocking 'tackle' by Rangers' Graeme Souness) is carried off the pitch at Easter Road on his Hibernian debut in 1986. (SNS Group / Alamy)

With Neil Lennon representing Celtic at a Celtic supporters function in Belfast.

Striker turned coach: George McCluskey (centre) celebrates as his young Celts win the Glasgow Cup.

Left: George McCluskey (patron of Project Zambia) presents a cheque to Aidan Donaldson (project co-ordinator) at the statue of Jimmy Johnstone in the Memorial Garden in Viewpark.
Right: Celtic ambassador and part of the match day hospitality team.

Celtic legend Bobby Lennox presents Aidan Donaldson with a cheque on behalf of Creetown and District CSC for Project Zambia. Also present with George McCluskey is Eddie McGaw (chairperson of Creetown and District CSC).

The McCluskey family today in Uddingston complete with the grandchildren.

The next generation of Celtic minded McCluskeys: Orlaith, Keira and Ruari.

during that period and would, subsequently, turn out to be of colossal importance during this enforced shut-down was the scheduled New Year's Day clash between Celtic and Rangers. This game, like many others, was a victim of the weather and after being put back was eventually played at Celtic Park on the very last day of the season.

The last league game that Celtic played in 1978 was against Morton and ended up in a 1–0 defeat for Celtic. That summed up their state of mind at the time. Celtic's league record in the 10 weeks from the middle of October until the weather stopped football was: Played 11 – Won 3 – Drew 5 – Lost 3. Hardly the stuff of champions. If ever a team needed time to regroup it was Celtic. And regroup they did. Celtic returned to the second half of the 1978/79 season a different team altogether. They beat Berwick Rangers 3–0 in the Scottish Cup when football resumed in the last week of February and re-commenced their league defence with a 1–0 win at Celtic Park against Aberdeen on the 3rd of March and put together an altogether different set of results until the end of the league campaign that reads: Played 18 – Won 14 – Drew 1 – Lost 3. So what had happened during those weeks that transformed an obviously failing Celtic team into one that would turn its season around in the most dramatic of fashions? Perhaps a trip to a place in the sun and with some serious Celtic history provided the answer.

So what do you do when the pitches are frozen solid and there's no football in Glasgow? Head to Portugal of course!

When the snow and cold weather came in to disrupt football at the end of December there was no real shock from fans, players or administrators alike. After all, if you play football or any other outdoor sport, it goes with the territory. When you happen to live in northern Europe and decide to play football in the winter months, then expect the odd game to be called off due to weather conditions. As postponement followed postponement it soon became clear that 'normal service' would not be resumed any time soon and steps would have to be taken to maintain the fitness and sharpness of the players in anticipation of the recommencement of the league. There is only a certain amount of indoor training you can organise without a squad starting to lose its momentum. Managers began to look at doing something different to counteract the negative effects of the enforced lay-off and many clubs went off to sunnier lands to training camps to get some football. It was almost like a pre-season in mid-winter with Spain and Portugal offering the best opportunities to keep sharp both physically and mentally. Celtic chose the latter as a base to rebuild.

In hindsight it was an inspired decision by McNeill to take Celtic away from the icy wastelands of Glasgow to the Algarve to train in the warm weather of Portugal. Getting away from Glasgow and from competitive football at a time when form had dipped gave the Celtic players a chance to have a long hard look at themselves and especially those who had been underperforming. Honest reflection was called for and given. The break also provided a welcome opportunity for Danny McGrain to complete his rehabilitation from a mysterious foot injury that had sidelined perhaps the most influential member of the Celtic team for more than a year. At that time the Celtic captain was one of the best full-backs in the world and his absence during most of the 1977/78 season and up until the restart of this season in the spring of 1979 was certainly felt by the Celtic team – as well as by the Scotland team at the 1978 World Cup in Argentina. His return for the final 18 matches of the 1978/79 season would be telling indeed. In addition to the welcome opportunity to train in the warmth of Portugal and regroup and refocus as a team, Portugal gave one huge lift to the Celtic squad. The manager was only too aware of what the surroundings meant to Celtic and he used them to great galvanising effect. It may have been almost 12 years previously that 'Cesar' had come out onto the balcony of the *Estadio Nacional* to lift the European Cup above his head and show it to the adoring Celtic fans on that famous night but for all Celtic supporters, that image and the story of the Lisbon Lions makes the hairs on the back of the neck stand up and the heart soar with pride. For a 21-year-old lad from a Celtic minded family from Birkenshaw this really was living the dream:

> When we heard that we were off to warm weather training we were delighted just to get away from the routine and freezing cold of Glasgow. With no games being played and the way our season seemed to be going just to get away from Glasgow was just what we needed. The decision to take the squad to Portugal was a master-stroke by the Celtic management. Not only were we away together to train and get ready for the second half of the season, it almost became a bit of a pilgrimage. We stayed in Estoril just outside Lisbon where the team had stayed in 1967 and played a match against the local team. We visited the stadium

where Celtic won the European Cup and I am sure that all of us relived that night in our own heads. You have to remember that quite a lot of our squad would have been young Celtic-daft boys in 1967 who were glued to the television set that day – the likes of Johnny Doyle, Mike Conroy, Tommy Burns and myself – and here we were, standing in the very ground where Celtic had won the European Cup, listening to Billy McNeill and Bobby Lennox taking us through the events of that day. There is no doubt in my mind that the squad who flew out from Glasgow the week before returned an entirely different group – and now a team with a mission.

The build-up to an unforgettable night at Celtic Park

Normality returned to Scotland as spring approached and winter released its grip allowing football hostilities to resume. The ten-week lay-off had in no way lessened the football public's interest in the season; indeed, quite the reverse. The break had only served to increase hope and expectation in the minds of the respective fans as they waited to see which team might kick on from the break. One by one the challengers fell behind with Dundee United being the last team to drop off the pace leaving Rangers and Celtic to battle it out over the latter half of the season. There was an almighty backlog of games and a Scottish Cup campaign to be fitted in as well. Rangers also had the added challenge of European football and had two quarter-final legs to play in March before exiting to German side Cologne. It was to be more or less two games a week from now on for everyone in Scotland. Resources would indeed be stretched – as would nerves.

Celtic went out of the Scottish Cup to Aberdeen following a replay very soon after the restart. In retrospect this turned out to be blessing as it meant that Celtic's sole focus would now be on the league. Rangers were still involved in other competitions and this meant additional games had to be played by Celtic's rivals. In the context of the titanic struggle that was emerging for the league title, the fact that Celtic had no distractions enabled them to gain momentum and to relaunch their league campaign. Throughout the coming weeks two sides went 'toe-to-toe' for the championship swopping the lead, sometimes twice in a week! It soon became clear that two games would take on crucial significance. Celtic and Rangers had to face each other twice in the final weeks of the season. Both games in May would be keenly fought and would have a massive bearing on the destiny of the league title. One of them in particular was to become a part of the Celtic story and George McCluskey would play a crucial role in that game.

The prelude to a glorious night in the East End of Glasgow

The run up to Celtic's final game of the season was most certainly not for the faint-hearted. Celtic won their first three league matches after the restart before losing their next game at Hibs. A couple of victories were followed by a defeat at the hands of Dundee United at Tannadice. The league challenge was still on – but only just. In April, George made his first league start since the previous November and scored a precious winner – a remarkable solo goal – as Celtic beat St Mirren 1–0 at Love Street. This set Celtic on a run of five wins and one draw as matches came thick and fast. There was little to separate the two teams as they entered the final month of the season. Celtic had a narrow advantage in terms of points but Rangers, because of their involvement in other competitions, had played fewer games than Celtic and would have the opportunity of turning those games into points in the home straight. Fifth of May was the first of the two games against Rangers and Celtic went down 1–0 to an Alex MacDonald goal at Hampden. The result was bad enough – indeed, massively damaging in a run-in to the title – and the very flat and deflated performance of Celtic didn't inspire much hope that this young team could turn it around in Celtic's favour. The impetus, it seemed, was now with Rangers. Yet this inexperienced Celtic team was not for simply rolling over and handing the league title to Rangers. Celtic still had four games left to play and everyone knew that in all likelihood they would have to win them all, anything other than a win would effectively hand the title to Rangers. There was no room for error. Two days after the defeat at Hampden, Dave Provan and George McCluskey scored in a 2–1 win at Partick Thistle on the Monday May Holiday fixture. The Friday saw Celtic defeat St Mirren 2–0 with goals from Bobby Lennox and George. Quite bizarrely the match (which was an away game for Celtic) was played at Ibrox. Love Street was also now under reconstruction and Ibrox (redevelopments almost completed) was passed by the Scottish authorities as fit to accommodate the crowd for this fixture. On the following Monday, Celtic played Hearts at Celtic Park and won 1–0 through a goal from Mike Conroy. The stage was set for a quite unbelievable climax to an extraordinary season.

Madness and mayhem as Celtic win the League!

For Celtic the game against Rangers on 21 May at Celtic Park was their final match of the season. It was actually the Celtic v Rangers match that had been originally scheduled for 2 January but had been postponed due to the weather. It was the last game of the 'catch-up season' for Celtic who were sitting top of the league on 46 points. Rangers, with two games in hand, were on 43 points. A win or even a draw for Rangers would leave Celtic looking for Partick Thistle or Hibs (or possibly both) to stop Rangers winning the league. Any number of permutations might decide the destiny of the Championship that season but there was only one that Celtic players and fans considered: win the game and we win the league! You really couldn't have made up a greater climax to a season that had see-sawed back and forward all year, a season in which momentum had started with Celtic and then switched towards Rangers, a season that had been disrupted like none other since the Second World War and now had come down to one final match. For Celtic, this was the last throw of the dice. Everything that had gone before would be decided in this 90 minutes at Celtic Park. You couldn't have written the script. George describes the mood among the Celtic players in the run-up to the game:

> We went into that last game of the season knowing that a win meant that we would win the league. It was as simple as that. I don't recall one single Celtic player – or fan for that matter – thinking about any other result. To an extent I feel that this gave us an advantage over Rangers. I guess that many in the Rangers camp would have been happy with a draw as that would effectively give them control over the title race and they probably thought that they should win their two games in hand. We knew what we had to do so the thoughts of any other result weren't even considered. Billy McNeill just kept drumming into our heads that if we beat Rangers on Tuesday night then we win the league. If you can't get motivated by that idea then you shouldn't be on the pitch.

Of course motivation is almost always a wonderful thing in any team and drives a player on to give everything he's got. There was one player for Celtic that evening who scarcely needed motivation when it came to pulling the green and white hoops on and running out against Rangers, but for whom that extra bit just might have been a little bit too much on this occasion: Johnny Doyle.

The game against Hearts in which Mike Conroy scored the winner and set up the league decider was played on Monday, 14 May. That was the 15th match that Celtic had played in seven weeks! In the need to fulfil the football programme by the end of the season all teams in Scotland were playing two games a week. The Celtic team then got a welcome break of a week due to a Scottish Cup Final replay between Rangers and Hibs. Celtic were able to use the break to recover from the punishing schedule and focus on the game. It was indeed a night to remember. The Celtic team lined out very much as it had over the past few games since the defeat by Rangers earlier that month (and five games previous). Tom McAdam was in his new position at centre-half and the line would be led by George McCluskey. The crowd was officially 52,000 which was a few thousand short of capacity for a clash between Celtic and Rangers. This was put down to a rail and bus strike in Scotland that evening and also the fact that some people who had bought tickets for the original fixture for January had lost them and didn't attend! George, however, (and many who were fortunate enough to attend that night) maintain that there were at least 70,000 in attendance. A walk-out by programme directors a couple of hours before kick-off meant that there was no television coverage of the historic game but some enterprising Celtic fans brought a camera into the ground and were able to record the game from the very precarious position in the gantry above the Jungle which does tend to confirm George's higher estimate.

With so much at stake it was an extremely tense and passionate affair from the moment the referee blew the whistle to start the game. Tackles were flying in and tempers were pretty much at breaking point. Rangers had set a side out that looked to contain a Celtic team in a game that Celtic simply had to win. The script did not go according to Celtic's plans. McDonald scored an early goal in the first-half for Rangers and that separated the teams at half-time. For Celtic fans it seemed that their team would have to do something remarkable in the second period. If things were gloomy at half-time for Celtic they were about to get worse early in the second-half.

We were a goal down and looking like we would have to score at least twice in the second-half to have any chance of winning the league. The ball was bouncing around the centre-circle when Alex McDonald won a free kick. There was nothing much in it and he wasn't badly hurt or anything, but I suppose, naturally enough, he wasn't too keen on getting back on his feet and having the game restart. We were all around trying to get him back up and there was a bit of pushing and shoving when suddenly in all the mayhem Johnny Doyle weighed in on the scene and booted the prostrate Alex McDonald in the rear. There was nothing vicious or nasty about it. It was done out of a sense of frustration. But he did it and it was wrong. I guess that Johnny had just lost it. Unfortunately the referee was about six feet away from it and witnessed everything. So off Johnny went and we were down to 10 men and a goal down as well. Yet I do not recollect any doubts or resignation in the Celtic team at that time. All I remember was all of us encouraging each other and feeling that we would turn this game on its head.

After the sending off of Johnny Doyle the Celtic team most certainly turned this game around. It was very much 'Attack! Attack! Attack!' as wave after wave of green and white shirts poured forward towards the Celtic end, pinning Rangers back. Roy Aitken equalised for Celtic in the 67th minute and the crowd went crazy. Suddenly the tide had turned in Celtic's favour. With 15 minutes to go McCluskey lashed a loose ball into the top of the Rangers' net from inside the box. Celtic fans were in seventh heaven... for all of two minutes. Rangers came up the park and a hitherto anonymous Bobby Russell fired a shot through a forest of legs past Peter Latchford into the Celtic goal. It was now 2–2 with a little over 10 minutes left and it was the Rangers fans who were in full voice. Yet Celtic responded to this setback in true Celtic style and, with pure passion and abandonment, set about Rangers once again. With five minutes to go George McCluskey picked up the ball in the Rangers box, skipped past a couple of tackles and struck a powerful goal-bound shot that the Rangers keeper, Peter McCloy, could only parry away back into play. It went straight into the face of the Rangers centre-half, Colin Jackson, and back into the net. Celtic Park went ballistic! The league title was now in Celtic's hands. Yet, true to the Celtic way of playing football, they did not 'shut up shop'. There was no time-wasting, feigning injuries, complaining to the referee, kicking the ball into the Jungle (where the fans, no doubt, would have wasted another bit of time before returning it), or any of the other antics that many other teams would have got up to. No, this was Celtic and they continued to play the Celtic way – attacking the opponents. As the game entered the final minute of the 90 there was still time for a final and definitive goal. McCluskey wasn't too far away from the action:

We broke forward and Murdo (McLeod) got the ball just outside the Rangers penalty area. I ran out wide and was shouting for him to give it to me but he wasn't for listening. Murdo thumped the ball towards the Rangers goal and I remember thinking that it was going over the bar into the Celtic end but it dipped and flew into the net. That was it: we knew we had won the league!

Wild celebrations were sparked off across Glasgow and in all the places where Celtic minded communities were found. Inside Celtic Park itself, it was absolute mayhem! George describes the scene inside the dressing room:

We had just come off the pitch and the fans were still going crazy. The dressing room is only about 20 feet by 20 feet and there must have been about 400 people crammed into it, all jumping about and screaming! My father had got in with a couple of his pals and we were all hugging and cheering and jumping up and down. Then Johnny Doyle grabbed me and he was roaring and bawling and greetin'. He nearly strangled me as he kept hugging me and saying 'Thanks, thanks – I let you down. I thought I had lost us the league. Thank you!' He was totally inconsolable and relieved and delighted all at the same time. He really thought that he had blown it for us all and he, being such a Celtic minded person, must have been devastated to have been sent off in such a crucial game. We were called to go back onto the pitch as the fans had no intention of leaving and we had to practically trail Johnny out with us onto the pitch. It was one incredible evening and I was probably too young and excited to understand that this team had written itself into Celtic's history.

The team eventually got away from Celtic Park some hours later and the celebrations went on into the early hours in the homes of the players when they returned triumphantly to their families and friends. The next day Celtic players returned to Celtic Park to come together one final time to reflect on what they had achieved before heading off for a break. George was one of the first to arrive at the ground and saw a car in the car park with his pal and team mate Johnny Doyle sitting in the front seat.

Billy McNeill had told us all to come to the ground to meet up before we went off for a couple of weeks until the pre-season training started. I was one of the first to get to the ground and I saw Johnny Doyle's car with him just sitting in it. When he saw me he told me to get into the car – which I did. He then grabbed me by the collar, looked straight into my face and said 'Listen George. Don't you tell one single soul that you saw me greetin' last night! Understand?' Of course I assured him that 'our secret' was safe and no one would hear a word from my lips that I had saw Johnny Doyle crying. I then went into the dressing room and one by one the other players arrived and everyone had the same story. Johnny grabbed every one of us as we arrived at the ground and made us swear that we wouldn't tell anyone that we saw him greeting last night. He even made people who hadn't seen him in such a state swear that they wouldn't tell anyone! But that was Johnny Doyle: a guy who loved Celtic so much – but didn't want people to think that he was soft!

The Celtic team that won the league in such dramatic circumstances that season did indeed write themselves into the history of Celtic and instantly became a part of Celtic folklore. Indeed, for years afterwards Celtic fans had a new song to sing. The disco anthem by Boney-M, 'Brown Girl in the Ring', was instantly translated by Celtic fans into 'Ten men won the league tralalalala!' And George McCluskey had played no small part in that magical season.

12

Real Madrid, How Tommy Burns Nearly Got us Killed in Spain and 'That Goal'

SOMETIMES A PARTICULAR goal is associated with a football player in such a way that it comes to almost define that player's career. It doesn't have to be remarkably skilful or stunning goal. It may not require the scorer running from the halfway line and beating four players before slotting the ball into the net, chipping the keeper from his own half or hitting a thunderbolt from 35 yards. Every outfield footballer could probably include an example of the above type of goal in his football *curriculum vitae*. Yet what makes a goal special – really special – is when it mattered and achieved something of significance. George scored many wonderful goals in his career but there is one goal that he scored in 1980 that is seen by many – and by George himself – as the most important goal in his career. Every time Celtic fans speak about George McCluskey, inevitably the conversation comes round to a day in May of that year – 10 May to be precise, when the young striker from Birkenshaw did something that many Celtic players dream about but few actually achieve: scoring the winning goal against Rangers in the Scottish Cup Final at Hampden.

A new challenge from a new direction

The season of 1979/80 begun with high expectations as Celtic fans who had witnessed such a dramatic climax to the previous campaign fully anticipated that this new season would see the still youthful Celtic team kick on and become something special. The Celtic squad for the new season was very much that which had proved itself the season before with George given the role of leading the attack, supported by Bobby Lennox and Murdo McLeod. Later in the season he would be joined by Frank

McGarvey who Celtic signed from Liverpool, while an outrageously talented youngster called Charlie Nicholas made his debut at the start of the season. The three strikers would come to form the main attacking options for an exciting free-flowing Celtic team over the next few years.

Domestically Rangers were finished as serious contenders for honours. Losing the title on the last day in such circumstances was a blow from which an ageing team would not recover quickly. It would be a number of years before the Govan club would emerge as contenders again and that would only be after a serious and, indeed, reckless spending programme would be put in place by a new chairman, David Murray. It was a strategy that would eventually bring this club to its knees. The new contenders would come from an altogether different and surprising source altogether. The rise of the so-called 'New Firm' saw a new and sustained challenge coming from the north east of Scotland in the form of Aberdeen and Dundee United. Football in Scotland was about to get even more interesting and competitive.

The term the 'New Firm' was adopted by the media as a catchy label for the two talented sides who emerged as genuine challengers for major honours during the 1980s. It was, of course, a play on the 'Old Firm' label that some used (and continue to use) to refer to Celtic and Rangers. It is a term that Celtic fans are rightly unhappy with since it suggests a linkage between the two sides that has no basis in reality. Celtic is an entity all on its own and needs no other club to help to define it. It also suggests that there is some 'cosy' relationship between the two clubs that accounts for the dominance Celtic and Rangers have exerted over the Scottish game for long periods. This is entirely untrue. Celtic is a wonderful club, with a remarkable and unique history, and whose achievements are entirely of its own making. It stands in need of help from no one. The rise of the twin threat from the north east owed much to two managers who put together two very strong squads of players who achieved much during this decade. Dundee United – under the tutelage of Jim McLean – won the SPL once, the Scottish League Cup twice and reached the Scottish Cup final on four occasions, the UEFA Cup final and the European Cup semi-final. Aberdeen, under the management of Alex Ferguson, went even further, winning three SPL tiles, four Scottish Cups, two League Cups and triumphing in the European Cup Winners Cup and the European Super Cup during the 1980s. His Aberdeen team at the start of the 1979/80 season was formidable indeed and included players such as Jim Leighton, Willie

Miller, Gordon Strachan, Joe Harper, Mark McGhee and Steve Archibald. During the next number of years these two teams would go head-to-head with the team from the East End of Glasgow.

The league campaign started off with a 3–2 home win for Celtic against Morton, with George scoring the opening Celtic goal of the season. He was fit, sharp and confident and relishing the 'number nine' role. His first league hat-trick followed in August in a 5–0 thumping of Kilmarnock and he scored both of Celtic's goals in a 2–2 draw against the 'new pretenders' of Dundee United in September of that year. Goals were also coming from all over the pitch as Celtic played with tempo and movement with the new central partnership of Roddie MacDonald and Tom McAdam in particular using the opportunity to join the attack with great effect. September saw four wins out of four in the league including a 2–1 victory at Pittodrie and by the halfway point at Christmas, Celtic were well in control and 10 points in front of Aberdeen, who looked out of the title race. Celtic's good form continued into the new year and by Easter it seemed that Celtic would have to drop points like confetti if any team were to catch them. Although Aberdeen had managed to knock Celtic out of the League Cup in October of the season, Celtic were having a good run in the Scottish Cup and a league and cup double looked very possible. Celtic were also beginning to emerge as a team to be reckoned with on the European stage. The season of 1979/80 would throw up a fascinating and closely contested between Celtic and one of European football's greatest teams ever – the mighty Real Madrid. It was a contest in which young George McCluskey would make a major impact. It also involved an incident in which George and his best pal and team mate, Tommy Burns, would have a close shave in Madrid. But before Celtic got to play the Spanish giants there was a visit to the communist state of Albania where the Celtic captain, Danny McGrain, almost had a close shave himself!

Tirana, beards, Tommy Burns and a tin of beans

In September 1980 Celtic were drawn against Partizan Tirana from Albania in the European Cup. It was a step into the unknown as Albania at that time was very much a closed society. Since 1945 Albania had been dominated by an autocratic form of communist rule under the iron rule of Enver Hoxha. It was, to all intents and purposes, a one party totalitarian state in which all opposition was suppressed and outside influences were viewed with suspicion. The Hoxha regime had issued numerous rules, regulations and dictates – some of them without any apparent sense or purpose – which had to be obeyed. One of the more bizarre laws concerned the sporting of facial hair. In Hoxha's Albania beards represented a grave national threat, with facial hair at the top of the country's banned list, just ahead of long hair, flares and rock music. Unsurprisingly there was a considerable amount of media attention trained on Danny McGrain (whose trademark beard had been a constant throughout his career). It was the first time he had been cast as a figure of western decadence, his appearance likely to corrupt Albanian youth. Speculation was that he would be forced to 'take one for the team' and shave it off – something he later said he'd been prepared to do. As it transpired no such request was made by the Albanian authorities and a familiar bearded Danny McGrain took his place in the team that played in Tirana. However, it was not facial hair that was foremost in the minds of most of the Celtic squad for that match; rather it was the vexed and important question of food.

It had been reported to Celtic that the quality of food in Albania might not be to the liking of the Celtic players and, to be on the safe side, the club urged the players to bring some 'emergency rations' with them. According to George this proved to be good advice as the culinary delights of Albanian cuisine did not suit the sophisticated palates of the Celtic lads.

I think that every single one of us found the food inedible. The soup looked like – and tasted like – warmed up lard and the fish suspiciously undercooked. We had arrived the day before the game so you can imagine we were pretty famished. We all headed up to our rooms to eat whatever we had brought with us. As usual I was sharing a room with Tommy Burns. By the time I got to the room he was sitting on the edge of the bed getting tore into a tin of cold beans! Apparently all he had brought with him was a tin of beans and a tin opener! His face was covered in tomato sauce and he kept saying 'I'm starving, George, starving' – with the odd swear word stuck in before he shovelled the next spoonful of beans into him. I don't know what took me aback the most – him swearing (which was not typical of Tommy) or the sight of his face covered in tomato sauce and his red hair to match. He looked just like a wean trying to feed himself! I took out me supplies (which Anne had packed). They included a loaf of bread, butter, ham and cheese, chocolate bars and biscuits and cans of fizzy drinks. Tommy just stopped eating and stared. 'Give us some, George', he said. 'I'll sell you some', was my reply. 'I'll fight you for them', was Tommy's response. Anyway we had a feast like two kids with both of us praising Anne for her foresight and him with a face covered in tomato sauce!'

Despite losing 1–0 in Albania, Celtic negotiated that round successfully defeating Partizan Tirana 4–1 at Celtic Park two weeks later. Yet there was more European drama to come later that season and, inevitably, it would involve the two friends who had shared so much together – including Anne McCluskey's 'emergency rations' in Tirana.

'Tommy's devotion to Our Lady almost cost us our lives!'

Tommy Burns' religious beliefs and practice are well-known and admired by many. Tommy was a daily communicant and was deeply associated with the Catholic charity SCIAF (The Scottish Catholic International Aid Fund). Tommy was seen by many as the public face of SCIAF and frequently launched its Lenten 24-hour fast appeal in support of its work in the Developing World. His face would be seen on billboards, on television and on the side of buses urging people to participate in the 24-hour fast as he did himself on numerous occasions. Tommy's Christian beliefs were not exclusive in any way as evidenced by his encouraging of Ally McCoist – a football rival yet a close friend – to co-launch the SCIAF Lenten campaign in 2008. This was not the only time the former Rangers legend found himself in a Catholic setting with Tommy Burns. Many Celtic fans who might have thought otherwise about Ally McCoist could not have been other than moved as this former Rangers footballer, in tears, carried the coffin of Tommy Burns into St Mary's Church in the Calton. The others who carried this great person into the church that day were former Rangers manager, Walter Smith, Danny McGrain, Peter Grant, Packy Bonner and, Tommy Burns' best pal, George McCluskey. Such was the regard for the Calton boy who loved Celtic and who reached out to everyone even in his departure from this life. In death – as in life – Tommy Burns transcended division, bitterness, bigotry and hatred.

Tommy's religious beliefs led him to a particular devotion to the mother of Jesus – Our Lady. His autobiography, *Tommy Twists, Tommy Turns: The Tommy Burns Story*,[14] contains a very clear piece of evidence of this.

14. *Tommy Twists, Tommy Turns: The Tommy Burns Story*, as told by H Keevins, Sportsprint, 1989.

Like many footballers and other sports persons, Tommy dedicated his story to his wife and family, to Celtic fans around the world, but then he added a third dedication – 'to Our Lady, the mother of Jesus.' This was typical of the man who, on discovering that he had been diagnosed with cancer, made a pilgrimage to Lourdes. But despite Tommy's devotion to Our Lady he did not go there seeking a miraculous cure for his illness. Rather, he went there to be close to someone he deeply believed in. Tommy Burns lived a very spiritual and prayerful life and turned to God often, especially when he had something on his mind. On one particular night in March 1980 he was troubled indeed and decided to try to find a church to pray in. George McCluskey accompanied him on that night which was to prove quite interesting and exciting indeed.

Celtic had achieved considerable success in the European Cup since Jock Stein's side dramatically won European football's premier competition at the first time Celtic had entered that competition in the 1966/67 season. Beaten finalists in 1970, Celtic also made it to two semi-finals in 1972 and 1974. Yet after that it seemed that Celtic had slipped down the European pecking order until in this season they reached the quarter-finals and were drawn against Real Madrid. Celtic had defeated Partizan Tiarana and Dundalk on their way to the quarter-final. Now Billy McNeill's team was up against one of Europe's most celebrated and successful clubs, which was packed full of international stars including Vincente del Bosque, Uli ('the Stopper') Stielike, Carlos Santillana (one of Spain's greatest strikers of all time), José Camacho and the English outside-left Laurie Cunningham. It was a formidable team indeed that this young Celtic team were confronting but there was a confidence in the Glasgow team that belied their lack of experience at this level and their youth. Passion and self-belief was at the heart of Celtic's renewed success and, besides, there was also the '12th man' factor to be taken into account. Real Madrid had played in many big games in noisy stadia before; but they had never played at Celtic Park.

The first game at Celtic Park on 5 March 1980 was one memorable European evening in the East End of Glasgow. Celtic lined out in the attacking formation which had proved so effective in the domestic campaign so far with George leading the attack and supported by Davy Provan, Murdo McLeod, Johnny Doyle and the seemingly endless Bobby Lennox. The official attendance that evening was 67,000, but there certainly seemed to be more there that evening according to George:

The ground was absolutely jam-packed that night. I know the official attendance was near 70,000 but it was probably closer to 90,000. After all, it was us against Real Madrid in the quarter-final of the European Cup and it was like the great days of European football were back at Celtic Park. I had played in a number of European games previously but this was something completely different. The Jungle was going absolutely crazy, in fact, every part of the ground was just a whole wall of noise! There was a genuine belief among the players and supporters alike that we had a real chance of beating Madrid. Indeed, on our day we felt that we could beat anyone in Europe. What we needed was a good result to bring with us to Spain.

Celtic started the match against the much-fancied Real Madrid team that evening with passion, with George McCluskey in particular giving the Real defence much to think about. His direct running at the defence and his clever lay-offs gave Celtic fans hope that this would be one of those nights that would go down in Celtic folklore. However, as the half progressed Real Madrid came more and more into the game with Laurie Cunningham in particular posing problems for the Celtic defence. George McCluskey was the main 'out ball' for a Celtic side that seemed to be increasingly put on the back foot. He was able, nevertheless, to set up a glorious chance for Bobby Lennox, winning the ball in the air and laying it into the path of the veteran striker who snatched at it and dragged the ball wide. The referee brought the first half to a close with the teams level at 0–0, thanks largely to the efforts of the Celtic goalkeeper, Peter Latchford.

It was a score that Real Madrid would have been more than happy to go back to Spain with for the second leg and one that Celtic would have to change if they were to have a realistic chance of progressing to the semi-final. Billy McNeill emphasised in the half-time talk that Celtic were giving Real Madrid too much respect and room and were sitting off them too much. He gave Murdo McLeod a more attacking role from the midfield and urged the two full-backs, Danny McGrain and Alan Sneddon, to get down the wings and provide more ammo for the strikers. These instructions were most certainly listened to as a completely transformed Celtic team took the game by the scruff of the neck. George McCluskey gave one of those man of the match displays that characterised his playing career. The greater the challenge, the greater the response from the lad from Lanarkshire. From the kick-off in the second-half the Celtic players poured through the much vaunted Real defence and started to unsettle the Spanish champions. In the opening minutes of the second period McCluskey collected the ball inside his own half, ran with it to the edge of the Real penalty box taking on the entire defence, before curling a shot towards the corner of the net which the Madrid keeper did well to save. In the 52nd minute the pressure paid off. Sneddon broke down the right flank and fired in a powerful shot towards the goal which Ramon, the Madrid keeper could only parry. George McCluskey reacted quickest to the loose ball and opened the scoring. He wheeled round to the delirious Celtic fans as a shell-shocked Real Madrid side shook their heads in disbelief. Things almost got worse for the Spanish team a few minutes later. McCluskey won a corner down the right, Lennox swung it into the box, McAdam headed it on and George glanced it into the net. Celtic Park erupted once again as it seemed that the young man from Lanarkshire had doubled Celtic's lead, only for the referee (for reasons only known to himself) to award a free kick to Madrid. Still Celtic piled forward in search of another goal, sensing that Real Madrid were there for the taking. Sure enough it came in the 74th minute. Like the first goal it was Alan Sneddon who was the provider, hitting a tantalising high cross into the real penalty area which was met perfectly by Johnny Doyle. Celtic continued to apply the pressure and, but for a couple of excellent saves from the Real keeper, would have run out winners by an even greater score-line. It wasn't to be, and 2–0 was the lead that Celtic would have to defend in the return leg in a fortnight's time in the stadium. No matter. It was a tremendous result for Celtic that night and George McCluskey had played no small part in it. He had scored against Real Madrid and was still only 23 years of age.

The return leg was played in front of a huge crowd in excess of 110,000 in Madrid with the same starting line-up for Celtic who were wearing their green away strip. Tommy Burns, who had been out of action since November 1979 with an ankle injury, came on in the second-half for George. Billy McNeill had emphasised to the team (and the press) that if Celtic could keep Real Madrid goalless for the first half then they would be in with a great chance of going into the semi-finals. But they would have to keep it extremely tight from the first whistle. Yet it was almost better than that for Celtic. Celtic were not overawed by the Spanish giants and, despite some shocking and cynical treatment of the Celtic players by their Madrid counterparts, the boys in green could have taken the lead as a number of chances were created. Tom McAdam almost scored with a volley which the keeper did well to save, George dragged a shot wide from 20 yards and Johnny Doyle clipped the bar with a shot-come-cross with the keeper beaten. As the minutes ticked away it seemed that Celtic would get to half-time with their advantage intact. In the final minute of the first-half disaster struck. The Celtic defence failed to clear a corner and from the ensuing scramble Santillana put the ball in the net. This completely changed the situation of the game and the atmosphere in the Bernabéu. Madrid hit a second goal on the hour mark meaning that the sides were now level. McCluskey's forward play was sacrificed as McNeill brought on Tommy Burns to try to strengthen the midfield. Celtic almost got to extra time but in the 86th minute poor defending by Celtic allowed an unmarked Juanito to head a crucial third goal from close in. Celtic hopes and hearts were shattered as the referee brought the game to an end. It had been a wonderful European adventure, and it shouldn't have ended that night.

The actual score-line only tells one part of the saga. The attitude and tactics of the Real Madrid side that night were cynical. It was not quite on a par with the night in 1974 when the other Madrid team – Athletico Madrid – came to Glasgow and covered themselves in shame as they set out to combat a wonderfully skilful and talented Celtic side by simply kicking them off the pitch. But it wasn't far off that disgraceful performance. In the Bernabéu Real Madrid could have been down to nine men in the opening minutes as both Bobby Lennox and Johnny Doyle were victims of brutal tackles that were straight sending-off offenses. Other than rewarding Celtic a free kick no further action was taken by the referee. This set the pattern for the rest of the game as the Madrid players took this as a green light to kick Celtic players all over the place. It was not a game for the faint-hearted as George explains:

It was simply the dirtiest game I played in during my entire career. The Real Madrid players set about us from the first whistle. A Madrid player rammed his studs into Bobby Lennox's leg in about the second minute. Johnny Doyle in particular was the victim of some really shocking fouls. It seemed that every time a Celtic player got the ball or went past a Madrid player someone came sliding in with a two-footed tackle or just simply kicked you. The referee gave us no protection whatsoever. Indeed, only one of their players was booked that night when two or three of them should have been sent off. I was the only other player who was booked that night too. It was halfway through the first half and shocking tackles were coming in from every angle. Johnny Doyle was being booted all around the park and the referee just seemed to keep giving the odd free-kick but totally ignored the Madrid players who were shocking that night. Then a ball was hit into space in front of me as they were trying to play us offside. It was a tight enough decision and I just ran on and clipped the ball into the Madrid net. The flag had gone up and the referee blew his whistle just as I was about to hit the ball but the striker's instinct kicked in and I knocked the ball into the net. Next thing the referee was booking me for that while the Madrid players where kicking lumps out of us all around the pitch!

The Celtic team went back to their hotel in pretty foul form. George and Tommy Burns always shared a room when travelling and the pair sat up talking about the great injustice that had been done to a Celtic team that could well have made it to the semi-final of the European Cup but for the shocking tactics of the Madrid side and a woeful performance from the referee. After a while Tommy said, 'George, I can't sleep with all this going on in my head. I'm going out to find a church and say a few prayers.' George, a practising Catholic and regular mass goer himself, decided to join him and so the two friends put on their Celtic tracksuits and set off into the Madrid night air in search of spiritual comfort. It must be remembered that Spain had recently come out of almost four decades of military dictatorship under Franco and was still a very unstable country. Certainly not the safest of places for two young footballers from Scotland to be wandering around late at night!

We just sort of walked around looking for some place that might be a church. The first couple we saw were locked and I was saying that we should go back to the hotel as it was too late to find one that was open but Tommy was determined to find an open church. I think that he must have thought that he had some sort of instinct or sixth sense that would guide us to one. Suddenly we saw some open gates and a big building that looked like a church with lights on. 'That looks like just the place', said Tommy, and both of us headed towards the building. We had taken a few steps inside the grounds and the next thing we knew was that we were surrounded by armed guards pointing machine-guns at us and shouting in a pretty agitated manner. You didn't have to be fluent in Spanish to know that they were not asking us if we were lost and needed directions! We were both frightened out of our wits and put our hands in the air shouting something about being Celtic football players and pointing to the badge on our tracksuits. The guys with the guns looked at us and pointed to the gate telling us (I guess) to get off the property and not come back. We didn't need them to repeat what their instructions or to ask them if they knew where the nearest chapel was. We just hurried back to the safety of the hotel thankful that nothing worse than getting kicked around the Bernabéu had happened to us that night! To this day I don't know what we had stumbled upon, whether it was a government building, some political party's offices or the residence of someone pretty important. I just know that Tommy's devotion to God and his desire to pray can sometimes be dangerous for your health!

Scoring the winning goal in the Scottish Cup Final

Celtic returned to domestic action the following week thumping Hibs 4–0 and followed that up with a 1–0 victory over Rangers with Frank McGarvey scoring on his first Celtic v Rangers match. As April commenced, Celtic had a comfortable lead over Aberdeen and the league titled looked destined to stay at Paradise. But April proved to be a month when Celtic's seemingly unstoppable charge towards retaining the SPL title came to grief. Incredibly, in the space of 19 days in April, Celtic lost twice in Dundee (3–0 to Dundee United and 5–1 to a lowly Dundee) and, crucially, twice to Aberdeen at Celtic Park. Whether or not this sudden and dramatic loss of form was as a result of the disappointment of the cruel way in which the European adventure had ended is a matter of debate. In the midst of the dropping of points throughout April Celtic put five goals past a Hibs team that included a certain George Best in a one-sided Scottish Cup semi-final. Momentum was now firmly with Aberdeen who went on to close down on the league title, winning it by a single point from Celtic. A season that had promised so much for so long was now in danger of ending without a trophy at Celtic Park. Celtic's season was to come down to one game – the Scottish Cup Final. The opponents? Rangers. For Celtic fans this was the stuff of nightmares; to finish such a promising season with nothing to show for the team's efforts while across the city in Govan a poor enough Rangers team would be celebrating a famous Scottish Cup victory.

On the face of it Celtic fans should have been going into the match with a considerable degree of confidence. They had by far the better team than their counterparts whose side finished a distant fifth behind Aberdeen, Celtic, Dundee United and St Mirren. Despite losing the league in the final couple of weeks, this Celtic team was a better outfit than the one that had dramatically won the title on the final day of the previous season while Rangers really had gone backwards. Celtic had also recently pushed one of the best teams in European football the whole way in that engrossing quarter-final encounter. Yet football is not always (if ever) about facts and rationality. Form going into a match is often an indication of how a game might unfold and Celtic's poor form would have given the Rangers fans and players more than enough encouragement to hope for an upset. Hampden on 10 May would be quite a test of wills and nerve for the more than 70,000 fans who packed Hampden Park that day and in bars and homes throughout Scotland and the world where the game would be watched with excitement and trepidation.

The Celtic team lined up in an attacking formation with McGarvey accompanying McCluskey up front and with Tommy Burns having now re-established himself in the midfield. A major concern for Celtic was in the central-defence where both first choice centre-backs, Tom McAdam and Roddy MacDonald, were unable to play due to injury. Roy Aitken and Mick Conroy were drafted into that area as an 'emergency central-defence unit' to combat the height and physical threat of Derek Johnstone. The two acquitted themselves very well and snuffed out the traditional Rangers' long-ball tactic without too much bother for the Celtic keeper, Peter Latchford. On the other hand, the Rangers defence was equally successful in nullifying the Celtic forward line and after the statutory 90 minutes the game was tied at 0–0 and extra time loomed. The first period of extra time brought no change to the score as both sides effectively shut down one another's chances for goals. It would take a bit of luck, a stroke of genius or a mistake to decide this game. In the 107th minute the game did change and George McCluskey became a piece of Celtic history forever. Some say it was a deflection or a piece of good fortune. Not at all. The best person to describe what happened is the man who put the ball into the Rangers net and won Celtic the Scottish Cup that day.

There was no doubt as the game went into extra time that one goal would probably win it. You're always afraid of making a mistake and conceding a goal because there's not an awful lot of time to get back at the opposition. Also everyone on the pitch was absolutely knackered and especially the forwards who had been running about for the guts of two hours. The idea of taking on two or three defenders or running into space was not happening for either team. It was going to have to be one of those moments of anticipating where the ball might be and hoping that you would be in the right place at the right time.

And so it was that early moment in the second period of extra time Celtic, attacking the Rangers end of Hampden, got a corner. Provan hit the ball into the Rangers box and it was cleared out only as far as Danny McGrain who struck a shot from outside the area that was going wide of the Rangers' goal. It was the young man from Birkenshaw who intervened and drove the Celtic fans crazy with delight!

Obviously I was up for the corner, as most of the Celtic players were. Davy Provan swung the ball into the box, it was cleared out, knocked back in by Alan Sneddon and cleared out again by Tom Forsyth. Danny McGrain hit a shot towards the Rangers goal but it was going wide. I was standing with my back to the goal but slightly to the left of the penalty spot. As the ball came in I put out my left leg (still with my back to goal) and directed it into the right corner of the Rangers net out of the grasp of the Rangers keeper, Peter McCloy, who had been diving the other way to cover Danny's effort. Suddenly it was total mayhem and delight as Celtic players piled on me to celebrate the goal! It may not have been the best goal I ever scored in my life but it was a very special one. It won the cup for Celtic and I am so proud of playing my part in that achievement.

George McCluskey may not have understood just how much of a place in Celtic's history he had won with his decision to steer the ball beyond the despairing Peter McCloy that day at Hampden. He was, in fact, the first Celtic footballer to score the winning goal in a 1–0 Scottish Cup Final victory; a feat only equalled by Joe Miller on a sunny day in May 1989. And the goal was also was significant for another reason which Celtic fans of a certain age often recall. After winning the match, the Celtic players went to celebrate with their supporters, as was the normal practice. Rangers fans responded by invading the pitch and running towards the Celtic end. A full-scale riot erupted on the Hampden pitch as mounted police attempted to separate the two sets of supporters and restore a semblance of order. Match commentator Archie MacPherson described the riot live on BBC Scotland in the most colourful terms: 'This is like a scene now out of *Apocalypse Now*... we've got the equivalent of Passchendaele here at Hampden.'[15] An inquiry blamed the trouble on the excessive consumption of alcohol, and soon after alcohol came to be banned from the terraces of all Scottish football grounds. So with one deft touch, George McCluskey won the cup for Celtic and is held responsible for getting drink banned from football grounds across the country. Quite an afternoon's work for the Celtic striker. What was becoming clear to Celtic fans at that time was that in George McCluskey, Celtic had a striker of great quality and vision and one who had that special X-factor that only the best of goal scorers possess: the ability to produce a vital goal from nowhere. Over the next couple of seasons Celtic supporters would see the very best of George McCluskey.

---

15. See T English, 'Old Firm Cup Final Memories', *The Scotsman* (8 May 2010).

13

Three Strikers and a Rotation System

GEORGE MCCLUSKEY WAS building a reputation for scoring vital goals. In the previous two seasons he had scored in the two matches that really mattered – when Celtic won the league with 10 men on the last game of the season in 1979 and the following year when Celtic lifted the Scottish cup against Rangers, who must have been sick of the sight of him already! As the 1980/81 campaign began, Celtic looked to build on the cup success of the previous season. Still smarting over being overhauled at the death by Aberdeen in the league, Celtic fans looked forward to putting their new rivals – press darlings at the time, one suspects due to the absence of a serious Rangers threat – in their place. Certainly Celtic took the challenge from the so-called 'New Firm' of Aberdeen and Dundee United very seriously indeed. Alex Ferguson had already proved himself a most capable and ambitious young manager who had assembled a squad that would play an important part in the Scottish international team during the next number of years. With perhaps not the same media focus or attention that Alex Ferguson attracted, Jim McLean had quietly put together a very formidable squad at Tannadice. Dundee United's longest serving manager had built a very successful side that, but for the achievements of Aberdeen, would (and should) have received more credit for its success, which was built around the solid defence of Hamish McAlpine, Richard Gough, Paul Hegarty, David Narey and Maurice Malpas, an excellent and lightning-quick midfield unit of Ralph Milne and Eamonn Bannon and a lethal striking partnership of Paul Sturrock and Davie Dodds. McLean's Dundee United side proved itself to be a team that could defend and was ruthless on the break. In both these sides Celtic would find plenty of challenges.

Many Celtic fans and others who followed Scottish football felt that Celtic lacked a cutting edge outside of George McCluskey. Celtic still possessed players of flair all around the pitch who played the football 'the Celtic way' and were prepared to go forward in the best Celtic tradition and contribute to the attack-minded philosophy that Celtic has adhered to throughout its history. Yet, outside of George McCluskey and Bobby Lennox, Celtic appeared somewhat lacking in direct goal threats. Billy McNeill recognised this also and it was the reason he brought in Frank McGarvey from Liverpool in March 1980, for what was then a record Scottish transfer fee of £270,000. McGarvey was a good footballer and on his best day a very good – even great – footballer. A life-long Celtic supporter from Easterhouse, he was extremely hard-working, courageous and determined and never feared showing himself in the penalty area. He had been a member of Alex Ferguson's extremely talented St Mirren side from 1977–79 where he was a thorn in Celtic's side on a number of occasions. Some may complain about a lack of consistency and incisiveness but McNeill thought that his effort and determination would be the perfect foil for McCluskey's sublime touch and the skills of a new Celt who was just breaking into the first team, one Charlie Nicholas.

The Celtic manager's judgement was proven to be sound as these three talented and complementary strikers very soon formed partnerships that defenders dreaded lining out against. During the 1980/81 season the three strikers would hit the net some 70 times for Celtic though they rarely started together. McNeill favoured playing two up front and in the four games that the three actually did start together, George tended to be given a wider, less direct, role. One important change was made to the Celtic team that year. Peter Latchford, who had been Celtic's goalkeeper since 1975, suffered a hand injury during the summer break of 1980, and his place was taken by a young Irishman from Donegal, Patrick 'Packie' Bonner. The big Irishman had been Jock Stein's last signing for Celtic and a valuable one he proved to be. He made the number one shirt his own and went on to make 642 appearances for Celtic (a record for a goalkeeper) and played 80 times for Ireland.

The season started with both McGarvey and McCluskey as the two preferred strikers and George would open Celtic's account for the season with a goal in a 2–1 win over Morton in the opening game. The two instantly struck up an understanding of each other's game and between them hit eight goals in the first three matches, with McCluskey's intelligent running and vision being complimented by the more direct play of McGarvey. One may have thought that Billy McNeill would have settled for this partnership for the rest of the season, but he had a selection problem in the form of Charlie Nicholas. The outrageously talented youngster from Maryhill was being talked about as the most exciting prospect of his generation and was never far off Billy McNeill's radar after excellent performances in the successful Celtic reserve side under Frank Connor the previous season. The manager's dilemma (and a wonderful one to have) was that he had three excellent strikers all fit and sharp and pushing for a starting place on the team. Despite his best efforts Billy McNeill could not find a design to his team that accommodated all three at the one time. McGarvey, because he gave that dimension of directness, determination and hard-work, was a constant throughout the season. Some might also suggest that, given that McGarvey had been bought from Liverpool for a record Scottish transfer fee, Billy McNeill was always going to start him. George, however, disagrees with that suggestion and maintains that faced with having three exceptionally good footballers vying for what were effectively two starting places it was inevitable that one of the three would end up on the bench. McGarvey was a totally different type of player than both Nicholas or McCluskey and generally selected to start irrespective of who his partner would be. He was a more conventional type of forward, always hard-working and in the box whereas the other two tended to anticipate the space where the ball might be hit into, made late runs into the penalty area, took on players, tried to create space, pass, move, collect the return ball and shoot. McNeill tended to play McGarvey up front with either McCluskey or Nicholas behind him. It was a system that George found difficult to adjust to.

Billy McNeill was always going to have Frank up front with either Charlie or myself. It really depended on how Billy was viewing our form whether Charlie got the nod or I started. There were a few games when he did start the three of us together but I guess that he just didn't fancy it and thought he had more options if he kept one of us on the bench. It was the first time that I was involved in a squad in which the rotation system was used. I was used to a selection system that if you were playing well enough then you were on the team and if you weren't playing well then you were dropped. Suddenly it seemed that you could play well one week and score but be on the bench for the next game. I suppose that that is inevitably the case when you've got a lot of players in form and looking to start a match. It didn't annoy me as you always had it in your mind that you would get another chance, and even if you were on the bench then there was a fair chance that you get on at some time in the match and that it was up to you to show the manager what you had to offer.

It certainly was a novel situation for the Celtic players and the strikers in particular. The system was established but the personnel in the front line changed often and not always because of injury or loss of form. A four-week spell in November and December of 1980 was a case in point. George McCluskey was brought back at the expense of Charlie Nicholas and scored four goals in five games including three crucial goals in three consecutive matches: a 1–0 win at Partick, a 3–2 win against Hearts and a 2–1 victory over Airdrie. These three matches gave Celtic a tremendous boost in its league campaign. McCluskey's reward? Back on the bench! Yet it was an important run of wins in Celtic's overall race for the championship. Three defeats and a draw in the previous three league games had left Celtic's title ambitions in danger of fading away. Following these victories Celtic kicked on and never looked back. From trailing Aberdeen at the start of December an impressive run of 15 wins, two defeats, two draws saw Celtic win the league in April at Dundee United with some games still to play. Celtic supporters and players alike didn't seem to mind this new rotation system so long as it delivered the league title to Paradise. In fact it was a season in which a domestic treble seemed possible. Two semi-final defeats at the hands of Dundee United put paid to that dream, but the league disappointment of the previous season was not to be repeated this time. There was no end of season collapse or last day tears. Celtic ran out comfortable champions six points clear of Aberdeen with Rangers and Dundee United a considerable way back. The three strikers had combined to score a remarkable number of goals and had allowed others such as Davy Provan, Tommy Burns and Murdo McLeod to contribute from the midfield. This rotation system looked to be the future as the new season loomed. Yet things in football do not always turn out as anticipated, and the rotation system would come to be abandoned for the 1981/82 season. It also was a season that would live long in the memories of those who had admired and followed the fortunes of the lad from Birkenshaw throughout his career. The new season would come to reveal just how good a footballer George McCluskey actually was.

14

Stepping up to the Mark and Winning the League for Celtic

THE SEASON OF 1981/82 was quite a remarkable one for George McCluskey. In the previous season George seemed to have been the player who was 'sacrificed' by the rotation system. In total he started in 14 of the SPL's 36 match programme fixtures as compared with Nicholas' 26 starts. Nicholas scored 28 league goals compared to McCluskey's 10. For some it seemed that the obvious pairing should be McGarvey and Nicholas, although advocates for McCluskey would argue that his goals/games ratio was pretty impressive and that Billy McNeill should look at a three-pronged attack system that would surely deliver results in true Celtic tradition. As the season of 1981/82 unfolded this became an academic argument.

The Celtic squad that set out to defend its title was (with the notable exception of the keeper) pretty much the same as the one that had won the title the year before, although in the new year a new talent would be revealed, as Paul McStay made his first appearance for his beloved green and white hoops, delighting Celtic fans as he would continue to for years to come. Like George McCluskey a few years previously, the Hamilton-born youth prospect was a member of Celtic Boys Club, and he burst onto the football scene in remarkable style when he hit two goals and was man of the match as Scotland schoolboys defeated their English counterparts at Wembley in front of a live TV audience in June 1980. Shades of 1973 indeed.

The season started as the previous one had ended with Charlie Nicholas being initially favoured over George to partner Frank McGarvey. The first few weeks of August were dominated by the Scottish League Cup group matches. Surprisingly Celtic went out at this early stage having lost their first two games, but a hat-trick for McCluskey at Love Street convinced the manager that he deserved a chance to start in front of Nicholas as the real business of the Scottish league commenced. George did not let this chance slip and scored twice in a 5–2 win at Airdrie during the opening game of the SPL. He went on to play every single match of Celtic's SPL, Scottish Cup and European Cup campaigns. He would come out of that season as the SPL's top scorer with 19 league goals. But such facts and figures cannot truly reflect the crucial role that McCluskey played in that season – keeping the league flag flying over Celtic Park.

Two injuries put paid to the rotation system favoured by McNeill and almost derailed Celtic's ambitions. Celtic made an excellent start to the league campaign, winning their first eight league matches on the bounce. By the start of December Celtic were still firmly in control. Any thoughts of rotating George McCluskey and Charlie Nicholas were put out of McNeill's mind due to the excellent form of George. He was simply playing too well for the manager to leave him out of the starting 11. He had established a very good and productive partnership with McGarvey and was scoring freely. If anything, it seemed that McNeill was more prepared to play the three strikers together than previously, although if he decided to leave one out it was Nicholas who would be sacrificed. George was now able to play to his strengths and talents. As a wonderfully gifted and intelligent footballer, George was able to make runs, anticipate where the ball would arrive, create space and score with ease. As well as establishing a successful partnership with McGarvey, George was also revealing an almost telepathic understanding on the pitch with his close friend, Tommy Burns. Time and time again Burns broke from the midfield, surged forward and hit a ball into space where George McCluskey arrived seemingly from nowhere to pounce on the chance. All those years of training and playing together had produced a remarkable understanding of each other's game. It seemed that Tommy Burns knew exactly the space George McCluskey would run into and that George knew where his great pal would play the ball into. Little wonder that George spoke of Tommy Burns as the player he most enjoyed playing with.

We'd come up through the ranks together and knew each other's game inside out. Tommy would often look one way but deliberately pass the ball the other. So if I'd see Tommy looking wide I'd make my run inside and if he looked left I'd go right. If he pretended he was going to shoot, the centre-half would move to block it but I'd know that he would slip the ball to me. I just knew where he'd hit the ball to and Tommy knew where I'd be.

A winter break and some bad luck

Celtic's progress towards retaining the league title was interrupted by another severe winter. It was not as bad as the one three years previous in the 'ten men won the league' season but, unlike that one, Celtic did not emerge from the enforced break a stronger revitalised unit. In fact Celtic returned from the football stoppage without one of their most talented players, a key player in their league win the year before. Charlie Nicholas' name would be missing from the team sheet for the rest of the season and it would have nothing to do with a rotation system or a sudden dip in form. You cannot play football with a broken leg.

Snow and ice meant that there was little enough football played in the months of December 1981 and January 1982. Celtic's last game of 1981 was against Dundee which Celtic won 3–1. A brief thaw allowed the Celtic v Rangers game to take place (a week after it had been originally scheduled for) with Celtic going down by a goal to nil at Ibrox. There would be no more competitive football until the end of January, although reserve games continued where playable. It was during a reserve match against Morton at Cappielow that Charlie Nicholas suffered a serious leg fracture which ruled him out for the rest of the season. Celtic had no option but to play with the favoured option of McGarvey and McCluskey and hope that nothing would happen to either of them.

From bad to worse

When the season resumed it was business as usual for George. He continued to score with apparent ease and regularity. He had also been assigned the role of penalty taker, which he carried out with great confidence and effect. Although Celtic were knocked out of the Scottish Cup by Aberdeen in February, their league form gave the fans confidence that they could see off the challenge of Ferguson's Aberdeen. They had, however, one problem as they entered the last two months of the season. On 31 March Celtic had beaten Dundee United 2–0 at Tannadice, with Tommy Burns scoring both goals for Celtic. However, the cost was considerable; Frank McGarvey's season came to an abrupt end. Like Charlie Nicholas, he too had broken his leg. It seemed that disaster had indeed struck and that Celtic were in big trouble with only one recognised striker still available and 10 games to go. Celtic's title hopes now rested almost completely on the shoulders of the lad from Birkenshaw. Celtic fans were in total shock to have lost two of their three main strikers. Celtic also had a huge tactical problem. The success of the previous season and much of this one had been built on the energy and stamina of Frank McGarvey and the sublime talents and vision of George McCluskey and Charlie Nicholas. Now two of those key elements were no longer to play any part in the league title quest and McNeill had to decide what to do. There was no point sticking George into McGarvey's role. He was a totally different type of player and would never be either a big target-man or a 'buzz-ball' in the box. And it would have been a waste of his talent anyway. Celtic would have a most difficult run-in to the title indeed and, if they were going to win it, George McCluskey would have to hit the best form of his career. But who was going to partner him up front?

With both McGarvey and Nicholas out for the rest of the season Celtic indeed had an injury crisis. Billy McNeill had to look at what he was left and turned to a young 20-year-old whom McNeill himself had signed from the Celtic Boys Club; Danny Crainie. A skilful player with a subtle touch and great close control, Crainie could play on either wing. He had made his debut from the substitutes' bench following an injury to Davy Provan in February of that year during Celtic's dramatic comeback against Partick Thistle, when Celtic came from 2–0 down at half-time to gain a valuable point thanks to goals from George McCluskey and Roy Aitken.

Following Frank McGarvey's injury McNeill moved Danny Crainie into a more central attacking position alongside McCluskey and the young winger-turned-striker proved to be a master-stroke on the part of the manager. Danny Crainie scored his first goal against Morton in a 1–1 draw in Cappielow and the following week he scored in the first minute against Rangers at Celtic Park when Celtic won 2–1. Suddenly Celtic fans were gaining confidence as this new Celtic 'emergency' partnership started to click and Celtic went on a roll of six wins in a row with both strikers scoring six apiece. Celtic were now starting to win with ease and on the first day of May they thumped Hibs 6–0 thanks to Murdo McLeod (two goals), Danny Crainie, George McCluskey, Roy Aitken and Tommy Burns. George was totally in his element in leading this Celtic team to another title. All they needed was to keep their nerve as they entered the final three games. Three points from three games would secure the retention of the title irrespective of what Aberdeen could do. Surely the disappointment of the 1979/80 season when Celtic threw away the league against Aberdeen in the final games could not happen again? Lightning had already struck twice this season when two of Celtic's best forwards experienced season-ending injuries through broken legs. But surely lightning cannot strike twice on two occasions?

'One man won the league'

As Celtic moved into the final three games, to be played over the space of 12 days, there was a quiet confidence in the Celtic camp. Celtic had two home games against St Mirren sandwiched in between a visit to Tannadice. Aberdeen had also three matches to play with the last one against Rangers at Pittodrie. Celtic had a vastly superior goal difference. All the cards seemed to be in the club's favour. The league title was theirs for the taking. Or so it seemed. One factor really began to tell on Celtic, however. The horrific injury list had shorn Celtic of some of its key players, and not only strikers, with Mike Conroy and Dom Sullivan also out. The Celtic squad was down to the bare minimum and McNeill had no choice but to use the wonderful but still very young Paul McStay in the final part of the season. On 3 May St Mirren surprisingly held Celtic to a 0–0 draw at Celtic Park giving Celtic fans a few concerns as Aberdeen closed the gap. Two points needed with two games left. Celtic went to Dundee United and the depleted (and exhausted) Celtic side was soundly beaten 3–0. Suddenly the gap was down to just two points with a game to go. The three goals conceded also weakened Celtic's goal advantage over Aberdeen. Celtic were still two points and four goals to the good going into the last match of the season. Celtic fans (and players) didn't need to use calculators to work out that if Celtic lost to St Mirren in the final game and Aberdeen beat Rangers by a margin of four goals or more then the league title that had been in Celtic's grasp for so long would go to Pittodrie. But Celtic fans reassured each other that their team would not be beaten at Celtic Park by St Mirren and, in any case, surely Aberdeen would never be able to put four or more goals past Rangers at Pittodrie?

Injuries, injections, Coatbridge Celtic and final glory!

As the tension mounted going into the final game of the season a new and extremely serious injury problem emerged at Celtic Park. The sheer volume of games played and the increasing intensity of each of the matches as the season came to a climax was having its toll on the sole remaining recognised striker left on the park. George had already played 42 games before going into this final match. He had been rested in only two matches – both in the Scottish League Cup – at the start of the season. He had led the attack all year and, especially since McGarvey's leg break. George was now reporting a serious knee injury just when he was needed most.

I had been carrying a knee injury for weeks and had been receiving pain-killing injections so that I could continue playing. My knee was giving me serious grief. I guess now with more attention to medical science and fitness I would have been rested and would have a lot of physio work on the cause of the problem to sort it out. But in those days the tendency was to give you an injection to kill the pain so that you could continue to play. It took the pain away but after the effects wore off there was hell to pay and often I found it almost impossible to get out of bed the next day. I suppose that if Charlie had have been available then I may have been rested a bit but the way things were that season I had to play every game, and the full 90 minutes at that. There was no 'George, give it an hour and if it's getting bad we'll take you off'. It was more 'If it's really bad, George, you'll have to get a pain-killing injection for Saturday'. I just had to get on with it but during that final week or two it was getting really bad.

Yet before George had to get down to the business of attempting to win the league title for Celtic, there was a small matter of Coatbridge Celtic Supporters Gala Dinner to attend to.

Celtic have a wonderful tradition of trying to facilitate supporters club functions by providing players (both past and present) as guest speakers whenever possible. George in particular has a tremendous reputation among Celtic supporters' clubs and associations for his willingness and generosity in giving of his time and hospitality in sharing his thoughts, recollections and humour by attending functions the length and breadth of Scotland, England and Ireland, as well as in America, Australia and Dubai. Nothing is too much bother for George when Celtic supporters are involved. He is a fantastic ambassador for the club he loves and gives so much for it. And there is nothing false or self-interested about this aspect of his character as his close friend Declan Leavey points out:

I was Chairperson of *Beann Maghadain CSC* in Belfast around 15 years ago and we were organising our first annual club dinner and trying to get a guest speaker from Celtic. George (whom I had never met or spoken to) phoned me and said that he was available. He didn't want any fee or any remuneration at all, just his flight and hotel room. He was brilliant and had time for everyone. George returned every time I asked him and has made so many friends in Belfast. He always remembers everyone he has met on previous occasions and always asks about how they are getting on. He is an extremely affiable and genuine person who also happens to have been a wonderful footballer.

Of course it's one thing for a former footballer to attend Celtic functions or for a current player to go during the closed season or if he is free due to injury. It is an entirely different situation when the player in question is about to play in the most important game of the season the very next day. But this is what George and Tommy Burns were instructed to do the night before the St Mirren game. In those days there was no flexibility or cancellations. Celtic had promised Coatbridge CSC that George McCluskey and Tommy Burns would attend its dinner dance, and Coatbridge CSC had advertised it on their posters and publicity. So on Friday 14 May the two friends set off to fulfil this engagement. Looking back on it George recalls:

Both of us would have rather been home resting before the match but, sure enough, we found ourselves heading down to Coatbridge to a CSC dinner dance. We both tried to convince each other that we'd only be there for an hour or so and show our faces, make a wee speech and pose for a few photographs with the people there and sign autographs, but deep down we knew that there was absolutely no chance of that plan working! People just wanted another photograph or have a chat about this game or a goal or a player. And sure, why not? After all, they were having a great time among their pals at a dinner dance. Eventually Tommy and I got away around 10.30 with some of the Coatbridge guys suggesting that we could come to their houses afterwards for a party! All we wanted was to get to bed and get ready for the game the following day. I just kept thinking that if I had a bad game there would be a load of people saying that I had been out all night with them in Coatbridge!

The next day the Celtic team arrived early at the ground knowing exactly what was at stake. Ninety minutes would determine whether or not the season of 1981/82 was to end in glory or bitter disappointment. There would be no sympathy for the injuries that had cursed Celtic that season. An expectant but somewhat nervous crowd of (officially) 40,000 awaited the final stage of the drama. Still, an early goal would help to ease the tension that hung over Celtic Park as kick-off neared. If the fans had known the full extent of McCluskey's injury as he prepared to get changed for the match then 'nervous' would have been replaced by 'anxiety bordering on despair'. George was limping very badly with his knee injury and a thigh strain. Today there would have been no question of him playing, but on that day Celtic simply didn't have a choice.

I was hobbling as I was getting changed and I came up to Billy McNeill and told him that I didn't think I'd be able to play, the knee was that sore. He nearly fainted and told me that I had to play, that there simply wasn't anyone else. He called to the club doctor and said, 'Doc, George's knee is goosed. Give him an injection.' So that was it then. I got an injection before the match and another at half-time. I guess that that's the reason that my knees give me a fair bit of grief today. But that game is one that I am delighted to have got through – pain and all.

To say that the Celtic supporters were jittery would be an understatement of considerable proportions. With every passing minute tension mounted as Celtic dominated play only to be frustrated by the St Mirren goalkeeper, Billy Thompson, who was in inspired form. Each time Celtic looked as if they were about to score, the Scottish international keeper pulled off a magnificent save. While it may have been last-gasp stuff for St Mirren, for Celtic fans things were beginning to look decidedly worrying as news from Pittodrie filtered onto the terraces that Aberdeen had put four goals past a hapless Rangers team in the first 20 minutes. The half-time whistle went with St Mirren – thanks mainly to an incredible goalkeeping display by Thompson – having resisted everything that Celtic had thrown at them.

Billy McNeill had headed into the dressing room a couple of minutes early to prepare a half-time team talk to both reassure and encourage his young side. He had gone to great lengths to keep the news of what was happening at Aberdeen away from his players. They were under enough pressure without having that in their minds. Every member of the coaching and management team, substitutes, any non-playing squad member (including injured players), ground staff, ball boys, security men, in fact all who were associated with Celtic and would have access to the players, were under strict instructions to say absolutely nothing about what was happening at Pittodrie. The Celtic players quickly made their way off the pitch and went into the dressing room. According to George:

> We all sat down. Billy asked me about my knee and I told him that it was starting to give me a bit of pain again. He called the doctor over and it was injection number two for me. Some of the boys asked the manager what was the score at Pittodrie. He told us that he hadn't heard but that what was going on in Aberdeen didn't matter. He pointed out that we had played really well in the first-half, that their keeper had pulled off some great saves and that all we had to do was to keep pressing forward, keep a positive attitude and goals will come. Just as we were about to go back onto the pitch the door of the dressing room opened and Frank McGarvey came in and announced, 'Here boys, Aberdeen are beating Rangers 4–0 at half-time!' Well, McNeill was furious, grabbed him by the scruff of the neck and pushed him out the door using some very strong language saying, 'You bloody idiot! I said no one was to tell the team what was happening at Aberdeen!' We just looked at each other and knew what we had to do in the second half. We would have to win the league ourselves. No one was going to do it for us. But that's the best way to become real champions.

The next 18 minutes proved to be a continuation of the agony that the Celtic fans had endured throughout the first half, Celtic continuing to press and come close only to be thwarted by the inspired Billy Thompson. So long as the score remained at 0–0 the possibility of a slip-up by Celtic was at the back of the fans' minds. Yet this young Celtic team was up for the battle of nerves and showed the character of true champions in a final half-hour in which George McCluskey threw away all inhibitions and his own injury and, with a blistering display of attacking football, led Celtic to a glorious triumph. In the 63rd minute Murdo McLeod surged forward across the halfway line and passed the ball to Tommy Burns who cleverly played it into space for George who timed his run perfectly. There was still a lot to do. In a split second George took the ball on his right foot, switched it to his left before drilling it low into the far corner of the net.

Not even Billy Thompson at his most inspired that day could do anything about it. It was a piece of pure class that the game and the season merited and it was delivered in style by George McCluskey. This instantly lifted the air of tension that had prevailed up to then and had the effect of liberating the Celtic players from the pressure. They then set about displaying the wonderful flowing football that had characterised much of their play that season. With Burns, McLeod and the young Paul McStay running the midfield it was only a matter of time before more goals arrived. 10 minutes after George McCluskey had sent the Celtic crowd into raptures a Davie Provan corner was met by the head of Tom McAdam and despite the best efforts of the St Mirren players on the line the referee judged, correctly, that the ball had crossed the line and awarded a goal. After that it was party time for both players and supporters as Celtic continued to play out the rest of the match in 'the Celtic way'. It was little wonder that a third goal was added before the final whistle and entirely fitting that it was George McCluskey who scored. As so often that year it was Tommy Burns who was the provider. The midfielder was in superb and confident form, picking up the ball just inside the St Mirren half, ghosting past several defenders before slipping the ball to McCluskey who had anticipated where it would be played into and in a flash slotted the ball into the net. It was a goal of a pure opportunist. George recalls the events of the second half:

Obviously as long as the game stayed 0–0 there would be that wee bit of doubt in your mind… this could still go wrong for us – especially as we all knew, thanks to Frank, what was going on at Pittodrie. Though, to be honest, I suspect that most of the tension and jitters were in the crowd. When you're playing you've no real time to think about what's happening elsewhere. Besides, you can't do anything about that. You can only influence what's going on in the match you're involved with. We just kept attacking knowing that sooner or later we would get a chance that could change the game. I was able to move much better in the second half and always felt that we were going to get the breakthrough. Tommy and I knew each other's game inside out and he slipped a great reverse ball right into the space I was running into. I took the ball on my right foot, switched it onto my left and hit it across the goal into the far corner. The third goal was also set up by Tommy. He cut in from the right, going past three or four defenders, and shaped to shoot. The centre-half tried to block him but instead of shooting he threaded a simple pass beyond him to me and I just turned and tucked the ball into the goal.

George even had a claim on a hat-trick that day. Celtic's second goal was claimed by and awarded to Tom McAdam. The big centre-half most certainly did meet a corner from Davie Provan with his head and powered it towards the goal where it was adjudged by the referee to have crossed the line before being cleared by St Mirren's Davie Walker. But did McCluskey get the last touch?

> Did I score a hat-trick that day? I scored the first and the third goals but I might just have got a slight touch on the second one. We got a corner on the right and Davie Provan swung the ball in towards the centre of the penalty area where Tom McAdam met it with his head. I was standing a couple of yards in front of the keeper and the ball just may just have brushed my stomach on its way to the goal. I joked with Tom afterwards that that was my goal. His reply was 'no way George are you getting away with that. My goal no matter what you say buddy.'

George may not have got a hat-trick that day but his man of the match performance won Celtic the league. For those who remember those heady days, the triumph of winning the title on 15 May 1982 was every bit as exciting as when Celtic did likewise some four years later against St Mirren at Love Street, 1986. Celtic fans and players alike celebrated joyously together on the pitch and Billy McNeill rightly singled his star from Birkenshaw out for special praise pointing out that 'he paved the way with a wonder goal [despite being] only 60 percent fit.'[16] Celtic had won the league and McCluskey had played a starring role in that triumph. Without his courage and determination to play through his injuries there is little chance that Celtic would have added the league title to its honours list. He was the leading goal scorer for the season and was afterwards acknowledged as one of the greatest strikers in Scotland. His contribution to the Celtic cause was acknowledged by Celtic fans everywhere. Quite rightly George was awarded 'Supporters' Player of the Year' by numerous Celtic supporters clubs and affiliations for his efforts and achievements that season. He was now in high demand. At the end of the season he and

---

16. In J Reynold, 'Celtic's nerves hold and Premier title is theirs', *The Evening Times*, 15 May 1982.

Packie Bonner were invited by the Celtic supporters clubs in Co Armagh as guests of honour to their annual celebration.

A visit to Ireland, a private mass with the Cardinal and a perfect rendition of 'The Johnny Thomson Song'

The pair arrived in Belfast on the Saturday and were picked up by the organisers and taken into the tranquil Irish countryside to where the function was to be held that evening. Well, it would have had been tranquil except that on entering Armagh a ceilidh band emerged from the side of the road with hundreds of welcoming supporters to walk them into the venue! A great night ensued and, naturally, went on into the early hours as those in attendance looked for photographs, autographs and snippets of first-hand stories from two very willing and affable Celtic ambassadors. The next day entailed a tour of parts of the countryside and a visit to a most distinguished and loved son of the County Armagh – the leader of the Catholic Church in Ireland and Primate of All Ireland, Cardinal Tomás Séamus Ó Fiaich.

To say that Cardinal Ó Fiaich was loved and admired by his flock would be a bit of an understatement. He was *adored* by ordinary Catholics throughout Ireland and beyond. A scholar and senior cleric, Cardinal Ó Fiaich was very much a man of the people and a lover of the poor and oppressed and his views over Ireland and its 'troubles' had brought him into conflict and disagreement with many powerful figures including Margaret Thatcher. He was also the most sociable and hospitable of people so when the organisers brought George and Packie to his residence (*Ara Caoili*), they were assured of a warm welcome. A simple throw away remark from George, however, produced a reaction from the Cardinal that surprised and delighted the visiting party.

We were introduced to the Cardinal and he seemed a really nice man, interested in how we had got on in Armagh and asked how we were enjoying ourselves. He also seemed to have much more than a passing knowledge about Celtic and football and set us at our ease. I then mentioned jokingly that I'd have to go to confession when I got back to Scotland because I had missed mass that day because the night had gone on so late. He replied, 'Oh, we can't have that, George. You coming to Ireland and having to go to confession for missing mass.' He then asked if we wanted him to say mass for us in his private oratory. I was totally taken aback by his offer and immediately accepted. So Packie, myself and the three Armagh lads were taken into the Cardinal's private chapel where the Primate of All Ireland said mass for us! It was a wonderful gesture. After that he brought us back into the reception areas where, after some refreshments, he offered to sing for us the only Celtic song he professed to know, 'The Johnny Thomson Song'! To our amazement Cardinal Ó Fiaich sang the entire song from start to finish. He wished us all the best on departure and sent me a lovely card a few days later, which I still possess and cherish.

Moving from Celtic before Returning Home

15

Paradise Lost – and a Loss to Paradise!

CELTIC FANS WOKE on 1 August 1983 shocked and saddened by the news that one of their finest players and one of their leading goal scorers over the past number of seasons had just been sold to Leeds United for £161,000. Rumours of a possible move by George from Celtic had been circulating around Glasgow for a number of months but were instantly dismissed by most of Celtic fans as simply 'newspaper talk'. Sure, George was 'one of us' and was playing for the only club he'd ever wanted to play for since he was a boy. He was loved by the Celtic fans and he loved them, and loved playing for Celtic. He had a young family and all his roots were in the wider Celtic family and in north Lanarkshire. He was only 27 years of age and pretty much at the peak of his powers. A little more than a year before, George McCluskey's name had been sung from the terraces at Celtic Park and he was spoke about with great affection and pride by Celtic fans everywhere. After all, wasn't he the reason that Celtic had won the title in 1982? It had been his best season by far and he was (in the opinion of many) arguably the best striker in Scottish football and was desperately unfortunate to have missed the cut for the 1982 World Cup. He had not suffered major injury nor experienced a dramatic drop in form that would make people question his ability or commitment to the Celtic cause. Nor had George, unlike so many before him and particularly since, decided to leave Scottish football in order to pursue wealth. George McCluskey was a Celtic boy in every sense of the word and so his decision to leave Celtic came as a shock to Celtic supporters throughout the world.

The coming of the 1982/83 season had looked so promising for McCluskey. Celtic's pre-season involved playing in the prestigious pre-season Feyenoord tournament which was held by the famous Dutch club at the Stadion Feyenoord. Celtic had won the tournament the previous year and looked to defend their title. They put a brave and spirited (but ultimately unsuccessful) defence of their crown, losing 4–3 to Feyenoord in a thrilling final in which George, Tommy Burns and Mark Reid scored for the Hoops. Despite the disappointment of losing, the tournament had been a personal success for both George and Tommy who were the two outstanding players throughout. In the game against Arsenal, George was in particularly good form and caught the eye of the Arsenal manager, Terry Neill. It was something that Neill would return to later that season.

So why did George McCluskey decide to leave Celtic?

The answer was quite simple. George (and many Celtic fans) felt that he was not being given the starts and role in the team that his ability and contribution merited. Despite McCluskey's outstanding contribution to Celtic's successes over the past number of seasons, and especially in crucial games, it seemed that he now wasn't getting the appearances that many (including himself) thought that he had earned. Coming out of the dramatic last day clinching of the league in 1982 it seemed that George's place on the team was assured. Indeed, his form at the start of the next season was promising and he was finding the net with ease in the Scottish League Cup group stage which traditionally opened the new season. George scored four goals in the opening five games of the season and it seemed that the return to fitness by Nicholas and McGarvey would herald a most exciting and free-flowing style of football that would see all three strikers with starting roles. However, as the 1982/83 league campaign unfolded it soon became apparent that the manager had different plans. With both Charlie Nicholas and Frank McGarvey available again Billy McNeill very quickly set out his formation with these strikers as his number one choice partnership and George all too often on the bench. Many Celtic supporters felt that Billy McNeill had unfairly favoured Charlie Nicholas and Frank McGarvey over George during the 1982/1983 season when the manager should have sought to accommodate all three in a system that would have excited the supporters and encouraged a brand of attacking football that very much in the Celtic tradition. One wonders how other teams would have coped with McGarvey, Nicholas and McCluskey, supported by Burns and McLeod. Many Celtic fans today still feel that this was an opportunity lost by the manager and that the complementary skills of this trio – all three at their best – would have been a thing to behold. But even in a supporting role, George McCluskey still revealed that knack of scoring the vital goal that really makes a difference. Fast forward to a Wednesday evening in September, Amsterdam.

Scoring a famous winner in Amsterdam and the mystery of Johan Cruyff's shirt – 'McCluskey – that was a great goal you scored tonight. I'll swap shirts with you.'

Footballers often swap shirts, particularly after European matches. Sometimes it depends where a player happens to be on the pitch when the final whistle is blown or who he lined up against. However, when a truly great footballer asks for an opponent's shirt then it can be said that the footballer must have achieved something quite special in the previous 90 minutes. It happened in Amsterdam in 1982 in the home team's dressing room. The 'truly great footballer' in question, Johan Cruyff – one of the greatest footballers of all time – agreed to swap shirts with George. How George McCluskey came to have the shirt of this incredible footballer (for a short time at least) has become part of the McCluskey family folklore.

The Celtic team that had won the SPL in dramatic circumstances in 1982 was drawn against Ajax Amsterdam in the first round of the European Cup. It was not an easy draw in any sense. The Dutch club had invented 'total football' in the 1970s, leading to many European successes that decade (including three European Cup triumphs) and had been the backbone of an international side that was desperately unlucky not to win the World Cup (beaten by West Germany in 1974 2–1 and Argentina in 1978 by the same score) was still a formidable footballing power. In their ranks they had players of genuine class such as Jan Molby, Jesper Olsen and one Johan Cruyff. Celtic had been held to a 2–2 draw by Ajax at Celtic Park two weeks previously. With two away goals to their credit only a win by Celtic or a high score draw would halt the Dutch champions' progress.

The game was held in front of packed stands, with more than 65,000 in attendance. It was played in the Olympic Stadium instead of the de Meer Stadion to accommodate the vast crowd and was the first full house for the Dutch side since 1974. McCluskey wasn't even supposed to travel to the game since he had picked up an ankle injury the previous week, but Billy McNeill decided that it was worth the gamble considering that he had to stack his side with attacking options if Celtic were to go through. Just after the half-hour mark the Dutch fans were silenced and the 3,000 travelling Celtic fans went crazy with delight as Charlie Nicholas beat two defenders and the keeper with an outrageous chip. Some who witnessed it would claim that it was the best goal Nicholas scored in his entire career. Unfortunately it was witnessed only by those who were in Amsterdam that evening as no television highlights were permitted in Scotland due to Ajax having JVC advertised on their shirts – a far cry from today when *not* having a sponsor on the jersey would cause quite a stir. Packie Bonner had an outstanding game in goal and made a number of crucial saves as Ajax poured forward in search the equaliser they needed to put them back in control due to the away goals rule. In the 65th minute the Celtic keeper was finally beaten by a cruel deflection from a cross by the Ajax winger, Gerald Vanenburg, which trickled past an unsighted Bonner and over the line. The match remained tied at 1–1 deep into the second half as a confident and unflustered Ajax team concentrated on running the clock down. With 18 minutes to go the Celtic manager decided that only a change could bring Celtic back into the tie, and so to the bench and the striker who had scored so many important goals for Celtic in an effort to change the game in Celtic's favour. Provan was withdrawn from the fray and McCluskey was brought on to accompany McGarvey and Nicholas up front. With five minutes to go the Dutch decided to shut up shop and took off Cruyff who spent an age leaving the pitch and ensuring that there would be even less time for Celtic to get a winner. With two minutes to go and facing elimination from the European Cup, Celtic, in true style, turned the game on its head. The man who scored the vital goal describes it as follows:

> Strangely the last 10 minutes of the game basically suited us because we were out of it if the score remained tied at 1–1, so we had nothing to lose. We simply had to get the ball up the pitch and score. My goal was one the three of us were all involved in – Charlie got it, passed it to Frank, who passed it to me. I drew the centre-half out and went by him. I struck it with my left foot and it went right across the box. I caught it sweet as a nut and the keeper had no chance of stopping it.

George's own account of the goal is typically modest. Many journalists and fans who were there that night viewed it as one of the best he was to score in his entire career and it led to unbridled joy among the Celtic fans as Celtic went through 4–3 on aggregate. The travelling Celtic support was praised by the Dutch police and football authorities for their sporting behaviour – as for the Ajax fans? Well suffice to say that for a second time in his career George McCluskey caused a riot among a section of the fans by scoring the winning goal!

There was much joy and celebration in the Celtic dressing room afterwards. After all, Celtic had just put one of the most famous and successful teams in Europe out of the European Cup and in Amsterdam as well. It was a considerable achievement for Celtic and George McCluskey was especially delighted since he had come off the bench and scored the winning goal. The Celtic goal scorer may well have felt that he had proved a point that he should have been getting a starting place on the team. After all, if he could score against Ajax then surely he was good enough to play more regularly. The adventures of the day were not quite over yet as George set off in search of something by which to remember this famous victory. He went into a silent and dispirited Ajax dressing room to see if any of the Ajax players were willing to exchange shirts with him.

Looking back on it now I might confess that it probably wasn't the best idea I ever had. I left one dressing room full of joy and celebration and entered another one that resembled a morgue. There was total silence. The Ajax players were sitting there just staring into space in total disbelief. They were stunned at what had just happened and just trying to come to terms with the fact that their European season was over. Needless to say there were no takers for swapping shirts with me. Just as I was heading for the door I heard a voice: 'McCluskey, that was a great goal you scored tonight. I'll swap my shirt for yours.' I looked round to where the voice came from and there was Johan Cruyff, lying down and getting his legs massaged by a physio and smoking a cigarette! He sat up, took off his shirt and gave it to me. So I left delighted that I had the shirt of one of the greatest players who ever kicked a football.

The shirt of such a legend is one that you might expect to see framed and in a special place in George McCluskey's home as a memento of a special night in which he scored a famous goal that knocked Ajax Amsterdam out of the European Cup and got the shirt of that club's greatest ever player. Sadly it's not to be seen. In fact it lasted only a few hours in the McCluskey family home. The culprit for its demise was the younger McCluskey boy, George's brother, John. George tells it as follows:

We got back to Glasgow the next day and were all, naturally, on a bit of a high. I went home to Birkenshaw and the family were all delighted to see me and get a ball by ball commentary of the match and especially my goal. I showed them the famed shirt of Johan Cruyff and passed it around. At the time John had finished playing for Celtic but was still playing a bit of five-a-side. He asked me if he could borrow it to play in the next day and said that his pals would be well impressed to him wearing Cruyff's shirt. I thought that it was a great idea so gave it to him with strict instructions to take good care of it and not lose it. At the time our Teresa was still a child and we had one of those safety fire-guards that was sort of box shape so that the whole hearth area was covered. We had all headed off to bed when John decided that he should wash it and have it ready for the next day. So he did that and hung it over the fire-guard to dry – and then he went to bed. The next day after training I asked John where it was and he told me that he hadn't seen it since the night before. We looked all round the house for it but without success with John swearing that he hadn't been able to find it that morning. It was a complete mystery and it was as if it had vanished into thin air... until my mother found the charred remains of an Ajax shirt in the bin. It seems my brother's attempt to dry the shirt had been too successful!

Painful negotiations and a decision to leave

The goal against Ajax proved to be one of the few highlights for the Celtic striker from Birkenshaw that season. All too often George found himself on the bench, sacrificed for a Nicholas and McGarvey partnership. Limited to five starts in the SPL, it is little wonder that George McCluskey could only manage two goals in the league. For someone who had been the top scorer in the SPL the year before and had been desperately unlucky not to show his skills on the biggest stage of football, the World Cup Finals, the situation at the club he had loved throughout his life had become impossible. George was incredibly frustrated, as were his many admirers. There is no doubt that Nicholas had a superb season that year which saw him score a total of 50 goals in all competitions (including 29 in the league). He also went on to win the Scottish Footballer of the Year and the Players' Player of the Year awards. Yet, for many associated with Celtic, these individual awards – merited as they undoubtedly were – did not make up for the overall honours won by the club that season. A 2–1 victory over Rangers in dreadful weather conditions (with Celtic fans enduring unremitting rain in the uncovered King's Park end of Hampden) in the Scottish League Cup in December 1982 was not a sign that greater triumphs lay in store for the 1982/83 season. Celtic were knocked out of the Scottish Cup in the semi-final stage by Aberdeen and worse was to follow as Celtic, in pole position for much of the season, began to leak points in the final 10 games and lost the league by a single point to Dundee United in the last game of the season. A dramatic 4–2 win at Ibrox for Celtic (having been 2–0 down) was not enough to defend their title. Dundee United matched Celtic by beating their city rival at Dens Park by 2–1. Throughout the league campaign the player who had been largely responsible for winning the league for Celtic the previous year had been left watching and waiting on the bench. Celtic fans debated about whether a decent run of games for George McCluskey could have changed the fortunes for a Celtic team that was clearly missing that extra something that he had brought to it so often throughout his career and especially in crucial matches. For many Celtic supporters that season there was a deep sense of frustration. After all, the previous season Celtic had won the league thanks largely to the efforts of the only main striker who was available. This season Celtic had all three strikers fit and yet Billy McNeill relied on keeping one of them on the bench. George could not spend another season sitting on the bench. Something had to change. Besides, his contract was coming to an end and it was common knowledge in the football world that he was unhappy and just might be open to a move away from his beloved Celtic.

It was common knowledge that I was unhappy with the situation at Celtic. Like any other footballer I just wanted to play matches and this wasn't happening for me at the time. I also was coming to the end of my contract and had been in to see the manager a couple of times about signing a new one, but only if I was satisfied with the conditions. Money was not my major concern. I wanted to play football and made that clear to Billy McNeill around halfway through the season. He assured me that I was integral to his vision of the future for Celtic but I was not convinced at all. I asked him how could he say that I was part of his vision for Celtic if he wouldn't even play me?

Shortly after this George was informed by an extremely good source that Arsenal had approached Celtic with a bid for £500,000 to sign him.

Arsenal needed a striker and the Arsenal manager, Terry Neill, had been impressed by McCluskey when he watched him in the earlier pre-season tournament in Rotterdam. George was interested in this news and went in to see Billy McNeill the next day to ask him if there was any interest in him from another club. What happened next continues to perplex George.

> Billy just looked straight at me and told me that no club had come in with a bid for me yet and that as far as he was concerned as manager of Celtic my future lay with the club and I would be a key player for his team over the coming seasons. I was (and still am) confused by this. Indeed, my confusion grew when the same totally reliable source came back to me assuring me that Celtic were well aware of Arsenal's interest in me and that the board had received a bid for me from Arsenal for the said sum.

All George could do was sit and await developments. The interest from Arsenal would surely strengthen his hand in negotiating a new contract with Celtic which would, he hoped, provide an assurance that he would be restored to his place leading the line in future campaigns. Word of a possible bid had leaked to the press and McNeill responded that he wouldn't countenance any sort of bid for George McCluskey. He was integral to the team and was going nowhere. George simply didn't know what was going on or what the truth of the matter was. Honest to a fault, he could have accepted being left on the bench if his form was bad or if the manager just didn't fancy him. But he had been unable to prove himself due to lack of games and the manager, who wouldn't put him on the pitch, was assuring everyone, including George himself, that his future was most certainly at Celtic and that other clubs were wasting their time in trying to get Celtic to sell him. George McCluskey's situation hadn't changed. He spent the rest of the season mostly watching from the side lines. Little wonder that his mind started to tell him that his future might be elsewhere. The closed season would see major developments that would lead the young man from Lanarkshire to a new club in a new league.

During the summer of 1983, Arsenal did indeed sign a Celtic striker, but it was not George McCluskey. On 22 June 1983 Charlie Nicholas departed the scene, just as many Celtic fans had been predicting for some months. A combination of football agents, the media, Nicholas himself and, perhaps, the Celtic board ensured that the 21-year-old prodigious talent was actively looking elsewhere. He was offered contracts by Man United,

Liverpool and Arsenal, finally choosing the Londoners and becoming the highest paid footballer in Britain. Celtic fans, already deflated by the loss of a league title they should have won to Dundee United by a single point, thus found their misery compounded by the departure (albeit expected) of Charlie Nicholas. This was not the end of the turmoil, however. Just eight days after Nicholas left for London, Celtic fans were rocked by the departure of another a Celtic legend who decided to go 'down south'. This time it was not a footballer but the manager, as Billy McNeill agreed to take on the managerial role at Manchester City who had just been relegated the month before! Turmoil in paradise indeed.

For the more suspicious (or maybe realistic) Celtic supporters, George McCluskey's exclusion from the starting line-up for much of the previous season had been part of a wider business plan to sell Nicholas for what was then a Scottish transfer record of £800,000. Nicholas received a signing on fee of approximately £100,000 and the then massive sum of £2,000 per week. Some believe that George was used in a cynical game to sell Nicholas to a big English club for a substantial profit and that his exclusion from the starting line-up for much of the season was due largely to a decision taken for business reasons to (as some put it) 'put Nicholas in the shop window'. Far-fetched as this belief may seem there could be some substance behind it. The board at that time was viewed with dismay and suspicion by many Celtic supporters for adhering to a policy that favoured short-term financial gain over footballing ambition. Some suggested that if the board had been in charge of the Sahara Desert there would be a sand shortage in two weeks! The transfer fiasco surrounding a player whose heart was set on staying with Celtic is evidence of this (perhaps) somewhat harsh assessment. George's contemporary striking partner at that time, Frank McGarvey, makes some interesting comments in that general direction in his autobiography.[17] McGarvey acknowledges the wonderful ability and contribution of Nicholas to a great and exciting Celtic team at that time. He also suggests that George McCluskey (in his opinion 'one of the most gifted strikers ever to wear the hoops') had to sit out much of that season to accommodate a McGarvey/Nicholas partnership. It was most certainly a successful one in terms of goals scored – even if not in terms of winning trophies – but it was not always sweetness and light. In a chapter entitled 'Charlie Isn't My Darling', McGarvey outlines the tension that

---

17. F McGarvey and R Espin, *Totally Frank: the Frank McGarvey Story*, Edinburgh: Mainstream Publishing, 2008.

existed between Nicholas and himself at that time. It was something that most Celtic fans were unaware of and one which McGarvey reveals in some detail. According to the former Celtic striker some Celtic teammates at that time appeared to favour Nicholas and would pass the ball to him even if McGarvey was in a more favourable scoring position. Whether or not this is true or (if so) whether favouring Nicholas was part of a larger ploy is open to debate. What would seem to be clear, however, is that everyone associated with Celtic was aware that Charlie Nicholas was a major asset who (like Kenny Daglish) would not be staying at Celtic for his entire career and, perhaps, George McCluskey's football career was secondary to getting Charlie Nicholas sold to the highest bidder. To this day George doesn't know himself exactly what was going on or if it was all just coincidence. When asked by the writer how he now deals with Billy McNeill after what must have been a very difficult and stressful time, George, in typical modest fashion, replied:

> I meet Billy all the time around Celtic Park and at different Celtic functions. We get on fine now but I do remind him of that transfer saga and say, 'Hey Billy. You sold Charlie Nicholas to Arsenal and now he's a millionaire. If you had have sold me first then I'd be a millionaire today too.'

But, for all that, McCluskey was now stuck in limbo with some serious decisions to make.

For many Celtic supporters this 'triple loss' (league, outstanding striker and manager) was something of a crisis. Yet 'you are where you are'. Celtic quickly moved to replace McNeill with the popular former Celt Davie Hay ('the Quiet Assassin') a week or so after McNeill's departure. One of the 'Quality Street Gang', Hay knew the club inside and out and was an ideal replacement for McNeill. Although Hay had departed for Chelsea in 1974 (against his own wishes) before George made his debut for Celtic they had played together on numerous occasions on the reserve team. Davie Hay certainly knew the talent that was already at Celtic Park and many thought that the new manager was about to re-establish McCluskey as the player who would lead Celtic to glory once more as he had on so many occasions in recent seasons. Indeed, despite the loss of Nicholas and McNeill many Celtic fans during that closed season were optimistic that this 'twin departure' would free up McCluskey from a system that didn't suit him and that he would come out at the start of the new season with all guns blazing in front of the Jungle in which he had stood on so many occasions as a boy and supporter. Any move from Celtic by George McCluskey – especially at this time – would simply not make any sense at all. So why did he decide to leave the team he (and his family) adored and go to England, to Leeds?

When your contract ends what do you do?

There was an awful lot going on behind the scenes than many of the Celtic fans were unaware of that very reluctantly led a wonderful gifted footballer to move from the club that he and his family loved to Yorkshire. In those days the manager would go to the chairman (Desmond White) to discuss new contracts, how much a player wanted and how much the club was prepared to pay. White had a reputation for doing things on the cheap and would not be rushing to give anyone huge pay increases. At the time George was one of the lesser paid players at Celtic. He was on £180 a week and felt that he was worth much more given his contribution to the team over the previous five or six seasons. The top players at Celtic were getting paid £350 per week. All he wanted was to be paid the same as the rest of the top players because that is the level that he was playing at. When you look at what players get today these figures must seem laughable. Yet this was what top footballers playing in front of crowds of tens of thousands of supporters were earning in the early eighties. To put these sums into context the writer was informed by one of George's closest pals, Paul Brannan, that a shift worker in the Caterpillar plant in Uddingston, with a bit of overtime at the weekend, would make the same money as George was getting from Celtic! A far cry from the riches that professional footballers are getting paid today. George's demand for a new contract that would deliver £350 per week could not be seen in any way as excessive or unreasonable given that a footballer's playing career was limited. Besides, Celtic players other than George who had not made any greater contribution to the Celtic cause over the preceding seasons were already getting paid this amount of money. All George McCluskey wanted was a new contract that reflected his ability and would secure a decent future for his family. With a new manager in place George hoped that he would be able to sign a new contract that would keep him at Celtic Park throughout the rest of his career. It was over to Davie Hay now.

To be totally honest I cannot praise Davie Hay enough for his efforts, openness and integrity. He had just come in as Celtic manager during the closed season and his first task was to sort out the team. He phoned me on many occasions and tried to get me to sign a new contract with Celtic. I was still keen to play for Celtic but I had to make sure that whatever new contract I might sign would give me the best deal for my own future both as a footballer and as a provider for my family. I was now 27 and had two children, Leenne and Barry. I was not asking for an outrageous sum of money and simply wanted what the rest of the top players at Celtic were already getting. Davie Hay couldn't have been any better in trying me to sign for Celtic and he continually stressed how much he wanted me to play a leading role in his team, especially since Charlie Nicholas had departed. The main problem was that he had to get everything signed off by Desmond White and it seems to me that is where the stumbling blocks occurred.

Clearly George could not speak highly enough about the new Celtic manager and the effort he put in to getting Desmond White to offer an honourable and realistic contract that would have tied down McCluskey at Celtic for the next number of years, which may have proved to have been his best years. Davie Hay himself knew exactly what he needed at Celtic and he most certainly needed a striker of proven ability who would not need a lot of time to settle. George McCluskey most certainly ticked all the necessary boxes. Yet dealing with the Celtic chairman was never going to be an easy task, as the manager very soon discovered.

I had promised Davie Hay that I would hold off looking for anyone else until he got back to me after he had talked to Desmond White. After a couple of days he called me on the phone and said, 'George, I can't believe what he [Desmond White] has just done. He told me that he would give you a new contract on £200 per week. That's nowhere near good enough. Do absolutely nothing right now. Don't talk to anybody. Don't think of moving anywhere from here. I'm going back to him and see what he will offer.' Well, a week or so later, Davie came back to me. He told me that Desmond White and the board had come back with a new and final offer of £300 per week which was still short of what I had hoped I might be offered but it might have been enough to entice me to sign again for Celtic except for the conditions attached by White.

The new Celtic manager was desperate to get McCluskey to sign and urged him to strongly consider doing so. Davie Hay realised that his hands were tied in relation to the financial aspects of the proposed contract but hoped that George's desire to play a leading role in his new Celtic team would be enough to persuade him to stay. Hay stressed the fact that with Nicholas gone from the scene he needed a striker like McCluskey to build the team around for the future and that he would be assured of his position in a system that suited his style of football. Unfortunately the new contract contained a clause that stopped George from signing on the dotted line.

It wasn't actually the money offered that stopped me signing a new contract for Celtic even if it wasn't as much as I had asked for or thought that I was worth. I was well aware that there were quite a number of football players at the likes of Rangers, Aberdeen, Dundee United and other Scottish clubs as well as Celtic who were getting more money than I was being offered but I was excited about what Davy Hay had in mind and would probably have put the financial issue out of the road if it wasn't for a major condition attached to the contract. Basically it stated that I would have to start the first 10 matches of the new season in order for the new contract to be implemented. Davy kept assuring me that I would start every game as far as he was concerned and that I should put that question out of my mind but I kept asking what would happen if I got injured or fell ill or something. I would have loved to have played under Davy Hay but not under those conditions. I guess that by the time the negotiations were over I'd just had enough. I had wanted a fair wage and a bit of certainty about my playing career and this just didn't seem to be being offered at the time.

And so it was that a very heavy heart George McCluskey ended his playing career with Celtic and moved his family to England where he would meet some fellow players from Scotland, some of whom were as Celtic minded as himself.

16

From Celtic to Leeds – into a Different World

GEORGE MCCLUSKEY'S TRANSFER to Leeds was not without incident or dispute. As a free agent who had refused a new contract, George McCluskey could be sold by Celtic without a lot of consultation. In the pre-Bosman era players were seen by clubs as assets to be transferred if the price was right. At the end of a player's contract the club still held the player's registration and consequently was able to insist on a fee for transfer. It could be argued that now the balance has shifted too much in the direction of the player (and particularly his agent), but in the 1980s if a club decided to sell a player then there was not a lot the player could do about it. Celtic put a price-tag on George's undoubted talents of £200,000 while Leeds were reluctant to go beyond £150,000. The final fee of £160,000 was settled by an independent football tribunal, making George the first Celtic player whose transfer was settled in such a fashion. George was awarded a contract worth £500 per week, almost three times his previous weekly earnings at Celtic. He now entered a new and different football world in so many ways. Playing football 'the Celtic way' in front of your own community became a thing of the past. New challenges had to be faced and a style of football adapted to in an altogether different environment.

George arrived at a Leeds club that had just been relegated from the top division. It was a club steeped in history and tradition which would have been known to all who followed football in those years. Don Revie's great Leeds team of the 1960s and 1970s had accomplished much in the recent past with players such as Norman Hunter, Johnny Giles, Terry Cooper, Mick Jones, Allan Clarke, Jack Charlton, and quite a large Scottish representation including Billy Bremner, Peter Lorimer and brothers Eddie and Frank Gray. Very much loved (by Leeds fans) and hated (by pretty much everyone else), Revie's side was built on skill, endeavour and not a short measure of physicality. They won several trophies during this golden era including two premier division titles and an FA Cup. They were runners-up in the English league on five occasions and generally there or thereabouts throughout the 1960s and much of the 1970s. Their greatest achievement during this period in their history was undoubtedly reaching the final of the European Cup in 1975 in Paris losing (unluckily in many observers' eyes) 2–0 to Bayern Munich. Going down to Leeds, George McCluskey would have remembered the famous so-called 'Battle of Britain' of 1970 when a wonderful Celtic team destroyed a much-fancied (by the English media) Leeds team both home and away in the semi-final of the European Cup. Due to the demand for tickets Celtic's home leg was played at Hampden in front of an official attendance of over 136,000 spectators.

These glory days at Leeds had come to an end by the time that George arrived. They had been relegated from the top division the previous season. Eddie Gray had been appointed player-manager and tasked with returning Leeds to the top flight as quickly as possible. A product of the Leeds youth system himself, Gray stabilised the side in his first season and turned to a very promising youthful squad to rebuild the team, including players such as John Sheridan, Neil Aspin, Denis Irwin and Scott Sellars. He realised that there were positions that the emerging talent could not fill and that players of proven ability and experience would have to be brought in. The Glasgow-born manager – who, like his younger brother Frank, was (and remains) an avid Celtic fan – would have been aware of the transfer situation at Celtic and jumped at the chance of bringing McCluskey's talents to the famous Yorkshire club. He also used his contacts and knowledge of the Scottish game to bring in midfield ball-winner Andy Watson from Aberdeen and Dumbarton midfielder John Donnelly. When George and his fellow Scots arrived at Elland Road they joined a large contingent from Scotland already there. In addition to the two Celtic minded Gray brothers, Leeds had on their team David Harvey, and Peter Lorimer who had returned from playing in North America (and University College Dublin) to the club with which he had achieved so much in the glory days of Leeds. George McCluskey's accent would certainly not be misunderstood by half of the Leeds team at least. And there was another person at Leeds who made George feel especially welcome, former Celt, Jimmy Lumsden.

Lumsden only made one first-team appearance during a four year association with the club, and that was in a qualifier for the Anglo-Scottish Cup against Clyde in 1978. Yet his value lay not in the first team but as a scout and a coach with the reserve team where he specialised in bringing on young talent to the next stage. George knew him well from those days and respected him greatly. 'Wee Jimmy' had moved to Leeds in 1982 as Eddie Gray's assistant and George was delighted to link up once again with someone whom players of his era would have regarded as mentor and friend.

> I was delighted that Jimmy Lumsden was at Leeds as I had known him from his days as reserve team coach at Celtic. He was someone whose judgement you trusted and you could always go to him for advice if things weren't going well. He was one of those people who would listen to you and who you knew was genuinely interested in you. He was great for taking young lads under his wing and helping them to move onto the first-team. He knew what a big move it was for me to go from Celtic to Leeds and also for Anne and myself to leave our families and friends behind. It was Jimmy who really sold the club (Leeds) to me and made the move from Scotland so much easier.

For the newly arrived McCluskey family this was indeed quite a move. Not only had George to get used to a new club, new opposition, new training methods and a different style of football, it was also a new challenge for his young wife, Anne. Everything was now different for the McCluskey family. For the first time George, Anne and their children were away from the extended family, friends and the community that they knew and had grown up with them. Things were indeed different at Leeds not least the challenge of not having the family support that George and Anne could rely upon in Scotland. Yet, as Anne recalls, Leeds made a great effort in making families feel included in the club.

> One of the things that struck me about Leeds United was just how family-oriented they were. For example on a match day the club provided a crèche facility so that the wives could go to the game or even go shopping in Leeds. And on a Saturday night the club provided a baby-minding service so that you could go out with the players and their wives if you wanted or if there was a Leeds function on. This made the move to Leeds so much easier. Today, of course, there is much more support for the families of the players but Leeds certainly put a lot more thought and effort into this even at that time and it did make you feel part of the club.

While Anne was able to settle at Leeds fairly quickly, life on the football pitch presented a number of challenges for the newly arrived striker from Scotland. Leeds had slipped into the English second tier and the challenge was to get to the top level as quickly as possible and that was the reason McCluskey had been bought by Leeds in the first place. Eddie Gray had also brought in another striker for the start of the 1983 season, Andy Ritchie, in the quest for promotion. But promotion was never going to be easy in a league in which the physical battle often took priority over the silky skills and sublime touch that McCluskey possessed. Most clubs striving to get out of that division would employ a system which would not suit his game either, playing a rigid 4–4–2 system with the ball being launched into the penalty area at every opportunity. For a player used to being part of a unit of three or four forwards breaking at speed, taking on players, laying the ball off and having the return threaded through into space or arriving at the precise moment to have a shot, this type of battering-ram football didn't suit. Besides, a forward like George McCluskey could only be as good as the players he played with and at Celtic he certainly had plenty of quality teammates such as Kenny Dalglish, Tommy Burns, Johnny Doyle, Murdo McLeod *et al* who were on the same wavelength as himself and who made each other even better footballers. At Leeds that was not the case. George sums up the type of football that typified the division at that time:

> I was never a big physical number nine who would be a direct target for crosses or someone would hold the ball up for the other forwards. Neither was I the type of striker who plays in the space behind the centre-forward. At Celtic we were all expected to make runs, play the ball quickly, take on players, anticipate where the likes of Tommy (Burns) would hit the ball into and look for opportunities to shoot. To be honest I think that had Leeds been able to get into the first division then I might have made a greater impact. Unfortunately, given the division that Leeds were in and trying to get out of it, meant that 'route one football' was the flavour of the day and that certainly didn't suit my style of play. Also, the midfield in that division tended to get bypassed which meant that you generally found yourself in a physical battle with some big central defender for a ball that would be launched in your general direction and so strength rather than skill tended to be a major factor in determining the outcomes of matches.

George recalls the type of football that was successful in that division.

When you played the likes of Wimbledon or teams like that you knew what to expect. The football would be unsophisticated and rather basic. I recall one game against Wimbledon in 1984 at their ground, Plough Lane, and it was the start of what became known as 'the Crazy Gang'.[18] They included players such as John Fashanu, Lawrie Sanchez, Dennis Wise and Dave Beasant. I was just personally glad that Vinnie Jones hadn't arrived yet at Wimbledon as he would have had the task of marking me! They had just been promoted the season before and came with a reputation of playing football based on one tactic – hoofing the ball up the pitch into the opponents' penalty area and attacking the keeper. All I can remember about that game was that every time Wimbledon got a throw-in anywhere in their own half, their back four would push out taking our forwards with them so as to stay on-side, the keeper, David Beasant, would get the ball thrown back to him, he would roll the ball forward about 20 yards up the pitch and launch it right into our box where our keeper, David Harvey, would attempt to punch as he got hit by a wave of four or five massive Wimbledon players! I swear that David still has nightmares about it! We got beat 4–0 and I think that I must have touched the ball about twice, including centring it! It was like watching a ping-pong game from the middle of the table with the ball being hoofed from one end to the other and it certainly did not suit my style. The problem with Leeds was that we were trying to play football in a division that was all about battering the opposition. In hindsight I probably went to Leeds at the wrong time and would have loved to have gone there when they were in the premier division and able to play football. I think that that would have suited me better. There is a certain irony that the Leeds team I played in kept trying to knock the ball around and play football and finished mid-table whereas the likes of Wimbledon played total 'route one' game – boot the ball up the park, kick and rush and all that – and they got promoted. It's a pity because Leeds were a great club who tried to play football in the proper way in a division that didn't reward skill.

---

18. This group of players, assembled by the Dons manager Dave Bassett, was famous for their uncomplicated style of football based on a no-nonsense direct approach. In 1988 an unfancied Wimbledon team shocked the English football world by beating classy Liverpool side in the FA Cup Final.

'All right big noise, Dundee United are no longer interested in you. Goodbye!'

George's Leeds career nearly didn't last too long. He'd only been at Leeds around six months when Eddie Gray called him into his office. He explained to George that Dundee United had come to Leeds with a very substantial offer to sign him and that the Leeds board were prepared to accept it. Gray asked George if he wanted to talk with the Dundee United manager, Jim McLean. George agreed and soon found himself on the phone with McLean. The United manager explained to George that he had been a big admirer of him and that Dundee United had wanted to sign him but reckoned that Celtic wouldn't sell him to a rival club so that's why they hadn't put in a bid for him at the time. However, now that George was at Leeds, McLean had put it to the board that now might be an opportune time to get George McCluskey to move to Dundee United. The only stipulation that McLean had was that all of his players would have to be prepared to stay in Dundee. George takes up the story:

I said that that wouldn't be a problem and that I'd already moved down to Leeds so moving to Dundee wouldn't be an issue. He then said, 'Right, the terms are you'll get a three year contract and be paid £170 per week and...' I said, 'Hold on a minute, you've not got the like of Narey, Hegarty and Malpas[19] playing for that sort of money.' Jim McLean said that that was the deal at Dundee United but if you played you'd get an extra £100 of appearance money. I said that that meant that all through the closed season I'd have to live on £170 a week and besides, I didn't think that there was any way that the likes of their top international players were getting that. And I told him that too. Jim McLean admitted that they got a bit more but the offer I was getting was the top one Dundee United were prepared to make. Well, I just told him that I was on £500 a week at Leeds and there was no way that I could consider going to Dundee for £170 a week and appearance money. I had hardly the words out of my mouth when Jim McLean interrupted, 'All right big noise. Dundee United are no longer interested in you. Goodbye!' He then slammed the phone down. I could have been an 'Arab'.

---

19. David Narey, Paul Hegarty and Maurice Maplas were all Scottish international footballers who played for Dundee United at that time.

Leeds fans on George McCluskey

I interviewed a number of Leeds fans from that era to find out what they, as Leeds supporters, thought about George McCluskey and his career at Leeds. These were genuine Leeds fans who had first started following Leeds during the glory years of the 1970s and had remained loyal to the 'Whites' or 'Peacocks' through thick and thin. One may have thought that their memories of the barren years of the 1980s would have coloured their assessment of those who played for Leeds during those difficult times but these supporters were fulsome in their praise for what they saw of George when he played for their beloved team. There is something refreshing about genuine football supporters who follow their team irrespective of success. Too many supporters today seem to be fickle to the point of making their allegiance contingent on success. On planet-football today money appears to guarantee success and that in turn generates media coverage which leads to the emergence of the new type of supporter who will follow his/ her team so long as they're winning things. Hence the appearance of so many replica-wearing supporters of the latest mega-football club. These Leeds supporters were nothing like this and it wouldn't matter to them what division their team found itself in. One suspects that you would still find them following Leeds if they were playing in the lower division of the Northern Counties East Football League. Perhaps it was the experience of knowing failure as well as success that gave my focus group that perspective of realism that only genuine football supporters can have. They fully understood the situation of the Leeds club at that time and the environment that George McCluskey found himself playing in. They appreciated what he was trying to do in challenging circumstances. The comments speak for themselves:

I have followed Leeds since the 1970s and have seen many top class players during that time. I can honestly say that George McCluskey was among the most skilful and technically gifted players I have ever witnessed in a Leeds shirt. To be honest he probably had too much skill for the type of football that was being played around him.

Fantastic touch and great movement. I remember being at Ninian Park in 1984 to see a late George McCluskey goal give Leeds a 1–0 win over Cardiff. The ball came in from a corner, broke loose and George was on it like a flash. Typical McCluskey goal, reacting quicker than anyone else in the box. That was more than 30 years since we'd last beat them. At least I can tell my grandchildren that I was there!

I would have loved to have seen George McCluskey play with the likes of Billy Bremner, Johnny Giles, Peter Lorimer (at his peak), or Joe Jordan, or with later players like Eric Cantona or Robbie Keane. I guess it was a case of wrong time, wrong league.

George was a great footballer with bags of talent and skill. He had terrific vision and intelligence too, which was a problem since he was playing in a Leeds team that lacked both. Sometimes he would get the ball, glide past three defenders and then hit the ball to where his team mate should have been running... only for the ball to go out for a throw-in. Then the crowd's going, 'Why did he do that? Can he not pass?'

'Then Peter Lorimer gets me in trouble!'

Yet playing for Leeds in the English second division was not a totally negative experience for George. Far from it. Apart from the manner in which the club treated the families of its players George also gained a lot from living in Yorkshire, a place set apart indeed. For a young man who had lived all of his life in Lanarkshire and among the wider Celtic family this was an interesting experience. Yorkshire people have a reputation of considering themselves a unique and separate, 'an independent country' as George put it. But he would say or hear nothing critical about Yorkshire people. George maintains that their initial apparent 'standoffishness' is only apparent and temporary and that when you get to know them and are accepted by them they are a wonderfully warm and friendly community. He also met some wonderful players at Leeds who became and remained firm friends. In particular George established a close friendship with Peter Lorimer who had returned for a second spell at Leeds. Lorimer was a household name for all Scottish football fans at that time. Throughout the late 1960s and 1970s the Scottish international winger/attacking-midfielder was a frequent and often spectacular goal scorer with a fearsome shot. Indeed, he was renowned for these strikes, with his shots reaching speeds of up to 90 mph. One penalty kick was apparently recorded at 107 mph.[20]

20. On Lorimer's career see P Lorimer and P Rostron, *Peter Lorimer: Leeds United and Scotland*

Although past the peak of his career, Lorimer still was a class act.

Peter Lorimer was one of those players I really would have loved to have played with at his peak. When he came back to Leeds for his second spell he was around 36 or 37 but still had a wonderful touch, great ball control, terrific vision and a shot that you just couldn't believe was possible. It's little wonder that Leeds fans to this day look back at him with pride and awe. He was also a very social person and sometimes after a game we'd go out for a drink together. Once he got me into serious trouble with Anne by keeping me out longer than we had intended and on return Anne made it pretty clear to me that she was less than happy having to mind the children while I was off 'galavanting' around the town. It actually was the week before my 28th birthday. I know this because (unbeknown to me) Anne had organised a surprise birthday party for me for the following week. There were a lot of family and friends coming from Glasgow who wouldn't be arriving until around nine o'clock on the Saturday evening. So she gave my 'partner in crime' from the week before [Peter Lorimer] the task of keeping me out until the people from Scotland had arrived! So after the game Peter gets someone to take his car and suggests that we go out for one drink. Naturally after the event of the week before I was somewhat reluctant to take him up on his invitation but he was very insistent saying that we'd only go for one or two drinks. As the evening drew on I was beginning to panic but he kept insisting that we'd be having 'just one for the road'. You can imagine my surprise when I arrived home at the appointed hour (excuses rehearsed in my mind) only to see all my pals and family waiting for me. One week Peter gets me in all sorts of bother by keeping me out, the next week he does the very same but this time under Anne's orders!

A visit from some familiar people

George and his family had left Scotland but still kept in close contact with friends, family and, of course, Celtic. Leeds was his new life and he was often visited by his family and especially his parents, John and Teresa, but this did not mean that he had cut his ties – personal and emotional – with Celtic. Despite his disappointment and hurt over his treatment by

Hero, Edinburgh: Mainstream Sport, 2002.

the Celtic board in letting him go, George McCluskey was not going to let this stop him following the club he had supported from boyhood and had played for with such distinction until his reluctant move to England. He still had (and has) enormous respect for the then Celtic manager, Davie Hay, who had tried so hard to keep him at Celtic. Having departed Celtic in 1983 for the second division in England George never thought in his wildest dreams that he would play again in a match that involved his beloved Celtic. Yet football, and life, has a habit of producing surprises and George did indeed play in a game that involved Celtic; but this time George McCluskey's name would be on the opposition team sheet.

The winter of the 1984/85 season had been severe both north of the border and in the north of England with the result that not a lot of football had been played in both jurisdictions especially since the start of the New Year. In order to keep sharp, clubs looked to play friendly matches which were organised pretty much on the spur of the moment and at short notice. Often these games were as a result of personal relationships between managers or clubs. Both the Celtic and Leeds managers had played together on the Scotland team during the 1970s and Eddie Gray had a great affection for Celtic. Given that, it was only natural that the two clubs agreed to play a friendly match. The game was played at Elland Road on 22nd January 1985 on a bitterly cold night in front of a crowd of 6,136 hardy souls including more than 500 Celtic fans who had somehow made it down from Scotland despite dreadful weather conditions in Glasgow that led to train and coach cancellations. The Leeds team that night contained two footballers who had played in the famous European Cup semi-final clash of 1970 when Celtic defeated Leeds both home and away: Peter Lorimer and Eddie Gray. The Celtic team that played at Elland Road that evening had quite a number of George's former teammates on the pitch including Packie Bonner, Danny McGrain, Tom McAdam, Murdo McLeod, Paul McStay, Davie Provan and, George's great pal, Tommy Burns. George's former strike partner, Frank McGarvey, had travelled down to Leeds but had taken ill and stayed in the hotel. Given the reported conditions that evening one suspects that the Celtic striker may well have been considered fortunate by some of those who actually played! George did not start the game but came on as a substitute in the second half.

It was an absolutely freezing night with sleet and rain coming down the whole night. I was coming back from a wee bit of an injury so Eddie let me sit it out for the first half. I was naturally thrilled to come on after half-time and got a great reception from the Celtic fans. Indeed, they applauded me every time I touched the ball and I was delighted that they understood that I hadn't wanted to leave Celtic for any selfish reason. The game ended up a 1–1 draw but the result didn't matter. And I ended up becoming someone who played for both Celtic and Leeds and who played against my former club.

George indeed is one of a very small group of players who has played for both Celtic and Leeds. This includes Bobby Collins and Mark Viduka as well as Liam Miller and Alan Thompson who were both loaned to Leeds during their careers. George McCluskey may well be the only ex-Celtic player who played against his former club, thus creating an additional bit of history.

Playing for Leeds and asking for a transfer

George's career at Leeds lasted three seasons and saw him play 73 times and score 16 goals. For those who are primarily interested in statistics McCluskey's goals/games ratio may appear somewhat disappointing, given his much greater strike rate at Celtic, where he scored almost one goal for every two games started. This statistic does not tell the whole story of George's time at Leeds. Certainly, and by his own admission, he found the style of football in the English second tier difficult to settle into and getting on the score sheet was never easy. George, as someone who had been brought in with a reputation as a proven goal scorer, was always under the spotlight and felt that the pressure was always on him. But, again, such is the life of a striker.

It seemed to take me ages to score my first goal with Leeds. In that particular division you never were going to get a load of chances. So I was always trying to get the crowd on my side and working hard at my game. It took me quite a while to settle in but after my first season – which was a real baptism of fire and getting used to getting battered all round the pitch – I was beginning to get to grips with the style of play and starting to feel a lot happier with my game. Then, in one particular match when I was just thinking that I was at last getting the Leeds fans on my side, Eddie Gray took me off. I was absolutely livid as I thought that I was having a good game. Being a striker is probably one of the most difficult positions on a team as if you aren't hitting the net then the fans notice. So when you start to show a bit of form you hope that the manager backs you. Getting taken off at that moment in my Leeds career really hurt me so on the Monday I went straight into the manager's office and let him know exactly what I felt. Eddie told me that he understood how I felt but that he had the responsibility of managing the team. Well I was still angry and told him that I couldn't see a future at Leeds and wanted to be put on the transfer list. Eddie Gray just looked at me and said that if that was my request then he would drop me onto the reserve team. So that was it. For the next number of months I was not playing in front of large crowds in the English Division Two but in front of several hundred supporters in the reserve matches. Yet during those months – and understanding that it was not as high a standard as first-team football – I was scoring for fun and playing some very good football. I think that during that period I scored around 30 goals in about 30 matches. Then one day I was going into Elland Road for training and a couple of the directors stopped me and asked me if I was prepared to reconsider my decision to be on the transfer list because I was playing so well. I thought about it for a couple of seconds and then went straight to the manager's office and told him that I had changed my mind and was now available for selection for the first team. Eddie told me that he was delighted and that I could now look forward to taking my place up front leading the line again. Yet just when I was beginning to think that I had turned a corner at Leeds, Eddie Gray was sacked in October of the 1985/86 season.

Eddie Gray had paid the price for not being successful in the quest for promotion. His successor, Billy Bremner, was a Leeds legend who had captained the club throughout its most celebrated period under Don Revie. Bremner had come from managing Doncaster and arrived with his own plans for the future and his own system for playing football, and George McCluskey wasn't a part of that system. The new manager set about building a new Leeds team and quickly moved on many of the young players who had been brought into the squad by the former manager and brought in more experienced ones in their place. He also removed the captain's armband from Peter Lorimer before 'retiring' him just before his

40th birthday at the end of the season. George and the new manager didn't see eye to eye and it was common knowledge that George had considered Eddie Gray's sacking wrong and without due respect for a man who had given Leeds so much. Soon enough it was George's turn to be moved on. Billy Bremner's approach was both brutal and total. The squad that Eddie Gray was building was decimated and scattered. On the last day of the season Gary Hamson, Terry Phelan, Denis Irwin and George McCluskey were all given free transfers. What continues to rankle with George is the way all this was done.

The season of 1985/86 had been a turbulent one at Leeds with Eddie Gray getting sacked and players coming and going in and out the door at a serious rate. I didn't see it coming but it now seems clear that Billy Bremner was already looking for someone to replace me as a main striker. He had made his mind up but somehow hadn't got round to telling me. The season had just finished and the players were expected to report in to and collect their gear before taking a couple of weeks break. The day before I was to meet with Billy Bremner I was told by Jimmy Lumsden that I had been put on the transfer list. I was absolutely shocked to hear this and extremely hurt that I hadn't been informed beforehand. So when I went in to meet him the next day I knew that I had been 'let go' and was going to be playing somewhere else the next season. You can imagine my surprise when Billy Bremner told me to go and get weighed so that the coaching staff would know what I'd have to lose when training restarted. I just looked at him with disbelief and told him exactly what I thought of him sitting there and talking about the next season and knowing full well that I was not going to be back at Leeds after the break. I stormed out and drove home where I told Anne what had happened and that our time in Leeds had come to an end. I could handle being placed on the transfer list and being told that I was no longer part of Billy Bremner's plans. What really hurt me was not being told the truth. I was now free to talk to any club I wanted and sort out something for the next season. Anne and I had to do some thinking and work out where we would go next.

But where to?

17

A Return to Scotland and a Brutal 'Tackle'

GEORGE NOW HAD to consider his options. His services were no longer required at Leeds. He was 29 years of age and still had years of football ahead of him. As a transfer listed player he was in a position of listening to any offers that came in. Soon enquiries arrived from a number of Yorkshire clubs including Chesterfield, Doncaster and Sheffield United and it is very likely that had he been willing to pursue his career in England bigger and more prestigious clubs would have made offers for his services. However, other considerations had to be taken into account. George McCluskey was a family man first and a professional footballer second. During the three years in England the McCluskey clan had increased in number with the birth of a second daughter, Natalie. The two older children, Leeanne and Barry, would be going to school and decisions had to be taken as to where the roots of this new generation would be laid down. Besides, George never took such major decisions about the family on his own and his wife Anne would have a major say on the next part of his journey.

I guess that we had some serious thinking to do and had to make a decision about where we wanted the children to grow up. Anne and I came from the same tight-knit community in Lanarkshire and from very close extended families. I had enjoyed my time in Leeds and options were beginning to emerge but, to be honest, Anne had her mind made up. She was home-sick and wanted to be back near her family again. It was important that the children would grow up knowing their grandparents, their aunts and uncles and their cousins. So it was very much a case that, whatever club I'd sign for next, it would have to be back in Scotland.

Unlike today's modern game in which agents would appear to have almost supreme control over their player's contract negotiations, back then a player in George's position would have had much more direct input into his next move. As someone who had been placed on the transfer list on a 'free', he was effectively in control of his own destiny and could listen to any offers. It soon became known that George McCluskey was keen on going back to Scotland. It wasn't long until his phone started ringing.

George knew that a return to Celtic was unlikely. Celtic had assembled a new strike-force in the persons of Brian McClair and Maurice Johnstone in the years since George had left the Glasgow club. Besides, George had already achieved so much for Celtic during his time there and he felt somewhere inside that there would be no return for a second chance. He had been extremely fortunate to play for his boyhood heroes and knew that he didn't owe Celtic anything and nor did they owe him. Sometimes players do return for a second spell at a club where they had made a name. Almost always it doesn't turn out as planned and more often than not ends in disappointment for the player, the club and the fans. The returning player will inevitably be judged by his highest standards and achievements. For example, for all his flair and talent, Charlie Nicholas' second time in the Hoops didn't match his first time there. Fans always remember your best games and can be unforgiving if you leave, return and don't match their expectations. Sometimes it is just best to leave what you achieved and move on.

Going to Hibs

If Celtic was not an option for George then going to play for Hibernian was not a bad second choice at all. In terms of the main reason for returning to Scotland – the family – it was most certainly a better location than heading up north to Aberdeen or Dundee. The McCluskey family were settled around Lanarkshire and that wasn't too far away from Edinburgh. George and Anne very quickly bought a house in Uddingston (which they still live in today) and were only a mile or two from parents, brothers, sisters and the extended family. They were back to their roots and George was less than an hour away from his new club. And it was not just location that was important about this move back north to Scotland. George McCluskey was extremely keen to do what he had done all his life and Hibernian Football Club was a pretty good vehicle to get on board at that time. Hibs had a reputation for playing passing attacking football which would suit George's style of play. The golden years of the 'famous five' (Gordon Smith, Bobby Johnstone, Lawrie Reilly, Eddie Turnbull and Willie Ormond) were long gone but Hibs fans still yearned for a return to the glory days when this forward line delivered league successes throughout the late 1940s and 1950s. The 'Turnbull Revolution' of the 1970s brought back memories of that golden era in Hibs' history. Under the management of the aforementioned Eddie Turnbull, the Leith club did win a trophy – the 1972 Scottish League Cup – when they defeated Celtic 2–1 at Hampden, as well as recording their most famous victory in an Edinburgh derby when they trounced Hearts 7–0 on New Year's Day 1973. During those years Hibs were undoubtedly one of the top teams in Scotland and would surely have added to their solitary trophy triumph were it not for their misfortune to be a very good football side at a time when Celtic, under Jock Stein, were revealing themselves to be one of the top sides in Europe and dominating Scottish football. By the time George arrived at Easter Road even the Turnbull years were a thing of the past as Hibs had slipped down the pecking-order with the emergence of the so-called 'New Firm' of Aberdeen and Dundee United.

In many ways George's arrival at Hibs was not unlike his move to Leeds. Both were clubs that had enjoyed a period of notable success in the past and had – especially in the case of Leeds – 'fallen from grace'. Their respective fan bases looked back at these 'golden years' with a sense of longing and nostalgia mixed with a disappointment at just how far their clubs had slipped backwards. Both were also in a period of transition when McCluskey arrived. At Hibs there had been a clear out over the preceding couple of years by the new manager, John Blackley. The former Hibs star and ex-international footballer was one of the 'Turnbull Tornadoes' and set about trying to mould a Hibs side in that fashion. He favoured a style of football based on passing, playing football the 'right way'. Blackley's first season as Hibs' manager had been reasonably successful. Hibs finished the 1985/86 season in mid-table and made the semi-final of the Scottish Cup and the final of the Scottish League Cup only to find their nemesis awaiting them, Aberdeen. Blackley had brought in Steve Cowan the previous season and a young John Collins was now beginning to show what a class act he would become. Also in the squad at the start of the 1986/87 season were defender/midfielder Joe Tortolano and one familiar face from George's time at Celtic was awaiting him at Easter Road, Alan Sneddon. The right-back, who had played alongside George on numerous occasions and had supplied the crosses for some of George's most famous goals (including George's goal against Real Madrid in 1980), had been transferred to Hibs in 1981. The young players who had been brought in by the previous manager, Pat Stanton, including John Collins, Paul Kane, Micky Weir and Eddie May, were now very much part of Blackley's new vision. True, Gordon Durie, Hibs' best player at that time (John Collins had not yet developed into the footballer who moved to Celtic in 1990), had been sold to Chelsea for £400,000 but the money had largely been reinvested into the team. John Blackley had used the funds to bring in Billy Kirkwood and Stuart Beedie from Dundee United, Willie Irvine from Stirling Albion,[21] Northern Ireland international footballer Mark McCauchy and George himself. George seemed to be joining a promising Hibs team, and his arrival from Leeds was seen by Hibs fans as bringing in that extra bit of class and experience. They awaited George's debut with anticipation. Little did they (or George) know what an explosive game that would be.

Making his debut for Hibs and 'that tackle'

Anyone who knows George McCluskey knows that he is an unassuming and modest guy who wouldn't seek out a fight. He's one of life's good guys and will always try to help others. On the pitch he was a wonderfully talented player who carried over many of his personal traits with him. He never shirked a tackle but he was not a footballer who would go looking for trouble. He most certainly could never be regarded by supporters or fellow professionals alike as a dirty player. Nor could he be accused of being a trouble maker, the type of player who will rush into an incident on the pitch and make things worse. His conduct and discipline were exemplary and he had never been sent off in his professional career. So it is certainly ironic that when you talk about George McCluskey's Hibs career most people will respond with one name, Graeme Souness.

It was truly a shocking incident and one that stays long in the memory of the football fans who witnessed it, and on the shin of George McCluskey who suffered it. The video is on numerous social media sites and in numerous football publications. Google 'ten worst/dirtiest tackles in football ever' and it will be there along with the worst tackles that shamed

---

21. It is important to note that there was another Willie Irvine at Hibs at that time. Like his namesake he was also a forward and had, incidentally, played for the Celtic youth team at the same time as George McCluskey. This particular Willie Irvine, however, had fallen out of favour with the manager and had been sent out on loan to Falkirk by the time that George McCluskey and the other Willie Irvine arrived.

the game of football. It rates alongside Harald Schumacher's reckless challenge on Patrick Battiston in the 1982 World Cup semi-final that left the French forward unconscious with a cracked vertebra and damaged teeth, or Roy Keane's horror tackle on Alf-Inge Haaland in 1997 which ended the Norwegian's football career. It's right up there with Ionel Ganea's shocking lunge at John Kennedy in 2004 that put the young Celt out of the game for two years and eventually led this most prestigious of talents to premature retirement. It also finds mention with Manchester City's Ben Thatcher's outrageous challenge on Portsmouth midfielder Pedro Mendes in 2006 in which Mendes was rendered unconscious, required oxygen on the pitch side and suffered a seizure while being transferred to hospital. It also 'stars' with Nigel de Jong's kick into the chest of Xabi Alonso during 2010 World Cup final. *The Observer* even lists the tackle as one of most outrageous moments in the history of sport.[22] So what was it that happened at Easter Road on that afternoon of August in 1986 that merited mention alongside such shocking sporting moments?

To get George to even talk about it was quite a task. It was not because it left any permanent mental scar on the man from Birkenshaw, although it most certainly has left a physical scar on George's right leg. George McCluskey's reluctance to talk about that incident comes from a principled position of integrity and decency. George simply doesn't want to give any notice or importance to what was a shocking and brutal attack on an unsuspecting victim. It has taken an enormous amount of persuasion on behalf of the writer to get George McCluskey to allow the episode to appear in this book.

George had made the move from Leeds to Edinburgh with a lot of publicity and carrying a fair bit of expectation from the Hibs supporters who were desperate to see their team mounting a serious challenge for honours. The first game of the 1986/87 SPL season for the Leith outfit was scheduled for Easter Road, 9 August, against Rangers. The Glasgow club had spent a decade in the football wilderness due to the dominance of Celtic and the emergence of the 'New Firm' and were without a title win since the 1976/77 season. Unable to compete with their arch-rivals, Rangers called time on the manager Jock Wallace in April 1986 and appointed Graeme Souness as player-manager at Ibrox. The signing of Souness from the Italian side Sampdoria was a massive coup for Rangers.

---

22. 'The 30 most outrageous sporting moments', *The Observer*, 31 October, 2004.

He had won 54 Scottish caps and been captain of a hugely successful Liverpool side in the late 1970s and early 1980s prior to his switch to Italian football. During seven seasons at Liverpool Souness won five League Championships, three European Cups and four League Cups. Aided by the five year ban on English clubs from European competition in the wake of the Heysel Stadium disaster and a large amount of finance, Souness was soon able to bring to Ibrox English international footballers, Terry Butcher and Chris Woods, who were subsequently followed by what appeared to be half the England team in the persons of Trevor Steven, Gary Stevens, Trevor Francis and Ray Wilkins. Souness himself came with a reputation of being a traditionally tenacious type of player, or what some people might call a 'hard man'. In contrast to McCluskey, who scarcely troubled referees on matters of discipline, Souness had a record to match the latter assessment of his physical style. Not that George McCluskey's thoughts were dominated by how Souness might perform, as the first game of the season loomed.

Naturally I was excited to go back to Scotland to start playing there again in familiar circumstances. I had loved being at Leeds but now this was a new beginning and a new challenge. I was delighted when the fixtures were announced and that Rangers at home was our first match. That meant a full house and a passionate atmosphere was guaranteed. I expected a bit of stick from the Rangers fans given my Celtic background and the fact that I had scored against them on a number of occasions. Obviously scoring the winning goal in the 1980 Cup Final would have made me a target for some of them but I enjoyed that thought. It meant that they still remembered me and what I had done. There was a lot in the press about Graeme Souness coming to Rangers and starting to sign some major footballers from England but I never took notice of it. I knew that I'd be playing up front for Hibs and was more concerned about my own game than about what the new player-manager of Rangers would be doing. Given my previous experience playing for Celtic against Rangers I expected it to be a pretty feisty encounter but surely nothing that I hadn't been involved with in the past.

It was feisty indeed and it turned out to be more than George (or anyone else) had anticipated. Easter Road was indeed a full house and George was being reminded by the travelling fans that he was not their favourite player on the pitch. Tackles were flying in and players were being upended as the game was played at 90-mile-an-hour speed. It was not a game for the faint hearted to play in or for the football purist to appreciate but that was not unexpected given it being the first game of the season. Hibs took an early lead through a goal from Stuart Beedie and Rangers equalised after the referee adjudged that Ally McCoist had been taken down in the box. Many thought that the Rangers striker had dived, including the Hibs keeper Alan Rough who was booked for his protests. McCoist levelled the score and Hibs, spurred on by a sense of injustice, roared forward as the game went up a notch and the noise from the crowd increased. In such circumstances some players can handle the atmosphere while others simply lose the run of themselves. Souness, making his Rangers debut in his home city of Edinburgh, probably should not have lasted for as long as he did. He launched into a crunching challenge on Billy Kirkwood almost directly from the kick-off after the Rangers equaliser and escaped with a booking which baffled most observers who thought that it merited an early bath and an entry into the competition for one of the fastest debut sending-offs.

The inevitable was, however, merely postponed. In the 35th minute Souness completely lost it. Already on a yellow card the Ranger player-manager launched another attack on Stuart Beedie in the middle of the park and all hell broke loose. Players from each side rushed in and in the angry melee Souness flicked out at an unsuspecting George McCluskey from behind. George had little chance to anticipate any danger as he was looking the other way at the time and there was at least one other Rangers player between him and Souness. This sparked off a mass brawl in the centre circle with almost every player on the park (with the exception of McCluskey who was lying on the pitch with a huge gash on his right shin, and the Hibernian goalkeeper Alan Rough) becoming involved. By the time order was restored the tally of cards shown in relation to the incident became the stuff of legend. Souness received his marching orders and every player on the pitch receiving a yellow card with the exception of Alan Rough who, already booked, chose not to get involved. Incredibly George McCluskey, who had been the victim of the assault by Souness and who lay bleeding profusely on the ground throughout the mayhem, was booked![23] To add insult to (literal) injury and to the sense of injustice,

23. A disciplinary committee subsequently overturned this booking.

Souness was dismissed as a result of receiving a second yellow card which meant that he only received an automatic one match ban from the SFA, while George McCluskey got 10 stitches in his right shin and was out of the game for a month. Stuart Beedie scored a second goal for Hibs who ran out 2–1 winners against a much fancied Rangers, but the result was incidental as the match has gone down in sporting history as containing a most disgraceful tackle that caused total mayhem on the pitch. For many football fans, this merely confirmed the 'dark side' of Graeme Souness' football nature and that he often crossed the line between being a genuine tough tackling but fair player and one whose actions, quite frankly, were not for the sporting field. The photograph of a seemingly unrepentant Graeme Souness walking off the pitch alongside a clearly distraught and angry George McCluskey who was being carried off with blood streaming down his leg told everything about what had happened. If many football fans viewed the tackle on McCluskey as truly shocking it seems that for some Rangers fans at the time this didn't seem to be seen as a shameful debut by their new player-manager. Perhaps getting sent off in your debut for a brutal foul on an opponent and sparking off a free-for-all on the pitch was seen by some as showing true commitment to the cause. Perhaps the fact that the player who ended up carried off was a former Celtic player may have increased the new player-manager's standing in some people's minds and hearts.

To this day many Celtic fans have a very strong opinion on this episode. Basically it goes as follows: George McCluskey was a very talented footballer who, during his days at Celtic, had inflicted serious damage to Rangers. Many of the Ibrox faithful would have remembered the goal he scored in the famous 'ten men won the league' match of 1979 and many more would have recalled that it was the man from Birkenshaw who scored the winning goal the 1980 Cup Final. And many would also have been aware of the fact that George McCluskey was as Celtic minded as you would get. So what better way to 'prove' your Rangers credentials and make a statement of your commitment to the Rangers cause than to single out the former Celtic legend for special treatment? It is certainly a theory that this writer subscribed to for many years and appears to fit into the received wisdom of many Celtic supporters (and others) for the past three decades. Yet it is an interpretation that George himself does not go along with and, given the fact that he was the victim and right in the middle of it all, it is only right and proper that his take on it should be given due weight and its rightful place. After all, he was the guy who was on the pitch and he has the scar to prove it.

To be absolutely honest I never for a second considered clashing with Graeme Souness or thought that the game would end up in headlines around Scotland and beyond. Up to then I had always respected Souness as a footballer and had watched him playing for Liverpool and Scotland many times. I know that some people think that Graeme Souness singled me out in order to ingratiate himself with the Rangers support but I can't see it that way. It happened all too quickly for any premeditated attack to occur. Souness had gone right through Stuart Beedie in front of the referee and I think that most people thought that he was going to be sent off as he already had a booking. There was a lot of chaos around him and the referee as players from both sides rushed in with a lot of pushing and pulling and shouting and all that. I was actually looking behind me when I felt this sharp pain right down my leg as Graeme Souness simply sliced my leg open with his boot. After that all hell did break lose but I could only watch in disbelief with blood streaming down my leg. I'll never forget being carried off the pitch alongside Souness who had been sent off and asking him why had he done that to me. He never said a word or even looked up at me. He was not a hard man and it is completely wrong to say that Souness had injured me in a tackle. There was no tackle. All he did was flick out at me from behind when I was looking the other way. For me that is not the action of a genuinely tough footballer or a true sportsman. I played against many 'hard men' in my day – the likes of Sergio Brio of Juventus – and Graeme Souness was not, in my opinion, one of them.

George McCluskey has not spoken to Graeme Souness since nor has Souness sought out George to apologise to him for what he did.

Yet listening to George McCluskey talking about this episode did reveal a great deal about someone who had always strived to play football the 'right way'. It was second nature to him throughout his entire football career and something he continually tries to pass on to his young lads at the Celtic Academy today. And part of this 'playing football the right way' that comes through is how George views the concept of a 'hard man'. To this day George McCluskey does not believe that Graeme Souness was a hard man. This may seem surprising to many given Souness' reputation and disciplinary records. Yet on this issue George is unremitting and unchanging. For many football fans a hard man is generally seen as a player who is physical, uncompromising and, often, outside the laws of the game. He is the defender who takes out the opponent without a second thought by kicking him into row Z. He is the midfield 'enforcer' whose main contribution and purpose is to impose his will and control in that vital area by whatever means are necessary. He is the big centre-forward who will act as a battering-ram in order to destroy defences. This type of player does not care how many or what colour of cards he picks up. It is not pretty or skilful but this is what he does. It is simply playing the part of a hard man. Yet for George McCluskey this type of player is not a hard man but simply someone who kicks real footballers all round the park. George has a different take on this altogether.

> To be honest I have absolutely no time at all for the so-called 'hard men' of football. I played against many footballers who were tough, rugged and uncompromising and not afraid of a physical battle. But they were fair and played the game the right way. People like Danny McGrain and Roy Aitken would run through a brick wall but would never ever deliberately try to injure another footballer. For me the genuine hardest man I ever watched or played football with was Jimmy Johnstone. He knew every time he stepped onto the football pitch at least one (but usually more) of the opposition had the job of kicking him off it! And yet he never hid or shied away from the challenge. He'd get lumps kicked out of him but get up again, look for the ball and look to beat whatever was coming at him. Now that is the mark of a real hard man.

It's unfortunate that this episode overshadowed George's three seasons at Hibernian where he scored 16 times in his 86 appearances for the Leith side. Yet (like his time at Leeds) these statistics do not tell the full story of how George McCluskey was regarded by Hibs fans who watched him during his time in the green and white of the Edinburgh club. Like many Leeds fans who saw George McCluskey as an exceptionally talented footballer trying his best to play football in a style unfamiliar to those who were around him, many Hibs fans of that time remember George as a football player of considerable class, vision and elegance who, unfortunately, was surrounded by players who were not on his wavelength. Despite McCluskey's best endeavours, the Hibs 'revolution' did not come about. Easter Road did not witness a return to the days of the 'Famous Five' and remained a mid-table team. Hibs fans, however, are quick to exonerate George McCluskey of any blame for this. Typical of the comments from Hibs supporters who had watched McCluskey at this time are the following:

> I thought that George McCluskey was probably our best player at that time. He had a great touch and vision. Just a pity that we didn't have another couple of players around him who could see where he wanted the ball delivered to. I could see what he was trying to do. Unfortunately some of his teammates couldn't!

> I was genuinely delighted when McCluskey came to Hibs. I had seen him a few times before when he played for Celtic and really fancied him to do something at Hibernians. I think however that he came at the wrong time and with different players he (and Hibs) could have done much better. George McCluskey was one of those footballers who needs to have players around him who link up, move the ball quickly, play it into space and, frankly, at that time we just didn't have too many players like that at Hibs.

> I really rated George McCluskey. By the time he came to us he mightn't have been the quickest player on the pitch but he more than made up for that with his touch and anticipation. He also had great anticipation where the ball might be going to and was always making runs into space, making himself available and so on. I think with better service he could have scored a lot more goals.

George's career at Hibs was quite similar indeed to his time at Leeds with one manager who fancied what George brought to the game moving on to be replaced by another whose football philosophy didn't require players whose main assets were silky skills, a sublime touch and anticipation. Hibs' financial difficulties were beginning to mount up around this time and these had the effect of restricting John Blackley's vision of a free-flowing Hibernian. Mid-table was the best he could manage with the team and in November 1986 he resigned to be replaced by Alex Miller. The arrival of the former Rangers player witnessed a distinct change in the Hibs style of play with a move away from the traditional attacking football usually associated with the Leith side with greater emphasis now being placed on the more defensive and, perhaps, physical aspects of the game. Many Hibs fans saw this as a betrayal of the Hibs philosophy of how to play the game and one Hibs fan from that era suggested to the writer that 'when Alex Miller came to Hibs, football went out the door and so did George McCluskey.' Certainly George (and other 'flair' players) found themselves slipping down the pecking-order with the new manager at the helm. George himself probably suffered more than most and made only four starts that season, with even appearances from the bench few and far between. It was little wonder that he was on the move at the start of the 1989/90 season, this time back to the town of his birth, Hamilton.

18

Paradise Regained – via Hamilton, Kilmarnock and Clyde

GEORGE'S TIME AT Hibs came to an end by mutual agreement as the 1989/90 season got underway. Hamilton Academicals came in with an offer of £35,000. It was a bid that Hibs were prepared to accept and a move that George was keen on. With the family now very much back in the original McCluskey 'homeland' there was little chance that the next move would take George, Anne and the children away from their grandparents, aunts, uncles, cousins and the rest of their extended family. A move to Hamilton had much to commend it. After all, Hamilton was the town where he was born and the region where all of his (and Anne's) family ties were living and only a few miles from where they were actually living themselves. Hamilton Academicals had been relegated from the SPL the previous season, finishing bottom by some considerable distance and scoring a paltry 19 goals in 36 games. The Hamilton manager, Jim Dempsey, had sought to build a team around talented youngsters such as Jim Weir, Paul McDonald and Allan Ferguson, but it very soon became apparent that they badly lacked the needed experience and fire-power. Many Accie supporters hoped that a striker of the class and quality of George McCluskey might help to address this problem. But, true to form, the actual signing of the contract was not without incident.

The Hamilton Chairman, George Fulston, cut his holiday short and flew back from Cyprus to meet with George and get the contract signed by all parties. Fulston had a reputation for being a straight-talking, plain speaking, no-nonsense type of chairperson who didn't like to be messed around in negotiations. When he saw a player he liked and wanted to sign it was generally a case of 'here's the contract, now let's get it signed'. Having come back from Cyprus early it was clear that he wanted McCluskey and was in no mood for any distractions or prolonged contractual negotiations. At that time George (like most players) didn't have an agent. He was accompanied by his wife, Anne, who was somewhat more forceful than George and was to take the lead in what proved to be an interesting encounter indeed. George's niece, Michelle, had been rushed to hospital the night before and required urgent medical attention. Halfway through the discussions between Anne and George Fulson, (George McCluskey having been reduced to the role of spectator as his wife and the Hamilton Chairman were disputing the details of the contract) the office secretary came in to tell Anne that there was a phone call for them from George's sister, Patricia. George took it and received the news that his niece had undergone an operation and was out of the operating theatre. What happened next is revealing about the values and priorities of George McCluskey and left George Fulston gobsmacked.

When we got the phone call from Pat telling us that Michelle was out of the operating theatre there was only one thing that Anne and I could do. We apologised to George Fulston and told him that under the circumstances we would have to postpone the contract negotiations and go to the hospital. Fulston was certainly taken back and less than happy. He started telling me that he had cut his holiday short to come back to Hamilton but I told him (in rather heated terms) that there was only one place that I should be and that was with my family in Yorkhill Hospital with my sick niece. We told him that we'd come back the next day to complete the discussions and walked straight out of the room. George Fulston just shook his head in disbelief and muttered something about not being one bit happy. I didn't care one bit if he still wanted to sign me or not. All I wanted to do was to get into the car and get to the hospital as quickly as possible.

This episode is hugely revealing of how George McCluskey has lived his life and how he views what is important. Faced with a choice between continuing with his contract negotiations or going to the hospital to visit his sick niece, George did exactly what he had learned from his parents from his earliest days, he put family first. One wonders what a modern footballer (never mind his agent) would make of this reaction. He would probably find it difficult to understand why any player and his (*de facto*) agent would storm out of a crucial meeting with the chairperson of a prospective new club. Happily, George's niece made a full recovery and the meeting did resume the next day. George Fulston had calmed down and Anne McCluskey was at her best, getting George a contract at double the wages he had been offered the day before. George Fulston later told George McCluskey that Anne had been by far the hardest person he ever had to negotiate with. George joked that he knew that only too well already.

George became an instant favourite with the fans by scoring a late equaliser against Falkirk at Brockville as Hamilton came from 3–1 down to draw 3–3. George's debut goal was somewhat uncharacteristic of the striker as it was the result of a diving header at the far post. He quickly established a very good striking partnership with John McGachie and for a time it looked like McCluskey's guile and experience might lead Hamilton back to the premier division. However, this was a time of considerable turbulence at Hamilton as managers came and went throughout the season with Jim Dempsey, George Miller (twice), John Lambie and Billy McLaren all occupying the manager's office at different times throughout the season. Unsurprisingly this disruption had an effect on the performance of the team which finished mid-table after a promising start. Furthermore, plans for the redevelopment of Douglas Park (as a result of ground safety regulations following the Taylor report) added to the general atmosphere of uncertainty at Hamilton as events off the pitch took priority.

The advent of live televised football added a new dimension to the 1990/91 season. League restructuring made for a division of 14 teams with only one place up for promotion. August saw George lead the line against Celtic in the Scottish League Cup in which Darius Dziekanowski's late strike proved to be the winner for Celtic. It was a season very much like the season before with Hamilton ending up mid-table again with George McCluskey proving to be Hamilton's main goal threat and leading scorer. The following season, however, proved to be a better one for Hamilton fans, even if it ultimately ended in disappointment.

A trophy, a great league campaign and disappointment

For many Accies supporters this was a season that was both sweet and bitter. Progress was being made in relation to the future development of Douglas Park which meant that the main focus of the club could now be on the team. The young and talented squad had now been playing together for a couple of years and were benefiting from the presence and experience of the Birkenshaw man. Many Hamilton fans felt that this could be a season that would see the Lanarkshire team return to the top division. Pre-season form was good with Hamilton beating Luton Town – who were in the top English division at that time – 2–1 with both goals being scored by George McCluskey. Former Celtic player, Billy Stark, arrived from Kilmarnock in October of that year and, as the players began to gel, confidence began to grow. In December 1991, the Accies won the B&Q Scottish Challenge Cup which is open to all non-SPL clubs, beating Ayr in the final 1–0 at Fir Park. This was a sign of things to come as the Lanarkshire side slugged it out with Dundee and Partick throughout the season for the (now) two promotion places and with only two games left one point separated the three teams. The penultimate match was against a Kilmarnock side revitalised by the recent appointment of a player-manager, one Tommy Burns. Sadly, for the Lanarkshire side, the reunion – albeit on opposing teams – of George and his great pal was not a happy one with the Ayrshire team winning 1–0 and doing Hamilton's chances of promotion serious damage.

Despite winning the final match against Meadowbank Thistle 2–0 at Douglas Park, Hamilton fell short of gaining promotion finishing one point behind the Division One champions Dundee and, agonisingly, behind Partick on goal difference by the slim margin of two goals! That was as good (or bad) as it got for the Hamilton team, supporters and George McCluskey. During his three seasons at Hamilton George McCluskey had contributed much to a team in transition and considerable turmoil. His three years at Hamilton saw him make 95 appearances and score 34 goals. For any goal scorer in any division this strike-rate – more than a goal in every three games – is pleasing enough and all the more so given the state of Hamilton Academicals at that time. George certainly provided a goal threat but he was a striker who relied on service to bring out the best in him and it simply wasn't there. The team wasn't quite good enough to get back to the premiership. At the end of the season of 1991/92 George's contract expired and Hamilton was still in Division One. His time at the Lanarkshire club was finished. Little did he know that one of his closest friends was looking for George McCluskey to do what hadn't been possible at Hamilton, to somehow get an unfancied team out of Division One into the SPL. A new challenge was put to George by none other than his great pal, Tommy Burns.

'George McCluskey got us up to the Premier League and he kept us there.'

George's life-long friend had moved to play for Kilmarnock in 1989 after leaving the club he, like George, adored. Many Celtic fans to this day still believe that, like George McCluskey, Tommy Burns was treated quite shamefully by a Celtic board that was more interested in money than integrity and ambition as it sold a still quite wonderful footballer to Kilmarnock for a paltry £50,000. Like George, the man from the Calton didn't want to leave Celtic and, again like George, his heart remained at Celtic Park despite his move to the Ayrshire club. Tommy arrived at a club that had just dropped out of Division One into the third tier of Scottish football and his presence and skill had the instant effect of securing Kilmarnock promotion to Division One in 1990. The main aim, then as today, was to get to the top level and more often than not it is the unfortunate manager who pays the price for failure. Football can be an unforgiving and even cruel business at times and when a manager cannot get the desired results from his team it almost always ends with the exit of the manager. And so it was with the then manager of Kilmarnock, Jim Fleeting, towards the end of the 1991/92 campaign. Indifferent results led to him offering his resignation to the Kilmarnock Chairman (and his own brother!), Robert, who accepted it and appointed Tommy Burns player-manager. Initially the Kilmarnock board had offered Tommy Burns the job in a caretaker capacity but the man from the Calton refused it demanding that it would be a permanent basis or not at all. Tommy Burns won that one and set about building a team that would challenge for promotion the following season.

The team that Tommy Burns inherited needed serious restructuring. He had been the catalyst for promotion from Division Two the previous season but Tommy recognised that this squad was too young and inexperienced and that it lacked players in key positions. In particular he looked at the forward line. He knew that he needed someone who was not only a proven striker but also one with the experience and ability to bring his young team to another level. Burns knew that his close friend George McCluskey was available and reckoned that he was the man for the job – the man to get Kilmarnock to the premier division. A couple of days after George's contract had expired a most familiar figure knocked on the door of the McCluskey's home in Uddingston.

The doorbell rang and there was Tommy standing there. He had heard that I was a free agent and had phoned earlier that day to ask if I'd be interested in talking to him about signing for Kilmarnock. I had said that I would be interested and so here he was. Of course it was straight into the home and he gave me a bag of sweets for the children and the usual greetings to myself and Anne that only this great life-long friend of the family could give. We then sat down and he explained that he wanted to get Kilmarnock to the premier division and that he felt that I was a key element in his plan. He then took a contract out from his coat pocket which I instantly signed. No questions asked (and not even by Anne who had given George Fulston such a hard time in my signing for Hamilton!) and that was it. I was now a Kilmarnock player. Tommy couldn't stay long as he was on his way to visit Jimmy Steele in Stonehouse Hospital in Larkhall. Jimmy had been a physio at Celtic Park and a real character and a true servant of the club for many years. It was typical of the caring nature of Tommy that he wanted to call in to see Jimmy in hospital. It was also typical of Tommy's ability to get lost once he would get outside of Glasgow. To drive from my house in Uddingston to Larkhall should be simple enough. You take the M74 for a few miles and follow the signs for Larkhall. It's only around seven or eight miles and should take you about 10 minutes. Tommy left my house around half past seven or eight o'clock at night and around half past one the next morning I got a phone call from Tommy's wife, Rosemary, wondering did I know where he was? It turned out that Tommy had missed the turn-off on the motorway for Larkhall and drove on.. and on. In fact Tommy drove almost to Carlisle before he decided that he must have missed his exit!

It was only the next day when Anne asked George how much his salary was to be that he realised that it hadn't crossed his mind to ask Tommy Burns about that rather important detail before signing. That reveals the relationship between the two. George trusted Burns completely and knew that he would never act in an unjust or unfair manner. It was not in his nature. All it took was a quick phone call to Tommy to confirm the details of the contract and that was everything settled. All McCluskey had to do was to try to keep his side of the bargain – to do his best to get Killie into the SPL!

George joined a Kilmarnock team that contained a number of seasoned professionals such as Bobby Williamson, (former Celtic) Danny Crainie, and Tommy Burns himself as player-manager, as well as group of talented youngsters. Burns recognised that to get out of Division One you needed experienced players who could go up against physically intimidating opponents and who would also help to bring the younger players along with them. He also recognised that experience on its own was not enough and that you needed something extra that might get you a goal when none seemed likely, would be a constant threat to opponents and, at the same time, an attacking option for your own team. In other words, to be better than the others you needed a player who could change games and Tommy Burns recognised this in his former teammate, George McCluskey, whose guile, touch, vision and, crucially, finish, were to prove invaluable in the campaigns that followed. Within the first couple of months in the blue and white stripes of Kilmarnock, George became a firm favourite with the Killie fans following an outstanding individual performance at Rugby Park against local rivals Ayr in the B&Q Cup. George emerged as the hero of the evening scoring a thunderous goal from 25 yards which proved to be the decisive score as Kilmarnock ran out 1–0 winners with McCluskey receiving a standing ovation from the fans as he came off after 79 minutes. The B&Q Cup, however, was not the primary target for Tommy Burns and the Ayrshire club. It was all about promotion to the SPL. The season of 1992/93 was a memorable rollercoaster with Kilmarnock chasing one of the two promotion places. Kilmarnock's fortunes went down to the very last game of the season with the Ayrshire club needing to take one point against Hamilton. Scenes of jubilation among the crowd of more than 12,000 packed into Rugby Park followed the final whistle as Kilmarnock had drawn 0–0 with Hamilton and secured promotion to the SPL. Tommy Burns had masterminded the return of Kilmarnock to the SPL after 10 years in the wilderness and he had done so with limited resources. George McCluskey had played a key role in this success, emerging as Killie's top scorer for the season with 11 extremely valuable goals. George McCluskey could now look forward to playing in an environment and in stadiums that he was all happily familiar with. The challenge for Kilmarnock now was staying up.

If winning promotion to the SPL for an unfancied Kilmarnock team was quite an achievement, Tommy Burns was now faced with the challenge of keeping his newly promoted team up. This, of course, is always the case for a newly promoted club in any division but for a team like Kilmarnock there was the added issue of league restructuring that had to be taken into account. The Scottish football authorities had agreed to the creation of a fourth tier in league football which would commence in the season 1994/95. In order to facilitate this three teams would be relegated from the SPL at the end of the 1993/94 campaign with only one to be promoted from Division One. The bottom five teams in that division would drop into Division Two and only the champions of that division would be promoted. The bottom eight clubs in Division Two would drop down to make up a new Division Three. Basically it meant that to survive in the SPL Tommy Burn's squad would have to finish in the top nine teams in the league. A tall order indeed for a club that a few years previously had been playing in the bottom division. Most football pundits – and quite a number of Kilmarnock supporters – saw little hope for Kilmarnock's SPL survival in such circumstances.

A further factor that was seen as another hurdle to Kilmarnock's prospects of survival in the SPL was the decision by the board to go ahead with a massive upgrade of the stadium. For a number of years various options had been discussed, plans drawn up, proposals made, obstacles and objections overcome about either redeveloping Rugby Park, which, quite frankly, was no longer fit for purpose – or moving to another site altogether. The decision was to remain at Rugby Park and to build an all-seater stadium with a capacity of 18,000. While the redevelopment work would not start until the end of the 1993/94 season the decision to carry this out meant that any serious funds for Tommy Burns to strengthen the team in the SPL campaign were simply out of the question. The manager made a very shrewd signing in bringing Billy Stark back from Hamilton during the closed season (adding to Kilmarnock's new nickname, 'Ayrshire Celtic') but apart from this he had to make do with what he had and a few younger players signed on the Youth Training Scheme (YTS) for unemployed youngsters. For many it seemed that Kilmarnock were in the eye of a perfect storm, having got into the top division in Scotland with a squad containing only a handful of players who were seen as being of SPL quality and at a time when priorities off the pitch might affect priorities on the playing front. One man who didn't accept the received wisdom was the Kilmarnock manager, Tommy Burns. He had not got his club to the premier division to go back down the next season. Nor had he brought his great friend to Kilmarnock just to get them out of Division One. This adventure hadn't yet run its course.

After an unsteady start that brought one win in the first three games Kilmarnock went to Ibrox to play the reigning SPL champions who had not lost at home in 17 months. To the utter delight of Killie fans (and disbelief of Rangers supporters and many others) the Ayrshire team won 2–1 with George's striking partner, Bobby Williamson, scoring the winner against his former employers in the 94th minute. The opening goal for Kilmarnock was scored by YTS youngster, Mark Roberts. In an interview Tommy Burns was asked what had he said to Roberts after the game, the manager quipped in his usual joking style, 'Son, get the kit hampers on the bus!'.

Throughout the season Kilmarnock amassed enough – just enough – points to give themselves a chance of staying up. Kilmarnock beat a Celtic side that was going through considerable turmoil at the time at Rugby Park and drew 0–0 with them at Celtic Park. They had a great Scottish Cup run getting to the semi-finals where they defeated only after a replay by a Rangers team that was beginning to dominate Scottish football at the time. With a little luck Kilmarnock could have reached their first Scottish Cup final since 1957 and only went down 2–1 thanks to a hotly disputed goal by Mark Hately with many maintaining to this day that the ball never crossed the line. Yet this 'gallant defeat' did not come without a cost. The two hard games against Rangers in four days in April had an effect on the Kilmarnock team and valuable points were dropped as the run-in to the main prize – SPL survival – loomed. Dundee and Raith Rovers were already down with any one of four teams, Hearts, Partick, St Johnstone and Kilmarnock, staring relegation in the face. Kilmarnock was the team most likely for the drop as they entered the final four games of the campaign. A great 3–1 win away to Dundee United gave some hope, only to be followed by a 1–0 defeat at Motherwell. This left Kilmarnock a point behind the other teams in third bottom place with two extremely difficult matches left, Rangers at home and away to Hibs. Against all odds and expectations (and with the bulldozers literally parked outside Rugby Park to commence restructuring the ground) Kilmarnock pulled off a shock result by defeating Rangers 1–0 in the last game to be played at the old stadium. They, and thousands of Killie supporters, made the journey across Scotland to Easter Road for the final game of the season needing at least a point to secure safety. A hard working team of experienced players, and especially Tommy Burns and George McCluskey who had experienced drama and tension in last day deciders at Celtic on previous occasions, helped to guide the more inexperienced players to an invaluable point via a 0–0 draw. With Hearts beating Partick Thistle 1–0 and St Johnstone winning by a similar score-line against Motherwell, three teams – Kilmarnock, Partick and St Johnstone – ended up with 40 points each with St Johnstone being relegated on goal difference. George McCluskey had played a key role both in the promotion and SPL survival of Kilmarnock and this is a point that George's best pal and the manager of Kilmarnock made on many occasions. Speaking to this writer, Tommy Burns stated in the clearest possible terms that it was George McCluskey who got Kilmarnock out of Division 1 and it was the same man who kept them in the SPL.

During the closed season Tommy Burns continued to work to build the Kilmarnock club. He had suggested that George might want to finish his career at Kilmarnock and come in as coach for the reserve team but George wasn't quite ready to hang up his boots yet. George still loved playing football and wanted to continue to do just that. Tommy had just moved on to manage Celtic in June 1994 when George got a call from Alex Smith, the manager of Clyde. He had heard that George was now finished at Kilmarnock and that perhaps he might want to come to Broadwood in Cumbernauld and 'help with the youngsters and pass on a bit of your knowledge and wisdom'. George had no hesitation and soon found himself playing his final couple of seasons in the third division as he sought to (in his own words) 'give these kids something that I had been given throughout my football career.' George played 35 games for Clyde between 1994 and 1996, when he finished a professional career in football that spanned 21 years in which he'd played 488 games and scored 141 goals. He gave the supporters at all six clubs he played for wonderful moments and memories but there was only one club that George McCluskey was (and is) truly identified with and that is the club he had supported and dreamed of being a part of since he was a boy growing up in Birkenshaw. So when a Celtic legend and former colleague contacted him about coming back to Celtic Park once again there was only one answer that a Celtic minded lad could give. After all, how could you say 'no' to the great Bobby Lennox?

'Hello George. Do you fancy coming back to Celtic Park to do a bit of work on match days?'

George had settled into life after football and was providing for his family through working as manager in a local company, happy to be able to go to the games at Celtic Park again. He was not forgotten by Celtic fans, or the club, and was kept busy representing Celtic at various supporters functions. Extremely affable, engaging and entertaining, it was no surprise that when Celtic decided to develop the hospitality side of the club it was people like George McCluskey who would be on the radar. George explains:

> It was around the time of the Fergus McCann era when Celtic Park had been rebuilt and for the first time in years there was a definite feeling that the club was going forward. Here we were with a brand new state of the art stadium and a team that was now able to challenge for honours after quite a few years in the doldrums. New people had come in and new ideas about how best to market the club in the new world of football were emerging. Bobby Lennox was put in charge of match day hospitality and set about assembling a team of people who would carry out the function of club ambassadors on match days and represent the club at official functions when required. I was delighted and honoured to be asked to come back to Celtic in a role which I thoroughly enjoy.

Not long after being invited onto the hospitality team by one Celtic legend, George was approached by another famous Celt who asked George if he might wish to help in another aspect of Celtic's development. This time it was his close pal, Tommy Burns, who approached him.

At that time Tommy Burns had just been put in charge of youth development by the new manager Martin O'Neill. It was a shrewd move by the Irishman. Tommy was already working at Celtic Park as Kenny Dalglish's assistant during the latter's short-lived tenure after John Barnes had parted company in 1999. Normally a new manager would change the whole previous management and coaching staff on arrival, bringing in his own men. But O'Neill – a Celtic fan from boyhood – knew what Celtic were about and saw Tommy Burns as a most valuable asset in his project to restore Celtic to glory and success. Youth development would be key to building Celtic in the long-term and who better to play a leading role in that than Tommy Burns, a man who lived and breathed Celtic. In turn, Tommy started to surround himself with like-minded people who were capable of inspiring and developing young talent so that they too might become the next generation of Celtic heroes. George McCluskey was an obvious choice for Burns to bring on board. Celtic minded to the core,

George had come through the ranks of the Celtic Boys Club, the Celtic under-age and reserve teams to play with distinction for the first team for almost a decade. Of a most caring and engaging nature, this was exactly the type of person who could instil and develop in these young footballers the qualities required to succeed in a wonderful but incredibly challenging sport. It was an opportunity that George McCluskey would not think twice about in accepting. George was about to put on his boots and Celtic gear and go to training again.

I was thrilled when Tommy asked me to become part of the youth academy. I love the hospitality work and meeting with people at Celtic park and telling them about the history of the club and what it means. But working with young lads to try to help them to improve and to watch them develop as individuals and a team is something altogether different and so rewarding. And it's not just about football. You always have to remind yourself that they're only young lads growing up, looking for advice and guidance. I was lucky in having wonderful dedicated coaches throughout my formative years including Tommy Cassidy at St Catherine's, John Higgins at Celtic Boys and all the staff right up to Jock Stein at Celtic, and, of course, my father when I was a 'Red Rocket'. They all kept me grounded and focused and they were all interested in me as an individual. I try to pass on those wisdom and values to the young lads I work with and, thankfully, most of them take it on board.

George started working with Miodrag Krivokapic with the under-13 squad, before joining Tommy McIntyre with the under-17s. In 2013 George McCluskey returned to Hampden where he had scored the winning goal in the Scottish Cup Final 33 years beforehand to see his young Celtic team beat Rangers to lift the under-17 trophy. Success at under-age levels continues and Celtic fans are excited to see young talent such as Kieran Tierney, Jack Aitchinson and Anthony Ralston – all products of the Celtic under-age system- moving through the ranks onto the first team squad. From cheering on Celtic from the Jungle, to scoring for Celtic, George McCluskey now seeks to bring the dreams he once had of playing in the Hoops come true for a new generation of Celtic hopefuls. George McCluskey did indeed play in the Hoops and for the Hoops. And he has now returned to the club he has always loved.

Postscript

GEORGE MCCLUSKEY HAS returned to the club he followed from boyhood and for whom he played with distinction for almost a decade. He now passes on a lifetime of knowledge, wisdom and experience to young lads who, like him some years ago, dream of running out in front of a packed Celtic Park wearing the green and white hoops of Celtic. He is now as happy at Lennoxtown training facility coaching as he was at Barrowfield under the watchful eye of people like Jock Stein. He is also a wonderful ambassador for Celtic who, as part of the hospitality team on match days or as a guest at events organised by Celtic supporters clubs throughout Scotland, England and Ireland, as well as America, Australia and Dubai, represent everything that is good about Celtic and the Celtic family. George understands the wonderful life that football – and especially Celtic – has given him and strives to pass that passion and joy to others in the Celtic tradition and those outside of it.

The values that were passed onto him by his parents, Teresa and John, and the community that he grew up in where he continues to live today are ones that he continues to live his life by. Family, friends, a sense of identity and generosity and acceptance of everyone you meet remain touchstones of George McCluskey's world-vision to this day. To say that George (and Anne) are family-centred is to state the obvious. They take great pride in their children – Leeanne, Barry, Natalie and Ashleigh – and the next generation who now recreate in the family home in Uddingston the same joy and laughter that a previous generation enjoyed when growing up in Birkenshaw. Leeanne's two children, Keira and Orlaith, and Barry's son Ruari are extremely fortunate and blessed to have the willing care and love of grandparents, aunties, uncles and cousins all around them. In addition to the benefits of a large extended family, the new generation of McCluskey grandchildren are being brought up in the Celtic tradition with Keira and Ruari both proud season ticket holders since they were able to walk. On match days they can be found with their parents and other family members in the North Stand where previous generations – including George himself – would have watched their own sporting heroes from the old Jungle.

A natural after-dinner speaker who is genuinely interested in other people, George has established an enormous network of friends throughout the world. He is particularly interested in maintaining and promoting the Celtic ethos of charity and uses his name and reputation to help others. George's friendships with people in Ireland have led him to become involved with the work of Project Zambia, a charity founded by the Christian Brothers in Belfast and of which he is patron. In *Celtic minded 2* [24] George wrote passionately and with pride about the work this charity does with some of the poorest and most marginalised communities in the Developing World:

> I am very moved by the plight of the orphans, AIDS victims and those who are struggling against all odds to improve their conditions and I'm delighted to promote the work of this charity whenever possible. It is a disgrace, a crime and a sin that in a world in so much wealth is flaunted – and in the modern football game as well – that people are still struggling from day-to-day and are dying literally every second from the lack of clean water, food and basic medicines. [25]

For the past 12 years George has constantly worn a Project Zambia wristband, only removing it whenever a new one is required. Listening to George speaking about those in need invokes an almost unconscious awareness and sense of the vision of Brother Walfrid and the foundations and history of Celtic. For George McCluskey concern for others is rooted in his upbringing by his parents, his sense of community and the values that formed him and which he seeks to pass on. They are values that also lie at the heart of Celtic. When considering what it really means to be 'Celtic minded', George came up with some very powerful and challenging thoughts:

> It is this sense of social conscience, of being aware that you are responsible for others – especially those in need – of knowing your history and the values that formed you, your family and your community that makes the 'Celtic family' unique and gives us an identity worth having. Perhaps that is what it means to be truly 'Celtic minded'. Perhaps that is the core of the criteria we should bring to bear when we consider those who are Celtic footballers, employees, trustees and supporters. [26]

Perhaps these are also criteria we should apply when we seek to identify

---

24. G McCluskey, 'Playing in the Hoops – Living for the Hoops', in J Bradley (ed.), *Celtic minded 2*, Glendaruel: Argyll Publishing, 2006, pp. 153–63.
25. ibid., p. 162.
26. ibid., p. 163.

genuine Celtic legends, those who wore the hoops with distinction on the park and represented the values and tradition of the club. These are qualities which George McCluskey has in abundance and are the reason we can truly say that when George McCluskey played in the hoops, he played for the Hoops and he played for us.